DANCING
WITH THE
DEVIL

A Journey from the Pulpit to the Bench

Christopher Geraghty

First published in Australia in 2012
reprint with corrections 2012
By Spectrum Publications Pty Ltd
a: PO Box 75, Richmond, Victoria, Australia 3121
t: (+61) 1300 540 736
f: (+61) 1300 540 737
e: spectrum@spectrumpublications.com.au
w: www.spectrumpublications.com.au

Cover Design: xy arts
Typesetting by Spectrum Publications Pty Ltd
Typeface: Times New Roman
Editing: Shona Weston

ISBN: 978-0-86786-172-3
ebook ISBN: 978-0-86786-151-8

National Library of Australia Cataloguing-in-Publication entry

Author:	Geraghty, Christopher, 1938-
Title:	Dancing with the devil : a journey from the pulpit to the bench / Christopher Geraghty.
ISBN:	9780867861723 (pbk.)
Subjects:	Geraghty, Christopher, 1938- Priests--New South Wales--Biography. Judges--New South Wales--Biography.
Dewey Number:	282.092

To
My other dancing partner
Adela Rosa Geraghty (nee Rodriguez)

"I think all we can offer heaven is human honesty. I mean at the gates of St. Peter. Hopefully it might be like salt to kingdoms without salt, spices to dark northern countries. A few grams in the bag of the soul, offered as we seek entry. What heavenly honesty is like I cannot say. But I say this to steel myself to my task".

The Secret Scripture. Sebastian Barry.

"The memory throws up high and dry
A crowd of twisted things".

Rhapsody on a Windy Night. T.S. Eliot.

CONTENTS

PROLOGUE

*"Memories are like timeless seashells scattered
over the beach of oblivion".*

In the new global Age of WikiLeaks, when all is revealed down to the most compromising detail in the interests of freedom of speech, when governments and organizations are intent on propagating spin and forging an iron cloak of secrecy, I am moved to record my memories of living as a priest in the gigantic institution called the Roman Catholic Church in the 60's and 70's of the last century.

What follows are Geraghty's memories – but of course, not all of them. And every time I paused to create a space of silence around me, more details came to me, more events and more of the characters who had come into and gone out of my life over the years. Faces from times past floated in and out of my half-consciousness. One thing led onto another, perhaps twenty or thirty years apart, as I was taken, frequently beyond my control, on a journey of remembering, and interpreting. In different moods, in different contexts, the same facts took on different colours. This floating world of memories is populated by angels and clerical ghosts, its landscape covered with mists and shadows.

I am writing as a wrinkled septuagenarian, drawing on my present memories as they come and go, and I am under no illusion. I have forgotten much of the detail of the long journey as I have lived it. I write in the present time, making a selection of events and personnages in the here-and-now, colouring them, and presenting them from my personal perspective. Of course, other old men will have different memories of the same events, or of the same personalities. Their remembered facts, passing through different filters, will be slanted in other directions.

Many of those who were involved in my life are dead. Some of those who are still living will surely have forgotten a particular event altogether. Others perhaps interpreted the experience differently at the time. I am telling it as I saw them, as I remember them.

Some of the names have been changed to avoid unnecessary hurt, to protect the innocent and to steer clear of defamation suits. I have been careful when telling of those who are dead since they are not here to protect their reputations, to suggest a different slant or deny my allegations. I see no reason not to speak the truth (at least as I see it), simply because some of the players have gone to God. If it were otherwise, history, including the Gospels, would never have been written.

This is the story of one man who passed through the Roman system and came out the other side. In part, it is a story of bullying and persecution. A story about a yearning for intimacy and a sense of belonging. About compulsory celibacy and the clerical way of life. About obedience, power and domination. About propaganda and a grab for freedom. About Jesus, the Church and a little man from Neutral Bay. It is a story which is at times painful, sometimes funny, at times embarrassing, but one which, by luck or by the grace of God, has a happy ending.

But it is not the whole story. Of course there were times of fun and laughter, of exultation, moments of satisfaction and feelings of friendship and achievement. In the years which I describe, I grew to adulthood, expanded my mind and slowly developed a spirituality to nourish my soul. I shared a life with many good men, a few holy men, some hollow men, with clowns and puppet-masters and sometimes with mad bastards.

I have no doubt that on reading this memoir some will think that I have lost the plot, my sense of humour and my faith. I don't really care what those people might think. There was a time when their opinion of me would have occupied too much space in my head, but I am over seventy now, and I feel I have earned the right to have my say. Some will undoubtedly shake their heads and dismiss what I say as the ravings of an angry, bitter ex-priest. They can say what they like. It is their right in a free country and once published, my book is out there for every man and woman to read and respond to in the context of his or her own life-experiences, values and prejudices. It is true, I was once, long ago, both angry and bitter. But as far as I am concerned, those destructive feelings didn't last beyond my wedding day in Toulouse, beyond finding a real job, signing a mortgage and witnessing the birth of my two boys.

In all sincerity, dear reader, I invite you to scrutinise what is reported and to bear in mind that wherever you stand, the whole truth is never told. I invite you to reflect openly, without rancour, on the events in the life of a Sydney priest who received his obedience training in the 50's and early 60's, who was ordained to the priesthood in July 1962 and who tried, ultimately without success, to live the life of a member of the clergy for almost fifteen years before taking flight and landing in another part of the universe.

I should not neglect to pay tribute to the people who have contributed to this memoir; my parents, my brother and sisters, my friends and my enemies, my teachers and confrères, my bosses and fellow workers. A special thanks to those who helped me through the writing stage; the retired priest and solicitor, Peter Marr and his wife and architect, Linda Coombs, Sharon Carleton, Kathleen Gilbert, John Challis, Oliver Freeman and my friend Neil Brown. They have each generously afforded me their advice and assistance, but let none of them bear any liability for the stories told, the stands taken, the criticisms made, or for the oversights, the memory lapses and the omissions. I am indebted to my wife and partner, Adela Rosa, for her patience and forbearance during the construction of this memoir. We have travelled well together on the earth.

chapter one

1991
A BLUNT JUDGEMENT

By 1991, I was on top of my little world. I was enjoying the company of a gentle French wife with whom I had helped create two healthy boys. We were reviving a heritage home which had fallen into ruin in McMahon's Point, near the magnificent Sydney harbour, close to the centre of the city. I had just returned from a successful day in court – another win, another happy litigant. I was in a good mood, gliding easily in the newly carpeted corridor, smiling at my clerk, a casual wink to the busy girl on the switch. The tension headaches which had plagued me during my clerical life had disappeared. My lifelong journey through the lands and forests of the Roman Church on the edge of the known world was just a fading memory. The Valium tablet bottles which I had kept just in case from my days of teaching in the seminary were at the back of the bathroom cabinet and covered in dust. After my law studies, I had landed safely on a reputable floor of successful barristers. There was plenty of work: everyone was busy. I had some interesting cases and a few colourful clients.

One afternoon I happened to be passing a colleague in the corridor as he was ushering two or three of his clients to the lift. It was the man who had encouraged me some years before to borrow a frightening sum of money to purchase a room on the eighth floor and who had helped muster the votes of the other barristers. Peter had welcomed me as a member of his chambers and I was grateful. Though I had been uncertain at the beginning, wondering whether I could make a success of barristering, nervous whether I would be able to repay the crushing loan to the bank, the move had proved successful. Together with a few of his other friends, I had been attentive to him over the few years I had been on the floor, sometimes visiting him in hospital or at home when he was sick. Life had been hard for him, but his friends had rallied to support him.

Peter was a prickly man behind his greying moustache. The devil had cursed him with a black, Celtic temperament and we all had to suffer. Before he became a judge, he was a formidable advocate in court and would strike at a difficult witness's jugular without warning and without mercy. I thought he was crusty and cankerous – someone to be careful of. For apparently trivial slights, he held grudges, but not against me or his close friends.

Without knocking, uninvited, Peter used to wander into my cramped chambers, sit himself down, light up a cigarette and spend valuable time while I played the role of the conversationalist. As I remember, he would hardly ever initiate a topic for discussion. He would wait, in silence, puffing out smoke, expecting to be amused, perhaps offering an occasional counterpunch or some black comment. To the world at large he could be rough, often aggressive, sometimes unpleasant, but within his circle of friends, though he tended to be rather taciturn, he could be generous and loyal. One of my confrères on the District Court, a man I came to love and respect, would not have a word of criticism of Peter spoken in his presence.

Peter and I used to spend a lot of time together – in chambers on the eighth floor, in restaurants, riding home in taxis after a busy day, even in Union Street where we were neighbours on the same line of terraces. I played the chatty character. I had the news and the gossip, and kept the conversation flowing.

As I passed Peter and his clients in the corridor, I uttered some flippant observation out of the corner of my mouth. A casual, passing remark. Nothing hurtful, not even smart, just a word or two to avoid passing in silence. He must have been in one of his dark, Celtic moods. Perhaps he misinterpreted what he had heard. With black, murderous eyes, through his bristling moustache, he spat back –

"and you're nothing but a fucking failed priest",

and he kept walking.

Nothing more was said.A sharp jab. A spontaneous flash of cruelty. But he had unwittingly scraped sandpaper over a wound which I had thought had healed. I was stunned, as though hit by a surge of electricity. My colleague ushered his clients to the lift and the steel doors of the lift-well banged shut. It was the end of our friendship. Once words of bitterness have been spoken, they can never be retrieved – and he never tried. A friend in the morning, a stranger after court.

A friend, a true friend, might have thought he had to confront me with the healing truth, however painful, that I had failed and I needed to accept this defeat in order to grow. I had spent a lifetime chasing a dream – years of prayer and preaching, miles of processions, pages of study, large baskets of sacramental bread – and now I was an advocate in a civil court, before a mortal judge, dressed in wig and gown instead of the heavenly, priestly robes. If I was a failure (and for years I believed I might have been), a true friend might have taken me aside and gently explored the territory where I had spent my past life. Perhaps he might have teased me with the reality of my peculiar past. He might have given me a playful clip over the ears, a friendly tap in the mid-drift. But this was a powerful blow in the face.

We never really spoke again. Oh, formally perhaps, as we passed in the street or on some social occasion, but our friendship was at an end. In those days, I was too brittle, too easily wounded. Unwittingly perhaps, yet certainly with a bad grace, Peter had pierced my armour and blood was flowing. He was not to know the powerful forces and twisted knots my education had generated inside me. He had not taken the time to walk a mile or two with me. There were some of my clerical confrères who considered that departing priests were Judases. According to them, we were damned eternally for betraying the eternal fatherland. Even some of my close friends in the priesthood already had me among the fallen angels in hell. A former friend had decided he would never speak to me again, though he too finally left the ranks and married – a few times. Cardinal Jimmy Freeman had scrubbed my name from the diptychs, with the observation that the diocese had wasted its money and resources on my education – and there was a modicum of truth in his remark.

For years after my departure, I had been troubled by half-remembered dreams flashing through my mind in the twilight hours.

Darby Mecham hovering like a grinning ghost; the odd Monsignor questioning me; the figure of myself dressed in white vestments celebrating the Eucharist; prostrate, face flat on the cold black-and-white marble in the College corridor; a sweaty meeting with his Eminence Cardinal Norman Thomas Gilroy. Phantoms had drifted in and out of the shadows of my dreams – old priests I had let down; Johnny Lander from Neutral Bay, Juddy McGlynn, Monsignor Charlie Dunne of Springwood, Dennis Ryan, an Irish compatriot of my father's, Paddy McManus and others; men I had admired, some of whom I later discovered could not keep their pure, Eucharistic, forgiving, sanctifying hands off the private parts of little girls and maidens; members of my class of '62, some of whom had drifted into madness; my dear mother and father, who were sad that I had not persevered, confused that I had been so unhappy among the saintly men of the clergy; parishioners from Avalon appearing suddenly from behind a screen and floating away.

Peter had no idea of the world I had escaped from, a world in which my unconscious was still trapped as though in deep mud. I had been struggling with feelings of failure and guilt. I had been a public celebrant of ceremonies one day and a faceless reject at the back of the church the next. I had "said" my daily Mass for more than 10 years; "said" my priestly prayers (the Breviary) several times each day; forgiven sins; counselled disturbed souls; buried soulless bodies and comforted the grief-stricken. Then gradually, an emotional tsunami had destroyed this world of grace and mystery and I was out on my own, searching for a new life. Peter could not have come near to understanding the interior struggle his colleague and friend had been engaged in and yet, like an awkward alien, he had waded into a foreign battle-field to swing his axe and inflict collateral damage.

I had to confront the fact that Peter might have been right. Businesses fail when they have to close their doors and vacate the premises. Marriages fail when one of the partners gives up and leaves the home. Failures are part of the human condition. On one level, it was obvious that I had failed. I had not persevered.

But was I "nothing by a fucking failed priest"? Even then, I did not think so. Now I am sure he was wrong.

chapter two

1962
MY FIRST PARISH

I began my life as a priest in the beach parish of St Aloysius in Cronulla with Father Jack Madden, who was old beyond his years.

In November 1962, full of grace and expectation, after twelve years of obedience training, I had been churned out of the seminary, cut, polished and buffed. Like the other junior priests, I would be organising and managing a youth club. I would be teaching without training, preaching without practice and delivering good counsel to sinners in the confessional without expertise. I would perform at social and public functions with dignity and humility, never embarrassing the institution, disciplined and under control at all times, delivering the formulas of faith without gloss or doubt, protecting the wealth of the Church and fostering a constant flow of vocations to keep our perfect institution in front of the field. To deliver this impossible load of expectations for the senior clergy, for the bishop and ultimately for God, I received a formal letter of appointment from Cardinal Gilroy.

In those distant days the priest was seen by himself and his flock, as a special messenger from God and the dispenser of divine mysteries. He was the representative of Christ on earth – God's interpreter and ambassador. Since he was invested with divine powers (to forgive sins, to make Christ present and to lay down the law), he was entitled to the utmost deference and respect. It was incomprehensible that a priest could be avaricious and greedy, jealous, unreasonable, lazy, self-indulgent, a thief or a sexual predator. We believed, and the people believed, that we enjoyed a status above the angels, forever cloaked in a graced aura of supernatural powers.

As I was launching my life as a priest in Cronulla, for centuries the celibate mystique had blocked in the minds of the faithful (and in my own mind), even secret suspicions about the sexuality of the clergy. Bishops and priests were asexual entities. Of course, they enjoyed no sexual activities. That was a given. They were not troubled by sexual desires. It would have been sacrilegious to have entertained a moment's thought about papal or episcopal sex. Though heaven knew (and I did not) that many of those who held those elevated offices, used to indulge themselves with great energy and fervour. The message handed down from parent to child, from nun to pupil, the message which I had received, was that we priests were somehow above ordinary mortals and I was ready, I was keen to live the message.

The parish of St Aloysius was thriving on the shores of Port Hacking, down-stream from Lilli Pilli, just a ferry ride from paradise at Bundeena. Father Madden, in his heavy black serge suit and a choking Roman collar, aided by his nervous curate, ministered to the Catholics, faithful and renegade who lived at the end of the railway line from Sydney.

The church building at Cronulla, which had been solemnly consecrated to St Aloysius had long since lost the battle to serve the local community. While the parish priest had looked on prayerfully, the area had expanded and changed. It was no longer a sleepy, isolated fishing community on the end of a long train ride from the city. New shops had opened and solicitors and accountants with empty saddle-bags, had ridden into town and set themselves up in businesses. New arrivals were building their homes in brick, and old residents, on land with splendid views of beaches and bays, were demolishing their fibro and timber homes.

The little wooden Catholic church had seen its day in the sun. It was something of an embarrassment to the new, up-market parishioners with sleek cars and fat bank accounts. The red and blue plaster statues of the Virgin Mary and the Sacred Heart, the noisy ceiling fans labouring under a hot iron roof, the old pews in which many of the scruffy Catholic school kids had recorded their initials, the worn carpet on the sanctuary, the faded brass candelabra, the wooden altar facing away from the people, the stained timber pulpit and the painted weatherboard walls no longer provided a suitable place of worship for Cronulla Catholics on the move. Yet the faithful packed in tightly every Sunday to endure the mumblings and ramblings of their unworldly parish pastor. The blond, sun-tanned teenagers had an excuse to congregate outside, pretending to pray, talking, some of them smoking and avoiding mortal sin.

Father Madden used to count the collection carefully after the Sunday services. He was determined to raise funds to build a brand new church worthy of the parish, a building dedicated to the honour of God, to the praise of St Aloysius, and to accumulate a little worldly glory on the side for himself. In the early 60's the institution was still strong. It was a force out there in the world, at a time when the profession of the Roman Catholic faith demanded regular Sunday attendance at Mass, when most junior priests like myself used to pass sleepy hours on Saturdays in a claustrophobic confessional, listening to lists of what I later came to realise were mainly constructed, artificial 'sins', often simply trivial weaknesses. Crowds of minor sinners used to turn up even on stuffy, hot, summer afternoons when the surf was running.

My new parish priest used to anchor his Roman collar to his shirt with winged studs. He wore elastic suspenders to support his black socks, silver cuff links, elasticised arm bands, and a battered black hat. His elderly housekeeper worked out the back in the kitchen and shuffled silently in and out of the parish priest's dining room, past the cedar sideboard with its large stained mirror. She served solid meals to her two priests at regular intervals throughout the day. A diminutive figure, almost invisible, in a perpetual black dress with a white lace collar, Mrs Keenan observed all and said little, at least to me, though I imagine she reported regularly to her boss. She knew every telephone call, every knock on the door, the exits and entrances of the clergy throughout the day and into the night.

Father Madden would preside at the head of the cluttered dining-room table. He carved the roast, served the soggy vegetables from his silver service and engaged in the same conversation almost every day. We never discussed politics, our philosophy of life, or theology. We didn't even talk about sport. Each day we touched on the fringes and paraphernalia of religion. Except for the grace recited rapidly, thoughtlessly and in Latin over the food, our personal faith and the content of our shared beliefs were out-of-bounds. That aspect of our lives had been decided and frozen in formulas centuries before. We could talk about the clergy. Grapevine gossip about important, powerful monsignors, about Charlie Keller up the road at Caringbah and about Bluey Gilroy are some of the things that would tickle his palate. Clerical stories involving characters dead or almost departed seemed to be repeated at regular intervals. He loved to be brought up to date with the latest gossip from St Michael's golf course, or the rumours circulating among the junior clergy. His face would light up with excitement when he heard news of minor scandals or clerical indiscretions. He used to giggle quietly to himself as he relished the morsels and tit-bits of clergy life, as he served the silverside or ate his bread-and-butter pudding.

One hot afternoon I came home to the presbytery to find my parish priest alone in the gloom of the dining room, curtains pulled shut to ensure that no light could penetrate the inner sanctum of the presbytery. He was sitting in front of a blank television set which was in a dominant position on the old sideboard. He was just sitting there, in the dark, on his own, in his clerical clobber, in the middle of the afternoon, looking forlorn. I thought he might have been depressed, so to make some light conversation I asked him if he wanted me to switch the television on. He roused himself, sat up straight in his leather armchair and answered in his drawly voice –

> "No, Father dear. You can't put the television on in the daytime when you're supposed to be out on the mission, pounding the pavements, visiting parishioners, conducting a census of the parish and going about your work. If you're not careful, you'll be watching the mid-day movie, or *Beauty and the Beast*, wasting time and losing your direction."

I knew what he was thinking. He had been given charge of a young colt from the seminary to train up and he didn't want him to get fat and lazy. He wanted him to develop good clerical habits while under his supervision. I took the message on board. Then he added as an aside;

> "I think we'll whip the television on at 4 o'clock (in twenty minutes time) and watch *Bugs Bunny*."

It wasn't long before I knew I had scored well in the lottery of parish priests. Others had not been so fortunate, though as far as I knew, none of the young ones were sent to assist the parish priest in his inner city parish where he was running one of the local brothels. One of my classmates, Father Steve Hyndes, had received his commission to serve in a parish in the western districts of Sydney, where the boss was running a huge regional housie game each week and raking in the cash. Thankfully, my new boss was not an entrepreneur. According to Steve, while he was not qualified to suggest any medical diagnosis, the parish priest he had scored was "basically an arrogant, ignorant arsehole in the best pedantic and dilettante tradition of the senior clergy". But there was no bitterness in Steve's assessment. He would double up with mirth as he shared memories of his former boss from Bankstown, who used to carry a revolver on his person and refine his aim by standing on the balcony and shooting rats in the school playground.

Compared to my friend Steve's problem, dealing with my boss was a breeze. Jack Madden could joke privately about his brother, Father Greg from Sans Souci, but it was clear he respected, reverenced and perhaps even feared the successful brother on the other side of the George's River. Jack's clerical life had been overshadowed by his brother. They had been ordained on the same day in St Mary's Cathedral but Greg was a little older, much less sensitive, rougher, gruffer, somehow more practical and down to earth. These seemed peculiar traits for Jack to admire in any "God-bothering" brother. While the older one could curse and swear, tell people to "bite their bums" (and worse), build churches, increase collections, order people about without care or scruple – my parish boss was far less assertive. He was not at all certain that he was a success as a pastor and thought of himself as a below average struggler in the vineyards. He seemed unsure of himself. Some parishioners thought he was a little odd, but those who knew him well thought he also had a touch of holiness. There was no denying that Jack Madden said his prayers every day, or that he was dedicated to his people. Over the years he had developed a special devotion to St Francis de Sales whom he quoted at every opportunity, often at the dinner table.

Father Jack was always worrying out loud about the folding money on Sunday's plate-collections, which he thought acted like a barometer to measure his success or failure. Even a slight, momentary, downward trend might plunge him into depression. Every Sunday he would count the two bobs, the single shillings, the zacks and tray-bits, even the pennies and half-pennies, roll them religiously in brown paper, fold the precious pounds and half-pound notes into bundles and wrap them with elastic bands, count, recount, tally and record. If the money was up on the week before, Jack would rub his hands together and rejoice, always with the same remark –

"The faith is strong today, Father dear."

His innocent curate was somewhat scandalised the first few times he heard his parish priest announcing the results of the Sunday opinion poll. But slowly it came to him that this was his parish priest's little joke. I was always a bit slow on the uptake. Father Madden was not only Catholic, conservative and careful, he was also a little mean – perhaps even more pennywise than Norman Thomas, his Archbishop, though that would have been difficult.

The house where we lived stood on a high piece of ground across the street from the old church. Some shonky builder had constructed a shaky verandah along the front and down one side of the building. It was cluttered with grimy junk. The interior rooms were dark, the paint was peeling from walls and ceilings and there were a few old prints in dusty frames (prints of the Sacred Heart, Our Lady of Lourdes and St Francis de Sales). The place screamed for a good coat of paint, inside and out and if money could not be "wasted" on paint and brushes, the verandah, the central corridor, the bedrooms, the dining room and especially the kitchen, needed a good scrub. We were living in semi-squalor.

Father Madden refused to spend the parish money on our living quarters, or on the purchase of the little round hosts we used to distribute at communion. Benedictine nuns were slaving away, putting food on their table and sandals on their feet with the proceeds of their cottage industry, which manufactured tiny white wafers for every parish church in Sydney and throughout Australia, except for St Aloysius at Cronulla and maybe a few other places.

One of the first pastoral skills I was to learn from my parish priest, was the parsimonious production of communion hosts. I was to become the parish baker. So Father Madden showed me how to mix the white, watery mush, and how to cook thin sheets of unleavened bread on a special hot iron.

"Don't put too much of the stuff on the hot-plate. It will only stream out when you close down the press, oozing out the sides and wasting the mixture. Just a little bit will do."

Once the white sheets had been cooked like plastic, prised off the hot surface like pieces of corrugated iron, I had to learn how to cut them out into tiny, round wafers with a special scissors-style utensil. This process was labour intensive, but it saved parish money and my parish priest was like many of his brothers – he placed little value on his curate's time.

The end result was embarrassing for a newly commissioned celebrant of the Mysteries like me. We were handing out thin, brittle hosts which seemed to have no substance at all, as ethereal as fairy floss, melting to nothing in prayerful mouths before they could be swallowed.

My new parish life in Cronulla was simple. As my seminary trainers had taught me, I tried to rise early so I could meditate for twenty minutes or half an hour before "saying" Mass and perhaps recite some of my priestly Breviary, but I was not very successful. When left to myself, I tended to fall away in the discipline department. The twenty minutes was soon reduced to fifteen, then to five, to every second or third day, until the practice was subsumed in a vague feeling of guilt. Though it had sewn an undercurrent of guilt and anxiety into the fabric of my life, the seminary had not succeeded in gouging a routine into my spiritual soul.

Mass was still in Latin – so too was the recitation of the Breviary. I heard confessions on Saturday afternoons and again in the evening for some hours. When the children returned to school in January, Madden and I used to hear hundreds of confessions, in and out, quick as a flash, lists of venial sins, made-up faults, as the children were regimented to prepare themselves for First Friday devotions. This sheep-dipping process occurred every month without fail and I had to struggle to maintain some devotion and concentration throughout this repetitive, mind-boggling ritual. I wonder whether those little children ever developed the habit of going to confession regularly, whether any of them now remain bound to the practice or whether our labour ever bore the fruits we were led to expect. I suspect the numbing routine proved as effective as my seminary training had been.

I prepared sermons. I gave classes in religion for Catholic boys and girls at State schools. I acted as chaplain to the ladies of the Legion of Mary and supervised a youth club with the loquacious John Russell as my deputy sheriff. I visited the sick and elderly, and was made to feel generally pretty important. Everyone called me "Father" and sometimes they invited me to their wedding receptions where I generally knew nobody and where I felt rather awkward. In those days I belonged to a jesuitically inspired group known as "The Pioneers", who had pledged never to consume alcohol in any form and who were making reparation to the Sacred Heart of Jesus for the sins committed by drunkards. At these functions and in general, the people treated me with respect. That's what the nuns and brothers had taught them and that's what the system had taught me to expect. Priests were different.

In the idyllic setting of a string of golden beaches south of Sydney, I spent some leisure time, afternoons after the midday meal, Saturday mornings, Sundays after the Masses, on the sand and in the surf. The main streets, the grassy areas above the beaches and the pedestrian crossings were crowded, especially on the weekends. Trains unloaded processions of passengers, with surfboards and sun gear, onto the beaches. Sun-tanned, sun-bleached beauties, brown-bronzed men, some with bulging muscles, the others with silken, soft flesh overflowing their scanty costumes, gathered on the sand, playing together and frolicking in the surf. It was stressful for a man of the collar, anonymous in his budgie smugglers, who had been taught to maintain a strict control over what he saw. But he was losing the battle. The pagan world of flesh and freedom definitely had its attractions. My flock, young and old, seemed to enjoy themselves without experiencing the irritating itch of a puritanical conscience. The Cardinal's commission had transformed my dark seminary world into a wonderland of sunlight and flesh.

When the gates were opened and we were released from the seminary into the parishes of the land, my colleagues and I were still young and immature beyond our years. Few of us knew the ways of the world. I certainly didn't. Physically, we were at our peak. Our brothers and mates out on the streets were ready and keen to perform. The wild testosterone bugs were dancing in our brains and raging in the pulsating muscles below the belt. We were frisky stallions who had been suddenly set free into a paddock of healthy mares, after a long and lonely period in airless prayer stalls. Danger was lurking.

I used to walk to South Cronulla beach, just at the end of the street, with my towel over my shoulder. Occasionally I would meet a parishioner. "Good afternoon, Father", and after the usual formal, reserved greetings between unequals, we would continue on our different paths. A swim in the surf, a sit on the warm sand for a few minutes. There was nothing to detain me unless I wanted to ogle aliens at play. It was tempting but I knew that trouble was there, just out of reach. They were having fun and they seemed so uncomplicated. The women, the mothers, the girls all seemed so attractive to a novice spiritual gelding.

It was early in my clerical life that I was drawn into a near-death experience which could have ended my career as a priest. Well, perhaps it was not so much a near-death experience as an event which set off alarms bells in my head – a solemn warning of my fragility and of the landmines waiting for me along the way. WARNING – keep off the grass – stay inside the railings.

My parish priest had a policy that he hardly ever answered the door himself. A blast on the buzzer meant trouble and over the years Madden had learnt to steer clear of trouble. His main pastoral concern was to avoid any disturbance to his quiet life, so normally his new curate had to answer the door and greet the stranger.

During dinner I heard the buzzer blow and went to answer the front door. There in front of me, looking up at me was an uncommonly pretty young woman with long blond hair and doe eyes. Two small children were holding their mother by the hand. With tears dribbling down her cheeks, she told me that her husband had recently deserted his little family. Lost and lonely, poor and helpless, without any visible means of support, the mother sobbed into her handkerchief as her waifs looked on helplessly, wondering what the matter was with their mother.

I ushered them inside the presbytery, onto the enclosed verandah where cardboard cartons were packed up against the wall gathering dust. I offered my best sympathy and understanding to the distraught mother – in my ankle-long black cassock and from a safe distance – I listened to her tale of abandonment amid the rubbish. My heart was supposed to have been trained to appear warm, but to remain cold and to hover at a distance. But now, so soon after ordination, my heart began to melt. As I sat listening to this attractive mother in distress, I felt the danger signs almost immediately rising up from the depths. I was shocked to experience that the flutter, the waves of fascination, the surge of emotion and the urge to protect, had come over me so soon, so easily. I knew I had to dance carefully on the edge of this encounter, or better, to dance out of the circle. I had to be steely cold and careful. I had to maintain an appropriate aloofness. I was, nonetheless, shaken to realise how easily distracted a young priest like me could be. Holiness was not as transparent or as pure as I had been led to believe.

Within a few days the pretty woman returned for another session of weeping, re-telling her tale of heartless rejection and exposing her ache of abandonment. She had obviously found the first encounter helpful. I began to feel important – someone was seeking out my ministry. I found myself wanting to drag her back from the edge of her despair.

But the old, cunning parish priest was not so other-worldly. He was not so besotted with St Francis de Sales that he did not recognise what was happening. An attractive and vulnerable woman was finding some comfort in her encounters with his curate and his curate was flattered. He was finding a certain pleasure in the company of this young, wounded mother. It was easy to be available to someone so much in need and so beautiful.

Without consultation, but with a knowing wink and a nod, Father Madden said he thought it best for him to deal with the mother of sorrows. Thereafter, contrary to his policy, he answered the door and spoke briefly with the woman, but she did not return for a second session with him. She disappeared immediately from my sight and from my thoughts within a week or so.

I reflected later that this had been a lucky escape. My parish priest had known more than his prayers and maybe, the withered housekeeper had had a hand in protecting me and my priestly promises.

chapter three

1963-1965
MORE AND MORE STUDY

L ife was good. I had arrived, blessed with success. I was proud to be wearing the Roman collar and conducting the sacred rites which I had seen Eris O'Brien, Johnny Lander, Dennis Ryan and others perform during my childhood – the same rites as those who had gone before me in the seminary were celebrating.

After a few months at Cronulla, Monsignor Jimmy Madden was on the telephone inviting me to present myself for a prestigious doctorate degree in theology. Rome had recently endowed the seminary at Manly with the privilege of conferring ecclesiastical degrees on some of its promising students. To be invited to join the ranks of the doctoral elite was an honour and a mark of trust from those on high. I was well on my way to glory.

I spent a little more than two years as a student-researcher with David Pegrem (now deceased), David Walker (later to become Bishop Walker of Broken Bay), Peter McIniery of Brisbane (also decceased) and a Sylvestrine Benedictine, Dom Alberic. From our narrow, individual cells in the Graduate House, each of us enjoyed our own breathtaking view straight down the harbour, across the heads over to Watson's Bay and beyond. Under God's orders and without the necessary training, we were expected to occupy our days, weeks and months on end in the lonely task of original research. We then produced a lengthy and scholarly written thesis and finally, presented the results of our work before a panel of judges. In addition, we had to attend a series of high-powered lectures which were delivered by the professors of the Faculty.

Father Julian Miller was one of those lecturing professors and a particularly flamboyant member of the Faculty. While he was an attractive personality with unusually liberal opinions, which he did not keep to himself, Julian was not blessed with an academic temperament. He lectured to all the seminarians on the twisted history of Christianity and the Catholic Church and, always with good grace and humour, he would entertain his listeners, sometimes touching lightly on the subject at hand.

Father Miller was also deputed to conduct intensive tutorials for postgraduate students. Once a week, at the front of the sandstone Gothic building on the hill, we would listen dreamily as one of us read aloud passages from Eris O'Brien's *The Foundations of the Catholic Church in Australia*. The baton would be changed from one to another as Julian observed a listener drifting off. I was often called on to do my bit. As I recall, there was no discussion, and certainly no attempt to evaluate the scattered material which was presented to us. We (academic neophytes) were scandalised at the time and affronted that valuable opportunities to learn were being wasted. Julian was simply bowling his arm over gently, with minimum effort, with no speed or spin. But on the second thoughts, which came to me in my later years, our professor was simply filling in time and "obeying" the ritual requirements of the Roman ecclesiastical statutes – they were not meant to be taken too seriously.

In other ways, Julian was a gust of fresh air through the corridors of Manly. He did not function on that formal, superior, clerical, wooden level which others tended to adopt. He was full of bonhomie and points of view with a different sense of values, and an ability, in a patrician manner, to "take the Mickey" out of the other professors and students. His sense of what was important, trivial, substantial, central, peripheral and inconsequential was beguiling. One would hear him speak with another professor, perhaps even a bishop, on such revolutionary topics as – English in the liturgy, more power for women in the Church, ecumenical liturgical services with Protestant communities, married clergy, voicing the "bleeding obvious" and giving expression to the dictates of common sense – careless of the reaction he was causing. He was not constrained by any sense of being a junior member of the team. In all respects, Julian was his own man and it was no secret that many of the older clergy and threatened bishops did not trust him.

Looking for a research topic was like fishing in a deep, dark well – I had no idea what I was meant to do. In the course of our studies, we had not been encouraged to exercise our own initiative. After many arid months, and in desperation, I wrote, in English, to my theological hero. Yves Congar was a Dominican theologian in Paris whom Rome had once considered a troubling heretic and who had been exiled to England, when the ecclesiastical heat was on him in France. In 1960 he had been summoned out of exile by Pope John XXIII to assist in the preparation of the Second Vatican Council and had become one of the giants of the modern Church. He was the author of countless books and scholarly articles. This internationally renowned theologian answered by return mail – in French, on a narrow, blue aerogram pointing me (a budding theologian at the ends of the earth) in the direction of St Irenaeus of Lyons.

As early as the second century, Irenaeus had developed a wondrous theological vision of the order and euphony which governed all things – the harmony in creation, in revelation, in the Church, between the message and figures of the Old Testament Bible and those of apostolic times. So soon after Christ's disappearance from the earth, he had developed lyrical, allegorical interpretations of passages of Scripture, witnessing to his belief in a mysterious unity within a baffling cosmic diversity. This ancient author saw the whole story, from the creation of the cosmos and our appearance on the earth to Jesus walking the land and the establishment of the Church, as one, coherent, harmonious plan which involved all visible and invisible reality, all in a continual process of evolution.

The Christian mystery of redemption has come to be presented, at least to many Western Christians, as a barbaric process whereby through dying, Christ repaid the heavy debt which man had incurred by sinning. Christ had appeased an angry God who had demanded satisfaction for the infinite insult of rebellion and disobedience. This was a primitive attempt, popular in the Middle Ages and among the reformers and even today among the fundamentalists and evangelicals, to explain and reconcile the baffling realities of evil, creation and redemption. This "explanation" of the Christian mysteries always seemed (to me at least) to be rather crass and ugly – resting on a horrible image of God.

As I was to find out, Irenaeus had had a different way of viewing the world. He believed that the whole historical process of redemption was characterised, not by any act of original sin, but by the original, pre-historic event of creation. His God was continually creating, evolving, and perfecting his work. Jesus was God's perfect creation and his promise for the future fulfillment of his work. His was a vision of redemption and of Christianity which could thrill the human spirit.

Yves Congar had introduced me to something important. The theological vision of Irenaeus was rediscovered later by other theologians, but in the early 1960's, I was part of an awakening to a cosmic and creational theology. Insights were more fully developed later by theologians such as Thomas Berry, Matthew Fox and Jurgen Moltmann, and expanded to embrace creation and the world, with an enthusiasm uncharacteristic of many Christians. These thinkers were able to present a religious dimension to beauty, sex, joy and wonder in a Christian world which had been tainted by a gnostic hatred of the flesh and the visible. Here, was an ideological basis for the forces of conservation and recycling – a launching pad to inspire a concerted opposition to the excesses of a consumer society, for those of us who wanted to live in the real world, among scientists and poets.

I laboured long and hard, on my own, in my narrow monk-cell at the Graduate House in an attempt to explore the cosmic Christology of Irenaeus – a subject which became the topic of my doctoral thesis. I was not a natural academic and though I had not been taught the skills of research, I was determined to succeed. Six months passed. I was trying to keep my head down, visiting the library, assembling a list of books which might be on the point, reading articles, recording ideas in an exercise book, preserving insights on pieces of paper, maintaining a rudimentary card system which I kept in alphabetical order in a cardboard shoebox. I wandered here and there, struggling to translate articles from French with the aid of a little pocket-dictionary, accumulating hundreds, thousands of pieces of paper. I was creating organisational and mental chaos.

Suddenly I was summoned to my thesis director, Dr Walsh, and summarily informed that he wanted to see a few initial chapters of my work within the following ten days. I doubled my efforts and began writing but without discipline or direction, stringing together insights and information scattered throughout my clumsy system. Within the allotted time, I delivered thirty or forty pages of sweated material to my supervisor and waited. Of course, I was keen to receive encouragement.

Dr Walsh invited me into his study overlooking the northern beaches. No words of encouragement. He had read my preliminary material – badly written and superficial – in a word, "atrocious". If this was all I could do in six months, I should think seriously of abandoning any ambition of continuing with my studies. Perhaps I should return to a parish. I didn't have what it took.

I was crushed. I had expected some encouragement at least. On reflection (and I am certainly not saying he was wrong), even if Dr Walsh could not in conscience have expressed appreciation, he might have examined my work more closely, critiqued it, analysed it and provided some guidance. Instead he clubbed me over the head with a few harsh adjectives and sent me away. My life was suddenly in crisis. Perhaps I was not up to standard. Maybe I should consider turning my back on further studies, returning to a parish and doing what I might be good at. Research was hard, and the academic life was lonely. I was tempted to give up. I suffered a period of gloom, lying on my narrow bed throughout the day, unable to do anything but gaze vacantly at the ceiling.

To his credit, after he had left Manly and the priesthood, Kevin Walsh wrote a brief note from the School of General Studies at the Australian National University where he was studying. He offered his sympathy on hearing that my sister was so ill, and passed on messages of encouragement about my lectures to young nuns at Lavender Bay. He said he was going through the agony of trying to write.

> "As I do so, I think of the way I so cruelly compounded the difficulties sometimes of those whose work I had a hand in, and I learned remorse. My own supervisors, one of them especially, are what I wasn't; and I learn from them too."

At the time, I had assumed that Dr Walsh had been a supremo – super-intelligent, strongly committed and experienced. I had been wrong. He was playing a demanding role on the clerical stage, but in his own world he was as fragile and inadequate as I was in mine. I came to admire his generosity and humility.

It took more than two years to complete my thesis study. They were long and lonely years, interspersed with occasional fun. We occasionally played golf, I played a few games of rugby with the college students on a grassed terrace overlooking Manly beach and from time to time I would accompany Peter McIniery on his daily, cross-country run to North Head. He was too fast for me and I would lag behind, lumbering along while he floated across the bitumen, circled the North Head area and ran back down the gentle slope to the Graduate House. We were exercising our bodies, learning to keep them under subjection and trying to cope with the boring routine of a student's existence.

The doctoral students from the Sydney Archdiocese did not receive a survival stipend from the cathedral. While the others were supported by their bishops, we Sydney-siders had no visible means of support. His Eminence, being himself a parsimonious fellow, did not believe in making it easy for his young priests. He was given to wagering match sticks in a game of cards with his sisters on Monday nights. He did not smoke, or drink, or own a car, or buy books – his only vice was praying.

While my colleagues in Sydney were receiving a living wage of fourteen pounds a month, I was expected to find my own way and beg for my supper. So after a few months I joined Brian Cosgrave's exclusive team of preachers who travelled from parish to parish on Sundays, preaching an appeal for money to support the *Propagation of the Faith* in Rome, as well as the work of overseas missionaries It was hard labour preaching with fervour and energy at every Sunday Mass. We were not welcome in some of the Sydney parishes because the collection tended to extract large amounts of available funds, which some parish priests resented.

As I developed my ability for extracting money and exploited my spirit of competition to do better each Sunday than the Dominican or Redemptorist preachers, I became one of Cosgrove's more successful employees and he paid me handsomely. Instead of the five pound stipend for supplying in the parish, the Propagation of the Faith organization rewarded my efforts with as much as twenty pounds for a weekend's work. For a short time, and in comparison with my classmates in the parishes, I was on clover.

Each weekend it was an education visiting different parishes in the diocese and observing how the clergy lived. I began to understand that young priests had to be able to survive in emotional squalor. By and large, the presbyteries were dark places, cluttered with old-fashioned, badly preserved chairs, beds, sideboards and tables. Rooms in drab colours, paint peeling off walls and, in some places, exhausted prints of paintings of religious or Australian subjects were displayed behind mouldy glass panels. I never saw an original painting in any of the presbyteries I visited. The guest-room in some of the places also acted as storerooms for cardboard boxes, empty bookshelves or a spare mattress. Conversation at the dinner table and in front of the television set was formal. Laughs were scarce – though, as I remember it now, I too, was a serious, little priest. Our business was sin and damnation: the spirit of frivolity, of fun and general gaiety was absent from presbyteries on Saturday evenings and Sunday mornings.

Back at the Graduate House, our daily routine was governed by morning Mass, three meals prepared and poked through the servery grill by phantom nuns, and the private recitation throughout the day of the Breviary. Apart from occasional recreation, my days were filled with study and research. For weeks on end, hounded by the dogs of failure, stuck down by depression, I would lie stretched on my bed, looking at the ceiling, wondering how I came to be in such a lonely, grey world.

At the end of the process, the seminary students decked in their cassocks and red sashes, gathered in the principal lecture hall. What was ahead of them might prove tedious, but it was better than lectures and real work. The established professors of the Theological Faculty processed into the hall in seniority, academic gowns over cassocks, followed by an archbishop or two, and the Eminence who acted as the Head of the Faculty though I suspect he had hardly read a serious book since his ordination. He was good at dressing up in his extravagant red robes and officiating at lengthy ceremonies.

Solemnly, I mounted the rostrum, seated myself under a large canvass of Our Lady ascending into heaven, and began to proclaim to the assembled undergraduates, graduates and staff, an eight-page summary of the result of my two-year study which I had painstakingly composed in Latin. I continued, in loud and pompous tones, for about forty minutes, undisturbed by questions, applause or objections.

When my presentation was complete, a few chosen members of staff asked a number of questions, again in Latin. Nervously, I answered in the mother-tongue of the Church. Monsignor Veech, the vice-president, made some unpleasant half-observations in the midst of huffs and grunts, before Monsignor Madden, as president of the Faculty, invited members of the student body to question me further. They sat with glazed eyes – none sufficiently informed to draft a simple inquiry. They were overcome with the solemnity of the moment, or perhaps with ennui. Then the assembled professors and dignitaries withdrew, pretended to discuss my case for a brief period, and returned to award a *"magna cum laude"* grading to applause, followed by cakes and scones.

I was a Doctor of Divinity and twenty-six years old. My whole life had been spent preparing for something special. But was this it?

chapter four

1965
A SECOND PARISH FOR A BEGINNER

After I had been awarded my degree, I opened an envelope from the Cathedral containing my new orders. I travelled north from Manly, up the peninsula, to take up another parish appointment. Instead of labouring in a cottage industry at Cronulla manufacturing altar breads, I was employed at Avalon, assisting my new boss, collecting, stacking and selling empty beer bottles.

As a schoolboy in Cremorne, I had used my homemade billy-cart to collect bundles of old newspapers from neighbours and sell them for a penny a pound to the fish shops at Neutral Bay Junction, or to the butcher round the corner in Spofforth Street. Seizing every available small business opportunity had been part of my growing up. Coming from a working class family, I had learnt the value of a penny. From the back of his horse-and-dray, I had assisted the bread carter to deliver his loaves and hot buns around the district. I had worked for Mr McLeod delivering heavy blocks of ice before Silent Night refrigerators came on the market. Beer bottles had also been a ready source of revenue. I used to sell them to the "bottle-o" as he made his rounds through the back lanes in his horse-drawn cart. I was trained and ready for anything, but I had not imagined that my vocation to the priesthood would involve a re-run of this small business activity.

I had landed in another beach parish. The jewel necklace of southern beaches from Bondi to Cronulla gave way to Bilgola, Avalon, Whale Beach, Palm Beach – strung together by a series of wind-swept, rugged headlands. The priests' house at Avalon was like the residence I had inhabited at Cronulla – drab and dilapidated and cold in winter, hot in summer.

My parish priests – Hughie Boland at Avalon and Jack Madden at Cronulla – had both been extruded from the same mould, both products of a decayed and rusty seminary system. Like a number of the students and priests of my era who had come to the seminary with one of their brothers, Boland had an older brother, Father Tracy, who was the parish priest at St Augustine's Balmain. Both of them were products of the old school, down to their braces and garters. Hughie was a man tough on himself, strict towards his curate and parishioners, tight with money, narrow in his theology and with a bleak view of a world full of pagans and heretics. He was blunt, at times to the point of rudeness, and a follower of the Roman way, even when he was dressed in gumboots and overalls – tall, awkward, military in his bearing, distant and shy, with balding reddish hair and a rather angry, penetrating, blue-eyed stare. He seemed most comfortable in his angular body when he was in his overalls stacking bottles or digging trenches.

We did not know one another. We had not met before, but he had heard about me from some of his colleagues. He was not certain he was happy to have an assistant straight out of Manly, one with airs and graces, with a theology degree, with new, perhaps revolutionary and revolting ideas. Life was going to be different for him in his little presbytery.

The presbytery was a simple fibro beach house which had been knocked together years before, in the sand dunes behind the beach. There was a cramped, laminated kitchen and an oblong lounge-room-cum-dining-room-cum-television-room which was the community area and which had a view through salted sliding glass windows over to the sand-hills of Avalon Beach. The one large bedroom, with two doors leading off the community area, was in a terrible mess – cluttered with piles of old papers and boxes spread everywhere, a desk at one end covered with musty receipts and scraps of yellowed paper which had lain there for decades, and a single untidy bed. Hughie had no filing system and no secretarial assistance.

At the back of the house, across a narrow corridor opposite the kitchen, was a tiny guest-room. If one stood in the middle of this space with arms extended, one could almost touch the adjacent walls. This hot fibro box contained another narrow bed and an old wardrobe. A bush outside had grown hard against the window obscuring the grimy view onto Central Road. This was to be the new curate's cell.

I threw my suitcase on the bed, unpacked some serious books from my VW, closed the ill-fitting door and began to cast an eye around my private space. Someone had, a century before, painted the walls a grey-lilac colour and, to avoid the cost of a different tin of paint, had brushed the ceiling over with the same colour. An unprotected light bulb hung at the end of a black cord from the ceiling, thick with dust. Covering the floor was a bluish grey felt carpet which rose in little ripples under my feet as I stepped around inside the room.

I was Avalon's first curate and as I later came to learn, the area where I would sleep and study, where I would prepare my Sunday sermons, had doubled as a kennel for the former parish priest's scruffy dog. After a few days I noticed that my pale priestly legs were covered in itchy hives. It usually takes a little time for mundane matters to register on my consciousness, as I am generally insensitive to my surroundings. Heat and cold pass over me without much notice. As a rule, I don't care much whether it is raining or the sun shines. But slowly it dawned on me that there was something not quite right in my new quarters. I stripped off the bed covers and the sheets and examined the blankets. After number forty-three, I stopped counting the fleas. Hughie had been on his own, batching in his large parish, building churches and schools on the cheap and not wasting much time or effort preparing to accommodate his new house-guest. The cell I had been allotted was unsuitable even for a humble curate, though it was not Bangladesh and missionary conditions, or a cave dwelling for one of the desert fathers, or martyrdom, and there were indulgences and graces to be earned by uncomplaining acceptance.

Within a few months of my arrival, Father Boland commenced a two-storey extension on the back of the old fibro building and with the aid of his faithful tradesmen, he completed it within record time. He always did things on the cheap and this new building was rather makeshift. To save the cost of an architect, Hughie had drawn the plans himself. He had engaged the discounted services of local Catholic tradesmen and worked with them as their labourer and he had chosen fibro as his building material of preference. On completion, I inherited two rooms, a bedroom and a study on the bottom floor.

In the meantime, I was occupying my narrow cell, sleeping almost side-by-side with my parish priest, with only a thin, fibro partition between us. I could hear him snore in the night, I knew when he turned over and, on occasions, I was almost blasted out of bed by the thunder of passing wind. Answering God's call to spend your life as a priest made some unusual demands. It was unnerving for a young priest to be living in such intimacy with a stranger.

I soon discovered that my new boss was an austere man. He hardly ever drank alcohol and he ate sparingly. He drove an old Rover bomb and dressed untidily. In truth, he was an eccentric senior bachelor who had given his life to the institution. While the local people mostly admired him (many even liked him), he was a distant figure in their lives. He seldom smiled and never laughed, or hummed a tune, or skipped, or danced. Had the people of the northern peninsula thought about their parish priest for a moment, hardly any of them would have understood him.

We batched to begin with, until Father Boland employed the services of an elderly widow from Condobolin whom he instructed to prepare and serve the same meals which we had been eating before her arrival. I forget the details of what we used to eat in the evenings – steak and kidney pie was on the menu – fish and chips from the local shop on Fridays, a shoulder of lamb, or smoked haddock with boiled potatoes and carrots. We always had the same luncheon fare – two wedges of tomato each, a few lettuce leaves and two or three slices of corn-beef washed down with a cup of tea. Wine was never served in the presbytery. As a special treat sometimes, in the late afternoon on a hot summer's day, we might drink a few glasses of beer. Father Boland made sure he counted the bottles and stacked them with the others down the side of the presbytery. We lived together in the presbytery in a frugal manner, just like I had lived my life in the seminary from the age of twelve, just like Boland had lived his whole life – military style.

The carpet in the communal area of the presbytery was faded and worn. The dusty, rusty under-felt was exposed in areas of constant traffic – for example, near the entrance, and the carpet in the area around the dinner table had stretched into uneven corrugations. There was an old television set at one end of the room with a few weary looking armchairs positioned strategically in front of it. Hughie used to sit there in full view, in the main room, interviewing parishioners, giving instructions in the faith and filling in marriage forms as I tiptoed past him to go to the kitchen or to my claustrophobic cave.

This house had been Hughie's home for a number of years, but apart from a few framed and faded holy pictures stuck on the grey wall, there was no sign of a personal touch. He had made no attempt to create a home for himself in Avalon, or to impose his personality on his living space – no paintings, no family pictures, no novels or poetry books spread about, no family heirloom, no piece of fine furnishing, no feature wall, no colourful curtains. We were living cheek-by-jowl in a wasteland just like all the other priests in their presbyteries throughout Sydney, and in fact throughout Australia.

Conversation at meal times was strained. Although Father Boland did his best to engage me in some table-talk, and although I tried to listen with a sympathetic and respectful ear, we were never really present to one another. Being a senior parish priest, Hughie shared the senior clergy's suspicious disdain for what they imagined was happening in the seminary at Manly. The students were revolting. They were taking the reform suggestions of the Second Vatican Council rather too seriously. He had heard rumours from other clergy and they were all wary of intellectuals like the priests on the seminary staff. Little did they know! They had heard that some of the riff-raff coming out of the seminary did not believe that Adam and Eve were real historical persons, or that the world had been created in six days. There was always some tension in the air.

My practice of body-surfing and sun-baking on the beaches of his parish also made my boss uneasy. He was disturbed by the shameless nakedness on Sydney beaches, by floppy flesh exposed. He imagined women in brief bikinis were like carcasses hanging on hooks in butcher shops. He did not visit the beaches himself, though on occasions over lunch he described, in lurid detail, the beach scenes of his imagination. The peninsula, where he was in charge of all things spiritual, was a danger zone, an area of temptation, of diabolical distraction. There was something ungodly, impure, something uncontrollable out there on the sand and in the tumbling surf.

I hesitated to tell my new boss that years before I had met him, I had first witnessed the intimate act of copulation in the sand-hills of his parish. I was on an altar-boys' picnic at the time. We used to travel each year in a double-decker bus from Neutral Bay to Avalon, under the close supervision of the priest in our parish, Father John Lander. We used to play cricket on the grassy area near the surf club, wrestle on the sand, and swim in the rock-pool. The sand-hills have since been cultivated and reclaimed, but in the 1940's the area behind Avalon beach was a sandy wilderness.

While I was chasing one of the other innocent altar-boys in the dunes, playing cowboys and Indians, I had seen a man with his pants down round his knees, grunting and pumping up and down on a girl who was not wearing any clothes on the bottom half of her body. I had no idea what was happening, but it looked awfully suspicious. Something to do with the virtue of purity. I diverted my eyes immediately. I knew instinctively that what they were doing was private and it felt like something forbidden. I looked back wondering what was going on there in the gritty sand, out of sight of the other little angels and our saintly guardian. I made no report to Father Lander at the time or to Father Boland twenty years later.

On at least one occasion, my conservative parish priest unwittingly scandalised me and it was some years before I began to understand and appreciate what he had done.

A pretty young teenage girl in the parish had fallen in love with one of the local lads who had a chronic drug problem. The couple were members of good Catholic families and when they proposed to get married, both sets of parents, who were good friends, went into a spin. In a panic, the two men, hand-in-hand with their wives, visited the parish priest for advice. (That is what people did in those old days before the Church was riddled with appalling scandals.) The local parish priest was an important figure in the district and they were thought to be wise and educated in the ways of the world. I had thought my boss was unworldly and inflexible. Many might have thought he would be the worst person to give any advice on such a complicated and delicate family matter, but they would have been wrong. His assistant priest, fresh from the seminary, would have been the worst of all councillors. Father Boland's advice was -

"Whatever you do, don't let them marry. Let them live
together. Let them bonk for all they're worth. Let's hope that
in a few months, in a year, they will have cleansed their
systems of this madness. The sexual passion will pass and
then each of them can continue on with their lives. A marriage
at this stage would be disastrous."

When both fathers told me what the parish priest had said, I was
shocked. How could a man of the cloth possibly give such immoral
advice, ignoring the sexual teaching of his Church? We had heard the
message from Rome – every act of intercourse, every intimate touch,
every arousing kiss outside of marriage, was a mortal sin. According to
the Church, the sexual act itself and the least sexual advance, every
sexual adventure was to be strictly confined within the matrimonial
home and restricted to married couples.

(Remember those distant days? The institution has a lot to answer
for. There must be many victims from the 50's and 60's who are
burning in hell. I wonder how the authorities will go about rescuing
these unfortunate souls and bring them home. They might have to
negotiate a prisoner exchange with some of their protected criminals –
the Vatican bankers and clerical paedophiles.)

How could this holy man in Avalon, in all good conscience, advise
this young couple from Catholic families to live in sin? I could not
accept it. When I was living in the presbyteries with Father Madden
and later with Father Boland, I was just a fledging priest, on my trainer
wheels. I had been force-fed on doctrine. I had lapped up the lectures
on sex which Monsignor Jimmy Madden had delivered in Latin during
our final year when we were already ordained deacons, when we were
considered mature enough to listen without the inevitable erections.
The sessions had been pretty tame – no pictures or diagrams, no four-
letter words or dirty stories, no adjectives or adverbs. Anyway, most of
the attendees could not understand Latin.(I remember that during one
of those hot afternoon lectures on sex, one member of the class who
was far from fluent in Latin, secretly tuned in on his earphones to the
final of the Rugby League competition.)

Now, looking back, I see the wisdom of Father Boland's advice. I am
still surprised, but glad, that an old priest like him could clear his mind
of the entanglements of crazy, petty moral imperatives and take a

common sense stand to solve a very common, but ticklish, problem. I wonder what other advice, unknown to me, he used to offer to his flock. I'd love to know.

Though Hughie proved a little difficult and somewhat suspicious, though he hated me coming home late at night, tiptoeing through his presbytery, past his window, and easing myself gently into bed within inches of him there on the other side of the partition, though life in the presbytery was formal and strained, my time in Avalon was often fun-filled and care-free. We were secluded at the end of the peninsula, far from the centre of town and the cathedral, with sun and surf, sand and sailing on Pittwater, gin and tonics on decks overlooking the Pacific, parishioners gathered on beaches under floral umbrellas, smeared with abundant oil. We were in paradise and those were heady days for a twenty-eight-year old bachelor.

It was in Avalon that I became a young adult and began to experience a sense of liberation and of personal identity. I also began to understand what I had signed up for and what I was missing out on. I was facing a life of loneliness, with no hope of intimacy, without a wife, without children of my own.

I recall a clear moment of illumination. One Sunday, I was standing tall in the pulpit, facing down a church crowded with young married couples and their restless children and the sparkling surf was beating the sand a few hundred yards away through the large, clear windows to my left. I was sufficiently relaxed to observe the faces of believers looking up at me as I stood there above them, in my flowing vestments, breaking open the jewelry box of the Scriptures and revealing their hidden treasures. I saw people listening to me with relaxed attention. I realised, perhaps for the first time in my life, that people liked me. These people liked me. From that moment, unconsciously, I began to put aside my constructed image. Rather than keeping people at arm's length and protecting myself from little jibs and criticisms, I began to relax my guard, to accept simple compliments gracefully, to receive the confirmation others were willing to offer.

It was easy to be popular in the parish at Avalon. Being so stolid and strict, Father Boland made it easy. I was the young blood who had launched the local youth club. I organised the rowdy dances on Saturday nights, arranging the live-bands and keeping control of the surfies on the verge of trouble. I enjoyed the heady feeling of being at the centre of the Avalon community – accepted, welcomed, treated as important and addressed by my new-found title, "Doctor Geraghty". I was stupid enough to think it was important and vain enough to be thrilled to hear others acknowledging my academic status. It was a sin to be so puffed up – but only a venial one.

I welcomed the natural warmth and admiration of the children at the local school. The nuns at the convent in their dowdy Good Samaritan habits were distant but respectful, and they trained the boys and girls to love their priests. The secret of success seemed simple – I did not talk money from the pulpit as Father Boland did; I never frightened the horses; I tried to give people what they felt comfortable with – no sackcloth and ashes, no heroic challenges, no locust and wild honey when people were eating strawberries and caviar, as many of them were, though certainly not all. I attended picnics across Pittwater, at The Basin, with the families of the members of the St Vincent de Paul, racing up and down Pittwater in speed-boats. I was interested in people and their stories. I smiled. I laughed. I listened. It was easy.

Boland was a man's man – hard, strong and reliable. He mixed, albeit awkwardly, with the men in the St Vincent de Paul Society, with Jack and Colin and the others, but he seldom drank with them and on the rare occasions when he did, he was moderate, verging on the monastic.

He avoided the company of women. He had no idea how to carry on a conversation with the offspring of Eve, with those who had different body parts and who painted their faces. What was going on in their pretty heads was a mystery to him – and to his curate. He was suspicious of women folk and awkward in their presence. They were unpredictable and dangerous creatures. They could catch you off guard and tempt you to do disgusting things. They could lead a good priest off into the bushes, and often did. We had to be careful because they all had that genetic link to Adam's wayward partner. It was better to have as little to do with them as possible. My parish priest seemed to believe in his heart that it really would have been better had God dreamed up some other method of procreation. The exchange of bodily fluids in the middle of the night was almost unimaginable, though some people had to make the sacrifice – thank God, not us. Happily our vows relieved us of such a revolting, sweaty activity.

Though I had lived a major part of my life in the company of men, almost exclusively priests and trainee priests, and only men drawn from a very limited cohort, I began to realise at Avalon that I enjoyed the company of women. They were easy to talk to. They seemed to share more easily. They were closer to the earth, more in tune with the realities of living, more radical, more open to change. They had more to say. They were fun. I was on a steep learning curve and I should have recognised the danger signs.

In retrospect, however, my personal life in Avalon turned out to be a struggle. Everyone else, except Boland and me, seemed to have a dancing partner. Some were moving in unison to the same tune, and others were completely out of sync. Some were still in love, others were dancing on one another's toes. Everyone else, young and old, seemed to have a companion to talk to on the beach or in a restaurant, someone to share with, to argue with, to laugh with, to look at.

I found myself under constant attack from unwelcome hormonal drives and urges. Pretty girls stretched out on the sand, in a circle on the beach, sun-baking, or screaming with excitement as they jumped through rolling, sparkling waves, wrapping their legs and arms around their partners as they floated together in the surf, preoccupied with each other.

I was all of twenty-eight, going on sixteen. Out of the hot-house and on my own, I was struggling with the forces churning around within me, confronting for the first time the life-long implications of the celibate decision I had made so easily in the ignorance and isolation of the seminary. I was surprised (and somewhat ashamed at the time, though I remember now with some amusement) to find that during Sunday Mass, sometimes at the most solemn moments of the celebration, my gaze fell, just for a fleeting moment, on the features, the face, the rounded shapes, the legs, the breasts and the buttocks of a young Avalon mother surrounded by her children. Some of the teenage girls in my youth club were obviously blooming and could easily attract the furtive attention of the local curate. I had to hold myself in check in case I came under their spell. I had to keep bringing myself back into the zone of my ministry, refocusing my mind on what I was doing, reminding myself of the burden I had accepted to carry.

I was not used to living among the female species. Suddenly they were there, in my face, all around me, whereas before, they had been away, out of sight, over there. Now I was in their company and I was expected to talk to them. I had not anticipated that I would be so distracted while I was delivering my homily from the pulpit or distributing communion. No wonder old Father Cusack had insisted that the Mosman ladies wear long sleeves in his church, that they should never enter his sacred space with their faces painted. He obviously could not stand the strain of the soft, silky arms and the temptations of lacey lingerie.

You might think my life in the paradise of the northern beaches had little to do with the Gospel. I would agree. As a young employee in the workings of a large institution, I was learning how to be part of the show, how to maintain some level of personal satisfaction and human happiness. At Avalon, I was an institutional man, charged with keeping the troops fed, the cattle quiet and providing a service which the people in the pews had come to expect of their religious leaders – Mass on Sunday, confessions on Saturday, classes for the poor Catholics who sent their children to the state schools, blessings, speeches, baptisms on Sunday afternoons, social graces, a steady boat, pious platitudes, no anger, no revolution, only the soft Gospel of acceptance and the message of "meek and mildness" – without the muscle or the sweat, without any terrible ambiguous ache in the stomach.

But unbeknown to me, I was not a company man.

chapter five

1967

A SEMINARY PROFESSOR

I can hear the Cardinal, Sir Norman Thomas Gilroy, dictating the letter to his secretary in his strained, throaty voice:

"Dear Father,
I have much pleasure in appointing you to the teaching staff at
St Columba's College Springwood.
Will you please speak to Monsignor Veech to learn of him
what is required of you?"

He probably did not know what he was asking me to do. I hope he didn't. Speaking to the Monsignor would not prove as easy as Norman might have expected, or as rewarding. Tom Veech was one of Norman's contemporaries, a colleague in the priesthood, a minor prince of the Church and his choice as the rector of his junior seminary.

In February 1967 I received an abrupt note from Monsignor Thomas McNiven Veech to inform me that I would be lecturing the seminarians at Springwood in liturgical studies and social ethics. Not a word of advice or encouragement for the new member of his crack squad. Just a short paragraph on a tiny page in his minuscule, spidery handwriting. I knew nothing about the history and theology of liturgy or about social ethics, but I knew Dr Veech and he knew me.

Tommy (Veech) had lectured me for a number of years in church history when I was a student at Manly and in early 1965, he had acted as an assessor of my doctoral thesis. His behaviour on the day I had defended my thesis in the *Aula Maxima* where he had been at his destructive best, remained in my memory. I am not claiming that criticism of my doctoral work was not warranted, it was. But the Monsignor seized the opportunity to mock and scoff, to scratch and wound. I should acknowledge that many others did not, and do not share my harsh assessment of this man. They thought that while he was probably an eccentric and a little peculiar, he was a refined, well-educated and extremely shy man. I do not dispute these characteristics, but personally I found him to be a most disagreeable and unpleasant person and we were destined to spend the next five years or so together in the mountains.

I was returning to my old haunts. In the 50's I had spent the first seven years of my priestly formation in this institution. I was not yet thirty years old when, as the new junior professor, I drove through the massive sandstone gates of St Columba's. I was excited to be commencing this new phase of my life. I felt I had been chosen. Being a member of the seminary staff, even the junior member, was a privilege.

Tommy Veech was in his mid-sixties when I caught up with him again at Springwood. After taking his doctorate in history at Louvain University in Belgium, he had lectured for years in the seminary at Manly, principally on medieval and renaissance periods and on the fathers of the early Church. He had been a gifted entertainer and much appreciated by the body of students. We were used to dry fodder which was hard to swallow and he had developed a very amusing lecture style. On several days each week, for fifty minutes, he would sit in the high tub in front of a class of a hundred young men and conducted an imaginary conversation with a principal personage out of the pages of our Church history. Tertullian, Origen (the famous biblical scholar who the historian Eusebius would have us believe removed his testicles in search of sanctity), Augustine, Jerome, Erasmus, Burchard (the secretive, scandal-mongering diarist who had recorded the machinations and conversations of the Renaissance popes), and Luther and his long-suffering friend Phillip Melanchthon – these monologues had been a welcome relief from the tedium of scholastic philosophy and theology.

At Springwood, Tommy Veech was the man-in-charge and the professors and students, all of us, could see that he conducted himself in a most erratic fashion. We witnessed his mood swings and his sudden, unpredictable outbursts. He had developed a most peculiar practice of rocking rapidly, rhythmically, back and forth on his heels and toes, bowing profoundly, straightening up suddenly, straining as though he wanted to stop but couldn't. He used to engage in this ritual dance on the edge of the football field, on the drive in front of the college, in the privacy of his own room, in the common-room before a blank television screen, behind a tree in the bushes, or in the chapel. We used to pretend that nothing out of the ordinary was happening, but we knew this was the bizarre behaviour of a most unusual senior cleric. The students had taken to calling him "Boo" after the strangely autistic character in the novel *To Kill a Mockingbird*.

Tommy had his favourites, and they could do no wrong. They were mostly sporting characters, usually gifted at rugby and perhaps a little off-beat. Vincent Kiss as a student, and later as a young priest, was one of the elect. And the Monsignor also had his pet hates, though it was difficult to comprehend why he would like one person beyond reason and dislike another. As far as I could see, his selection was founded on whim and trivia – the cut of someone's jib; whether someone addressed him unexpectedly; whether a boy was too keen, or too docile, too casual, too anxious to please; his manner of walking and of talking; whether he was soft in the Rugby forwards, or not elusive enough in the back-line. Where you went to school also seemed to be important – GPS schools carried weight.

I should confess that I was never a member of the blessed, or even of the unwashed, faceless crowd who were able to pass under the enemy radar. I was one of the disliked. I arrived at Springwood at the end of February ready to begin work and apart from a few non-descript words in the first few days, the Monsignor did not address more than a word to me for approximately six months. It was as though I did not exist. He was determined to put me in my place from the start – at the bottom of the heap. He would watch me as I went about my work, but he chose not to speak to me until he was good and ready.

Though the Monsignor may have had good reason to dislike me, I was not the only seminary resident to suffer from his cold shoulder and his outbursts of spleen, as the following story shows.

St Joseph, the husband of Mary, stood frozen on a pedestal in the shadows, at the top end of the main corridor. The pillar of plaster was five foot tall and clothed in colourful vestments, more in the style of the Middle Ages than of Palestine in zero A.D. Joseph held a blossoming white lily in his right hand as a symbol of his purity, a sign of a haunting celibacy in his marriage, and from the look on his painted face he seemed inoffensive, even apologetic. There was a diminished level of testosterone flowing through him and he appeared far too old to be married to a teenage virgin. The bushy beard seemed to suggest that this fellow would have been too worldly-wise to uproot his little family on a whim or a dream and flee with a newborn and its mother, to brave brigands and the elements and settle as a refugee in Egypt. He had the air of a man well passed his prime, too old to be interested in sex. (But does the urge ever disappear?)

This statue of Mary's partner had guarded the ancillary, double door entrance at the end of the corridor since before my arrival at Springwood as a boy in 1951. He had stood there, silently, protecting the secrets of students who came and went in the shadows.

Then one morning, as I strolled through the corridor to breakfast, I noticed the pedestal was vacant. St Joseph had disappeared. He had stood there stationary a long time. Perhaps he was sick of guarding the entrance in silence. For years we had taken him for granted. Perhaps he had had another dream in the night and disappeared on his own business, or simply returned to heaven.

Tommy Veech and his assistant, Lennie Wholahan, were furious when they discovered that St Joseph had "done a bunk" in the middle of the night. I confess I had to feign a level of shock when I heard that students had kidnapped the saint, carried him in procession to one of the dormitories and laid him to rest, stiff in some student's narrow bed. They had tucked him in tight with blankets up over his grey beard. This was a major terrorist act. The authorities immediately launched an inquisition. Rebellion was afoot. They were determined to uncover the plot and punish the offenders.

Monsignor, apoplectic with rage, summoned all the students to an extraordinary general assembly in the chapel and threatened the guilty with dire consequences unless they confessed. No one came forward, of course. He encouraged the innocent to report what they knew and expose the culprits, and themselves, to the wrath of their fellow students.

Peter Marr (known to his friends as "Darcy") knew everything about the assault on St Joseph and, as a tough footballer and a product of an exclusive GPS school, the Monsignor had a sneaking regard for him. He was the Master of Ceremonies in the college and the leader of mutinies. As a school-boy he had boarded at St Joseph's, so he knew the drill. When the Monsignor, merely on suspicion, accused him of being involved, naturally, he denied everything. But the inquisitor was not satisfied. (They never are.)

Angrily, Veech informed his official MC that he (Peter) knew who had done the deed and ordered him to name the guilty. But like any respectable criminal Peter denied being in possession of the relevant names, pleading "not guilty" of the charge of misprision of felony. The authorities simply did not believe him. Instead of placing him on the rack or condemning him to trial by fire, the Monsignor refused to speak to him, sent him to Coventry and maintained his silence punishment for over six months.

The cold war within the seminary had serious repercussions. Being the Master of Ceremonies, Peter Marr needed to know, on a daily basis, classified information which could only come down from the top on a need-to-know basis. The rector would send a messenger to Peter to inform him that he wanted to see him. When Peter arrived at his study, the Monsignor would pass a note under his door.

"Bishop Thomas will be here for Mass tomorrow" or

"The Cardinal is coming on Wednesday."

Not one spoken word passed between them. No eye-contact. Just silly-buggers.

After a few weeks Peter began to see the amusing side of the Monsignor's behaviour and thought he would join in the game. He answered the rector's cryptic notes by scribbling a note of his own in reply, on a scrap of paper –

"Thank you, Monsignor. I received your message."

He would sign his note and slip it back under the door.

Apparently, all the students knew that Tommy was mad but I didn't know they knew. Believing they were simple seminarians like I had been in an earlier generation, I thought that they looked at us all, especially the Monsignor in charge, with pious reverence and respect. There were serious things I didn't know about Monsignor Charlie Dunne when I was a student for seven years under his regime at Springwood and which I only came to know much later. The professors were on the top table, eating their specially prepared food from the silver service and the best china, while the students were down in the galleys, eating porridge and bangers off cafeteria plates. I did not realise the new students were scrutinising us through a 60's lens, coming to their own, unflattering conclusions, amusing themselves with our idiosyncrasies and the boss's crazy outbursts. I did not realise at the time that the students had concluded on the evidence that their leader was "captain rats".

Stranger still, as I recall, I didn't know that other members of the staff, some of the senior men, had come to the same conclusion. The state of our leader's mental health was not discussed in my presence. I had observed that others were cautious in his presence, that they were reticent to express an opinion, paying court to the boss, avoiding his company and then relaxing when he disappeared at night into his cubby hole. But no one, in my company, as far as I can now remember, proffered an opinion on the Monsignor's ability to govern.

I learnt in later life that the neophytes at Springwood, and at least some of the priests on the staff, knew what I knew – that Tommy often tumbled over the edge of sanity. Years later, at a funeral in Canberra for one of the students I had taught, without provocation on my part, one of the mourners approached me. He told me that when he had informed Monsignor Veech that he did not think he had a vocation and that he was leaving, the Monsignor immediately flew into a rage. He rocked back and forth violently on the spot and in a vicious tone of voice, shouted –

> "You and your kind are not worthy to tie the laces of the
> noble men who have gone before you. You are rubbish. Get
> out of here."

The poor seminarian withdrew in confusion. As he closed the door and began to walk away, he heard the rector huffing and puffing, throwing objects about in his room and sighing loudly. In the minds of some, perhaps in Cardinal Gilroy's mind, or some other bishops, maybe among senior parish priests, colleagues of Tommy, every aspirant who gave up the fight, who threw in the towel and returned to the world, was a reflection on the calibre of his trainer. Veech did not want to be seen as a failure.

The same ex-seminarian said that he and other drop-outs had visited the college years after it had closed, after the flood of vocations had dried to a thin trickle. They were surprised to find one of their old teachers living there like a hermit in retirement, alone. Dr George Joiner, before he became the parish priest of the Gosford parish, and then of South Strathfield where, without permission, he demolished a heritage building in the dead of night, had reluctantly taught in the seminary for more than ten years. George was happy to see them and they talked of earlier times. In fact, in contrast to the veneer of barbarism he had cultivated as a professor, there was a hint of tears in his old eyes. He confided to them that he had been unhappy at Springwood while they were students there; that he had tried on a number of occasions to escape; that he had asked the Cardinal to move him, without success; and that at the time the man-in-charge had been completely mad.

I had come to the same conclusion and so had the students. I wonder how Tommy had come to be in control of so many lives – mine included. I suspect it was simply that he had been the next in line. He had the seniority. Maybe he hadn't even indicated an interest in the position. Perhaps he was ordered to leave his job teaching church history to the students at Manly (a position where he had been entertaining as well as harmless) and to take on a job for which he had had no training or aptitude.

I don't blame him for the mess which resulted from his appointment – for the lack of direction, for the system's failure to adapt to the modern world, or for its cold resistance to the reforms proposed by the Second Vatican Council. He was himself a victim of the system. In the end the responsibility rested on the shoulders of the eminent office worker at the Cathedral, who had been his superior and who had posted him there in charge.

chapter six

1967

THE FIRM IN ACTION

One of my first close-up glimpses as to how the global institution worked, occurred when Cardinal Norman Thomas Gilroy visited us at Springwood.

The 1917 Code of Canon Law required every bishop and archbishop to visit his diocesan seminary regularly. Cardinal Gilroy had to personally supervise the education of the students in his diocese and acquire some insight into the character, piety, vocational aspirations and progress of each of them. It was his duty to inspect and assess every aspect of the administration of the seminary, to ensure that all the Vatican regulations were being observed faithfully. The bishop was the institutional auditor. For example, he was forbidden, among other things, to admit into his seminary anyone who could not prove, by a valid birth certificate, that his parents had been married at the time of his delivery – bastards were not welcome among the clergy (though the system seemed quite proficient at producing them).

The bishop also had to make sure that each of his candidates could function as a male member of the species, even though he was forbidden to do so. I don't know how my bishop, Cardinal Norman Gilroy, completed his task. He did not conduct a physical examination of my private equipment, nor anyone on his behalf. During my years in the seminary, I only ever saw one student dressed in his birthday suit. He used to insist, contrary to strict regulation, on drying his balls in public, for all to see, after a shower. I could personally vouch for his legitimacy but as for the other students, they used to conduct themselves "with due decorum and modesty" behind doors and under dressing gowns, at least as far as I knew. From time to time some of us had entertained the uncharitable thought that because of their effeminate ways, a few girls had infiltrated the system. I suppose it was possible that a number of ring-ins had got in under the wire, but it was the bishop's responsibility to ensure that only those with the essential appendages were ordained.

It was also the bishop's responsibility to make sure that the students recited their morning and night prayers in common every day; spent some extended time in mental prayer (at least half an hour); participated in the *"Sacrificium Missae"*; that they approached the sacrament of penance at least once a week, and "refreshed themselves frequently on the Eucharistic Bread"; that they engaged in spiritual exercises annually for several "continuous days"; and carried out the other equally onerous duties which controlled our daily life.

To carry out these duties, and accompanied by his secretary Neil Collins and later Ian Burns, His Eminence used to visit us at Springwood religiously, every month or so. The secretaries used to chauffeur their boss in their own car because, in the true spirit of poverty, Norman Gilroy did not own a motor vehicle (not at least until he inherited a Daimler along with a huge property in the eastern suburbs from the fabulously wealthy Reschs Estate). Ian Burns drove a VW beetle and his boss used to ride beside him in the front because, with only two doors, it was undignified to be seen, eminent bum in the air, scrambling into the rear seat. From sheer devilment, Ian used to push the front passenger's seat up as close as possible to the dashboard to make it as inconvenient as he could for his august non-paying passenger. The Cardinal would ride all the way to Springwood and back, in his flash cassock, his ruby ring on his finger and a gold cross hanging around his neck. With his delicate hands almost under his chin, clutching the passenger's handle above the glove-box – he never made a complaint.

On a hot afternoon in December 1950, the Cardinal Archbishop, with Monsignor Charlie Dunne on one side of him and Bishop Jimmy Carroll on the other (all decked out in their finery), had interviewed me when, at the age of twelve, I had been accepted as a seminarian to study for the priesthood. Norman Gilroy had been my bishop through the long years of training and had regularly questioned me (and all his other students), as the Code required – about my health, my piety, my obedience, the quality of the food I was given to eat each day and about my spiritual life. The questions were always the same and so were the answers. The same set of questions for everyone. He ran to a formula. He had developed a satisfactory ritual which, like *Craven A's*, never varied. We had all been in awe of him. He was the boss man, remote from us earthlings, exercising the heavenly power of life and death. There was no way I was going to complain about my treatment, even if I was being kept on starvation rations.

Gilroy had ordained me at St Mary's Cathedral in Sydney and signed my faculty sheet with his neat, enlarged signature, giving me the breathtaking power to preach and to forgive sins. I was nervous in his presence and always on my best behaviour.

Norman Thomas was a Prince of the Church. A figurehead and a churchman to his boot-buckles – cold and distant. His old bones were clothed in a ghostly alabastral, wrinkled Irish skin, in a red cassock, capes and cloaks, a tall hat and a gold ring. He was, at the same time, both more than human, and less. He spoke as though through a thick oily film, with an exaggerated, slow articulation and modulation, somehow metallic. Smiling behind his yellow teeth, he spoke in a type of studied sing-song monotone which had a sexless, perhaps even an effeminate quality. While the leader who turned up at Springwood appeared among us in his fancy dress, red robes, wearing a gold cross on his breast which was hanging from his neck by a heavy, gold chain, with buckles on his shoes – the man in this iron mask was more like a corner-shop tradesman. He was pennywise and puritanical, but enveloped in opulence.

Those were the days immediately after the Second Vatican Council. Priestly training had been on the agenda, guidelines had been published and seminaries were supposed to be on the move, responding to the demands of the modern world. I was not long at Springwood as a teacher before I began to realise that the place was not functioning as it should, even for a Roman seminary. I was young and impulsive by nature, but I was also keen to fit in and make my contribution. I was anxious to please my superiors. However, I could not fail to see that the man-in-charge of us was unstable, perhaps a little mad, and that the members of his staff were too nervous and too well-trained to challenge him. All of us, young and old, even the experienced ones, had been drilled to a slavish and unquestioning obedience. We kept our heads down and went about our daily work as though everything was normal. But it wasn't. I guess the same happens in many families and in professional associations, in schools and large companies. Incompetent surgeons continue to operate with impunity under the noses of critical theatre sisters and anaesthetists. The same thing certainly occurs in politics and among judges.

Soon after my appointment to the staff, and driven by the requirements of the Code of Canon Law, his Eminence visited our Springwood retreat in the mountains. I could see that the students had grown restive and the place was rumbling with discontent. A few of the staff, keen to train men for a contemporary ministry, felt frustrated with the system and the man-in-charge. Some of the promised reforms, embraced by the Fathers of the Second Vatican Council, were being introduced into the establishment reluctantly, piecemeal and with heavy feet. The old system, which had been devised by the Fathers of the Council of Trent in the sixteenth century, was on its deathbed but still gulping for air. It was hard to give up the old ways.

His Eminence stayed among us for three days, praying in private, celebrating highly stylised liturgies in the chapel, presiding at meals where he graciously tinkled the table bell, thereby permitting the students to talk while they ate. On most days we all ate in silence, except when the Great White Father was among us, or on some other special occasion such as Easter Sunday, Pentecost, the Feast of Sts Peter and Paul, or of St Columba. Talking was reserved for special occasions.

While he was with us at Springwood, enjoying the country air and our hospitality, his Eminence might have felt free to enquire as to how I was settling into my new life as a professor in his little seminary. He had sent me into the mountains with his episcopal blessings. How was I coping with the work? What kind of things was I teaching his students? Did I find the place too isolated? Too cold? A little too regimented? What had I been doing on my day-off? Did I sometimes catch up with my classmates? Did I get to see my parents regularly? What films had I seen recently?

Had he engaged me in such a conversation, I might have been immediately on the alert. Why was he checking up on me? Had he heard something on the clerical rumour mill? Who'd been in his ear? Despite the name his parents had given him, it was not normal for my Archbishop to be interested in me or in what I was doing – unless it was bad. The barriers between us were high. He was living in a different world. We all belonged to the one huge institution and we each had our own role to play, but the gulf between us was vast. Norman showed no interest in me whatsoever.

There was no way I could have casually observed –

> "I see you've just had a hair-cut, your Eminence. Where do
> you go when you are in Sydney? My father cuts my hair and I
> cut his. I learnt the art from Mick Kelly here in the
> barbershop near the recreation hall."

No one ever talked to the Cardinal in such a familiar tone or on such a mundane level. Anyway, I should have known that my Archbishop did not go to the barber. A special Catholic barber came to him, and only when he was summoned. I wonder, did the barber keep the clippings just in case Norman Thomas was one day canonized?

There was no way I could have asked this august man how his sisters were; or whether he had slept comfortably in a strange bed; had he been warm enough; did he find the Springwood weather too chilly; did he need to get up several times in the night.

If I were to utter the simple words; "have you heard ...?" in the presence of the assembled staff, the Monsignor in charge and the other subservient members of the clergy, everyone would have frozen on the spot. What was Geraghty going to say? Who does he think he is? Does he know what he's doing? Let's get the Cardinal out of here and on the road so we can get on with our lives.

I waited impatiently during the three days in the naive expectation that this remote figure would call us together for a frank discussion about what we were all doing in our remote hide-away. Morale was low. Knowing what I now know about myself, Tommy Veech must have been having hot sweats and palpitations for fear that I might blab some outlandish, baseless criticism of his regime.

On the morning of the third day, minutes before his departure, while we sat bleating platitudes in the common-room, as he waited for his ordained man-servant to bring the VW around to the main entrance, as we waited to say farewell before rushing off to breakfast, I thought I half-heard his Eminence saying in his artificial, throaty voice –

"I couldn't help but notice ..."

Immediately he had my attention. This was the moment I had been waiting for. At last, the big boss was leading us into the discussion which I had been expecting. He had waited till the finale before launching perhaps only a brief exchange. We were all gathered – the one in charge, his trusty lieutenants, senior men and us few insignificant juniors. We waited, each attentive to what the Eminence was about to say, hanging on his every word.

"I couldn't help but notice ... how shiny the students' shoes were during Mass".

Shiny shoes –
spick and span –
sleepy heads and plastic bread –
rows of men from narrow beds –
silver buckles, oily smiles –
laced-edged shirts and empty mouths –
no joyful singing and no laughter –
aching members kept on ice –
nothing nasty, life is nice.

As I sat there in the circle of clerics, an angel from another world was whispering in my ear. But I was distracted, thinking of other things. Since childhood, I had longed and longed to share in the magic of that broken-down system.

As far as I could see from the regular visits he made to our seminary, our Cardinal did not question what he was doing, or what was really required of him by the international organization or by his superiors. He did not like change. He liked the sparkle of military discipline. He did not look for change. He supported without question the old system, tried and true. The modern world and the Second Vatican Council were just a passing phase.

The job God had given to his eminent servant was to continue to inject new blood into old veins, to train and twist young bones to feel at home in a decaying skeleton. Raise the flag; salute the sovereign; belt the anthem out; do your duty and trust in God that all would be well. There was not going to be any problems on his watch.

Gilroy was like all of them – the bishops and archbishops and most of their parish priests. They didn't get it then and they still don't get it now. They continue to live at the bottom of the garden, among fairies and bogeymen. When Ted Kennedy left his post in Redfern to go to God, the Archbishop of Sydney (who was a Roman paratrooper from Melbourne) couldn't see that if he moved into the area with a sympathetic team of men and women to serve the many aborigines who lived there, he would have been a champion on the Sydney scene within months. Instead, his decision to foist a foreign group of conservative Neo-Cats on the community attracted criticism and derision from the unwashed mob and from the pews. If he had espoused global warming and climate change and married the cause to a theology of creation and redemption, he could have captured the attention of the nation. Instead, Cardinal Pell had to rush to the fringe of the debate, turn his back on the almost unanimous opinion of scientists and join the ranks of the reactionaries.

They can't see or hear. They can't read *the signs of the times*. They can't dance or sing. They can't laugh and they can't cry. They think they're infallible. God help them.

chapter seven

1968
CONFIDING IN FATHER SUPERIOR

My first year back at Springwood on the staff was a year of learning and a time of reflection. I was teaching myself to be a teacher – learning from my mistakes; selecting topics to research; assembling bibliographies; accumulating information; trying to communicate it in such a way as to inspire students to search for answers and insight; learning to set examinations and to mark the answers fairly. Teaching is an art, like fighting, like surgery or breaking in horses and I was on my own, acquiring the art as I went along and experimenting by trial and error on the reluctant students. At the same time, I was also learning to reflect on what I was doing, on my priestly vocation, on the seminary system and on training young men to be priests for the modern world.

The next year, when I returned from holidays in February 1968, I was ready to discuss my role in the training program with Monsignor Veech. During the Christmas holidays I had sought advice from friends. I had described my life in the seminary over the previous twelve months to them – my feelings, my impressions of the place, how the students were responding and particularly how the Monsignor had been treating me – no warm words of welcome; no advice on my arrival on his team. He had not spoken to me for at least the first six months. As far as he was concerned, I hadn't existed. Then, but for an occasional passing or mumbled pleasantry, he had not included me in any conversation for the remainder of the year. I had waited long enough for our dialogue to begin. "Speak to Monsignor Veech to learn of him what is required of you", was the Cardinal's direction to me. So I did.

I knew our encounter was not going to be pleasant, so I summoned my courage and visited the Monsignor in his tobacco-stale study at the end of the verandah overlooking the quadrangle. In my own mind, I was not going there to criticise him or his seminary, or even to make a minor contribution to his training program. My intentions were pure, but I had not sized up my opponent. As a junior once again, at the bottom of the institutional pecking order, I was conscious of my position, but someone had to occupy that space. I wanted to inform my father superior how I had been feeling as 1967 had progressed. Because there were some things which prudence dictated I should not say, some feelings I could not flesh out because of the touchiness of the top-dog, I was forced to be more obtuse than I would normally have been.

In retrospect, I should have paid more attention to my plan of attack. No, on further reflection, I should not have gone there at all. The advice I had received over the holiday period proved bad. Anyway, as it turned out, I had to be prepared to allow some of the Monsignor's vicious, bodyline bowling to strike me on the chest, or to pass over my head, through to the keeper, without being tempted to play at it. For prudence's sake, I left some of his harsh allegations, some of his cruel observations unanswered. There was no meeting of minds, no communion of aspirations. Our "dialogue", which mostly took the form of a diatribe and which lasted about one and a half hours, was a disaster.

I began by telling the old man that I had not been happy or relaxed in his seminary. I was blunt. I knew no other way.

St Columba's was not a home for any of its inhabitants. I had been living under constant tension in the world he was controlling. I had felt uncomfortable, under pressure to be someone I could not be, to play a role foreign to me, and furthermore, my presence in his college was only tolerated. Any contribution I might be able to make was considered unacceptable. I felt I was required to disappear quietly into the system.

I complained that no one had taken the trouble to introduce me to my work as a teacher in the seminary. The Cardinal had sent me a short, formal letter of appointment; I had had no face-to-face interview with anyone; Archbishop Jimmy Carroll, who was in charge of education and seminaries, had not contacted me to discuss the diocesan policy on priestly formation and to let me know how I would fit into the overall picture. Was there any policy? Did anybody know what we were doing, where we were heading?

Despite my requests on my arrival in the early part of 1967, the Monsignor had made it clear that an interview with him was not necessary, or desirable. He had penned a brief letter which he had considered sufficient. I thought this behavior strange from those dealing with "important" work, which would later prove disastrous.

I had started the race off a long handicap. I had not received any training in teaching and I had had no experience. The subjects I had been given to teach were foreign to me. Liturgical Studies had never been taught in the Sydney seminaries before, so I was breaking new ground and Social Ethics was a vast field of acquired and sophisticated knowledge which was completely new to me.

I also told the purple Monsignor, who was by now huffing and puffing, bouncing back and forth, goading and scoffing at me, that on many occasions during 1967, his seminary had been the last place on earth I had wanted to be. The whole year had been a trial to my faith. My awkwardness and inexperience were obvious to the students in class. At times of stress and loneliness, I had wanted to turn the key in my blue Volkswagon and drive away. Though my heart was choked with indignation, I was unable to tell our leader that those under his control and supervision, among whom I numbered myself, were precious and valuable; that he should not presume on the faithfulness and loyalty of others (he had no right to do so); that good intentions did not excuse his bad manners; that the faith and obedience shown by one human being, did not excuse the lack of courtesy in another. However, despite my natural reticence and my years of educated reverence, he was getting an earfull. I told the very reverent Captain Quigg that my contribution to the college was belittled by the secrecy which surrounded his decisions and which permeated his establishment. A good deal of my information about the daily life of the college came from the students, especially from members of the student representative council who met regularly with him for "discussions". I was puzzled why the rector himself could not pass on information to me and the other members of the staff. Obviously he did not consider me as a player on his team. Information circulated in the institution on a strictly need-to-know basis and the staff in general, particularly those in the junior ranks, did not need to know.

In the early part of 1967 a number of the Springwood staff had joined with teachers from other seminaries throughout Australia, at a conference in Melbourne. I had been present and keen to contribute. It had always been part of my character – I liked to be involved. When we had divided into discussion groups, being a young pup and without daring to volunteer, the members of the group had appointed me as their secretary recorder. Later, at the plenary session, the recorders had to inform the assembly of the principal points of discussion and recommendations. I had been nervous making my appearance among the ranks, but I did my best.

Tommy Veech had been harbouring a grudge against me since that conference and probably for years before that. Trying unsuccessfully to control his rising anger, he blurted out that I had made a fool of myself and embarrassed him in Melbourne.

> "I had no idea what you were going to say next. For such a
> young, inexperienced person, you had far too much to say.
> You should have remained silent and listened. You
> demonstrated far too much confidence. I was embarrassed to
> sit there and listen to you, wondering what the others were
> thinking of you."

Now the gloves were off. Veech moved in, knuckles bared. He was not using this occasion as a counselling session, or as an educational interchange. He never made a contribution to the conference, or to any meeting I ever attended. He preferred to sit off-stage and observe the foibles of mankind. He avoided meetings and was uncomfortable in the company of others. When circumstances forced him to attend a meeting, he would sit at the back, head down and slanted to the side, not uttering a word. On the occasion in question, he had not sought to share his acquired wisdom with the conference participants – a wisdom gained over many years on the seminary staff. Had we all done as he did, the conference (like our community life in the seminary) would have been a non-event. Tommy was not a contributor – only an observer, a keen observer, sometimes a vicious observer, and at times, when he felt like it, a rather good mimic of others. In pursuit of his love of Rugby, he used to travel down to Sydney to watch a GPS game on the odd Saturday afternoon, or put in an appearance at the college Rugby League games at Springwood – dressed in his cassock, his prayer-book in his hand, hiding behind a bush, off there in the distance, hoping no one was aware of his presence. He would creep away before the game ended, to avoid being noticed, for fear that someone might talk to him.

I could see that the Monsignor was trying to hold himself in. He told me that it was important to understand that it took years to build oneself into a position of trust and decision-making within the system. The prudent exercise of responsibility demanded years of experience rather than a familiarity with any formal, structured body of knowledge. He said that one learnt the system after a period of time, by osmosis, and that I had a long apprenticeship to serve.

"What we are doing here will become clear after a while."

Observation time and living time introduced a junior team-member to the arcane workings of the seminary. But I privately thought that perhaps time, isolated time, slow time, was the agent which dulled awareness, permitting fossilised clerics to exist in a supernatural vacuum, to suffer the sores and scars without treatment, eventually without notice. I accepted that experience was important, but some people, no matter how long they spend in the system, never acquire the experience which gives rise to wisdom. Some people's minds are twisted and locked shut. Besides, freshness, enthusiasm, energy and new eyes were also important.

According to our rector, the overall plan of seminary training could not be spelt out. However, he claimed, after living at Springwood with senior men such as himself, I would grow to understand the plan and the aim of the system.

"What do you want to be? A dean of discipline or something? Overnight?"

Looking at me across the desk, with cold, hard eyes in a flushed face, he promised me a successful "career". I should not be impatient. To develop "a satisfactory career" demanded experience born of time and patience.

Though I did not say so, despite my naive youthfulness, I did not agree. Stupid me! I did not agree that I should view my role in the seminary as a *career*. I regarded the life I had chosen as a calling to be lived out in a community of other believers. The other members of the clergy were not my professional colleagues – they were my brothers. The Monsignor was not my boss, but my father superior to whom I was bound in faith, love and obedience, and he bound to me in love and respect. "Career" was not a concept which described what I thought my life was about.

Then, uninvited, Tom Veech began to "discuss" my friends. He did not approve of them. The priests with whom I was supposedly associating, should be avoided by someone in the elevated position I occupied. My friends were not loyal to the organization, they were not true churchmen.

Even now I have no idea to whom he was referring. I was not mixing with the larrikin crowd at the golf course, or with the senior men who went to the races at Randwick, or the mob who attended massage parlours for recreation. Many of the clergy in Sydney had been generally critical of the seminaries and critical of the lecturers who had been appointed there since they themselves had graduated. They were, almost to a man, narrow, practical pastors, challenged by ideas, hostile to theology and to intellectual pursuits. I was not mixing with these clerics and Veech had no cause for alarm. My friends were not drinking to excess, or watching pornography, entertaining female friends on their laps, coupling with male or female partners, interfering with boys, plotting to overthrow the Pope or to undermine the power of any cabal of monsignors.

I didn't realise Tommy knew who my friends were. I saw my classmates, Michael Bach and Lex Levey from time to time and often spoke with them on the telephone. Before his early death in March '69, very occasionally I saw Peter "Beau" Ryan at his brother's pub in Willoughby, or in his parish at Eastwood. I might have had a beer or two with him. I regarded Neil Brown as a close friend and still do. I used to call in on him on the odd occasion at Concord before he went off to teach Moral Theology at Manly. So, who was Boo talking about?

In those days, my friends, like myself, were all boringly conservative members of a tamed group of young priests. As far as we were concerned, there was no revolution in the air, at least among those of us who had been ordained in the early 60's. We were the last members of the old, reactionary guard before young priests and seminarians moved into their full rebellion mode.

Even though I was a teacher in his system, I was being kept in the dark and did not know that Tommy's old friend and ally was already on the ropes at Manly. After my class had left the major seminary to join the ranks of the junior clergy, the student ethos and morale had "deteriorated". They had begun to wage war on the authorities. One morning at breakfast, Monsignor Madden had unfurled his starched breakfast napkin to find a hand-written note of demand – "We want maturity, not maximum security". Rebellion was in the air. It was the year of the Paris riots and protest delegations from Manly had been visiting the Cardinal to complain about the system and the man-in-charge. Jimmy Madden was under attack at last. His old regime was limping along, on its last short legs.

Unbeknown to me, for some years young priests had been meeting secretly in presbyteries in Sydney, exchanging ideas, talking revolution. Murray, McBride, Butcher, Messenger were meeting regularly with Roger Pryke and Ted Kennedy. Discontent was on the rise. There would be a nationwide gathering of priests meeting for a week at the Coogee Bay Hotel late in 1969. Four hundred would assembly at St Joseph's College in Hunter's Hill in May 1970.

The rector at Manly would be gone by early 1969 and Veech had been joined with him at the hip, as they stood together propping up the skeleton of a system well past its used-by date. Tommy could see what was happening. His world was collapsing. His friend was going down and he was going to be next. The 60's had hit the seminary at Manly, and Springwood would inevitably come under siege in due time.

The friends I was associating with and whom Boo was frightened of, were only figments of his tormented imagination. They did not exist but enemies of his world certainly did exist. They were at work, and Tommy knew it. As the junior teacher, as the youngest, I represented the enemy. Mine was the face of danger. Though I was not plotting or planning, I had my own ideas and they were critical and threatening. Who knew what trouble I might be fermenting in Sydney?

The Monsignor was offended because I considered myself free to attend "suspect" meetings in Sydney – harmless gatherings of friends or the diocesan senate of priests. When he told me he did not like the group of clerics who were gathering at those meetings, I was amazed. I had no idea how he could have known what we did, where we gathered, who else was there, or how I spoke or voted at the meetings. Maybe he had had his tea-leaves read, or perhaps he had paid a fortune-teller to read his palm. Apparently I was a major figure in his pending collapse.

Our encounter was beginning to "hot-up". He was warming to his task, defending himself and his position in the rat-pack. He blurted out that I was an "impertinent upstart". (I had not heard that expression since Mother Eulalie had used it to describe one of her tarty girls at Neutral Bay in the early 1940s.)

Like John Howard's famous attack on his Aboriginal brothers and sisters, Boo's unexpected outburst seemed to frighten him a little. He withdrew his insult almost immediately, though it was clear his heart was not in the retreat. His original, sudden bluster was what he truly believed. He thought that I was over-confidant, too overbearing, unwilling to accept criticism and in pursuit of kudos. Maybe he was right but he was making a mess of this encounter.

On reflection, I can understand why he thought this and his opinions were not without some basis. Others, not just him, have thought that I was too cocky for my age and status. I was probably very annoying. He observed that I "ran hot and cold"; that I was unstable; my interests were too varied and changeable; that I went out too much; and that I sometimes appeared depressed – and at least some of what he said had some substance. He criticised me for my many trips to Sydney. I told him I was unhappy at Springwood, that I did not feel "at home" in his cold, clerical world. It was nowhere for any normal person to live.

Veech's contribution to our 'conversation' was not however entirely a front-on attack from beginning to end. At one stage he asserted that the lifestyle of seminary professors should be ascetic; that we should seek seclusion. We were meant to be scholars and bookmen, not public relations people. We must find our contentment in the silence and loneliness of our studies.

I suspect that Boo might have been trying to advise me to slow down. I was hyperactive – too frenetic. Maybe, just maybe, he was wiser than he appeared but he was unable to communicate across the barriers which separated us. Perhaps he could see that something was wrong, that I hungered for approval, that I was too conscious of what others thought and too anxious to please. After all my years in a broken system, I now had to find my true self, my authentic self, and I couldn't do that out there in the world, in a rush, always performing. I had to have time to reflect and to allow my soul to expand.

I had spent years training to conform to what others considered to be the model of a good priest. Learning to suppress my personal needs and desires, living out the dictates of selfless love and service and thereby becoming a nobody. Maybe Boo saw that I could never be happy or successful until I broke free of the world in which I had grown up and he wanted to warn me to slow down and settle into myself before it was too late. I doubt it and it doesn't matter now, but whether he knew it or not it is now clear to me that, that is what I had to do if I was ever to enjoy an authentic life.

Suddenly the Monsignor changed his tack again and began to flap around in the shallows. He attacked me for not working in the grounds of the seminary. The other priests did. It was true some of them worked hard in the grounds and particularly on the development of the new football field, which they were carving out of sandstone down in the valley and to which Tommy was especially wedded – a huge area which has long since returned to the wild. But not everybody felt the need to engage in regular, physical hard labour. I did not. I had never enjoyed digging and shovelling even as a student, though in those days it had been compulsory. Now that I was free (I thought I was free), I had no intention of swinging a pick, shovelling dirt, or chipping away at sandstone to amuse myself. If I wanted some physical activity, I would play tennis, or go for a long run in the bush. I would do what I liked, not what Tommy liked me to do. I did not regard the seminary as a Gulag camp like it had been when I was a student. Maybe it still was for the students but it wasn't for me.

While at last we had come to the truth, I was not so sure this meeting had been a good idea. I could not escape. I had cornered the tiger and had to accept the deep, throbbing scratches.

As though shocked by his outbursts, Tommy seemed to take a few paces back to retrieve a more dignified position as would befit a Monsignor. He admitted he was "a very cold fish" and he gave me to understand that he knew in his heart he was unfriendly.

But these concessions were only a momentary lapse and soon he was on the attack again. He asked me, sarcastically, how I had got on with Father Boland at Avalon Beach and seemed pleased when I admitted that Father Boland and I had not altogether "hit it off". We had not ended up as buddies. However, he was not pleased to hear I had felt relaxed and at home with Dr Harry Davis at the Graduate House. My observation produced a cynical, knowing smile. Harry was obviously not on Boo's Christmas card list.

With his mad eyes ablaze, he told me that questions regarding priestly celibacy were not suitable for discussions in class and that I was not to presume to initiate such discussions among the students. If they wished to raise questions, they should be referred to their spiritual director. Celibacy and other delicate questions were taboo. Once the cat had escaped from the sugar bag, it was hard to trap her again.

I was flabbergasted. In my stupidity, I had thought this important matter needed to be discussed regularly and fully, with young people whose entire life might be ruined by their hasty, over-generous choices.

We parted – our discussion had not gone well. This had been a bad move. I was too young and he was too old. I had assumed we had been living in the same hemisphere and I thought we had been sharing a common world-view. I hadn't realised Tommy's head was in a different space. He was bogged in the mindset of stale traditions, of hierarchical structures, of entrenched power and authority. In a moment of boyish innocence, perhaps stupidity, I had communicated a little of my frustration to a hostile and vindictive, minor prelate. I had given him a strategic advantage. He might have been guessing before: now his suspicions were confirmed. My visit had given him the opportunity to pour out some of his pent-up resentment, while I had not made one dent in his shell. He had defended his position in the institution like an angry sea serpent, hiding in his dark cave, darting out to bite and poison, retracting suddenly out of range. I had no doubt I would hear more of this.

chapter eight

1968 AGAIN
ANOTHER ROUND OR TWO IN THE RING

"........ Do not let me hear
Of the wisdom of old men, but rather of their folly,
Their fear and frenzy, their fear of possession,
Of belonging to another, to others, or to God.
The only wisdom we can hope to acquire
Is the wisdom of humility: humility is endless."
East Coker – Four Quartets. T.S. Eliot.

Some months later, towards the end of June in that famous year of '68, I was involved in an even more unpleasant meeting.

I had not been coping well with constant headaches and bouts of depression. Dr Jim L'Estrange from Naremburn, had prescribed Valium and suggested that I try and reduce my work-load for a few months.

It was wintertime and icy in the mountains early in the morning. I was huddled over a radiator in a reception room downstairs, sitting near a frosted glass window-pane which was clouding my view onto the sandstone quadrangle. I was reciting my Breviary, in Latin.

The Monsignor suddenly appeared as if from nowhere, holding his old tobacco-stained Breviary in his wrinkled tobacco-stained hand. He was dressed in his heavy serge cassock with purple piping tattered around the edges, with a row of frayed purple buttons down the front, chin to ankles. As his opening gambit, the rector inquired whether I felt well enough to take my turn and celebrate the community Mass in the chapel throughout the coming week. I was deliberately distant. I told him that I was feeling better but that I had been sleeping a little longer than usual. He seemed anxious to relieve me of my standard priestly duty and pressed me for further information about my health. I replied politely. He tried again. When I simply repeated that I was OK, he had to come directly to the point.

"What has the doctor said?"

I told him that I had been prescribed a mild tranquilliser for a few weeks, that the doctor thought I had been overdoing it and working too hard, that I was too self-critical, setting standards for myself and others which were unrealistic. He had also observed that, in the light of his experience with other religious groups, he thought I was having problems in the community. In addition, my sister Maureen had been gravely ill.

This information did not appear to please the Monsignor. He became visibly upset and began to throw his rhythmic hibby-gibbies there in the parlour. He was shaking, rocking back and forth on his heels, bowing and straining to straighten up as though trying to control rolling spasms. It was obvious he was angry.

"Your problem is with me, isn't it?"

"I've never said that, Monsignor", I replied.

His outburst had startled me. I was not ready for it, or in the mood to deal with it. I had never complained, to him at least, that he was the problem, but he had not misread the signs. Anyone could see that his hovering presence and particularly his ignoring silence, had upset me. I had interpreted his consistent disregard as a put-down which only reinforced my feeling of isolation. I was haunted by memories of my time at Springwood as a young seminarian, fighting for acceptance. None of us had ever been good enough.

Veech insisted.

"You are blaming me. You're blaming me for your health problems."

His attack demanded a response. He was flushing me out.

"Well, it's no secret Monsignor that I find you difficult to deal with."

Now he grew more agitated and angry and went on the offensive.

The previous Thursday had been Manly Day – an annual occasion when the students from St Patrick's major seminary used to visit us at Springwood for a grudge football match.

> "What time did you get home on Thursday night?" he snapped.
>
> "Late," I replied.
>
> "That's no answer. What time was it when you came in?"
>
> "Two o'clock."
>
> "I forbid you to enter the seminary again at such an hour. You're to return at a reasonable time and not be creeping into this religious establishment at some ungodly hour of the morning. It did not pass without notice that you rose very late on Friday morning to say Mass."
>
> "Friday was a holiday" I replied, "and there was no need to be getting up at any regulated time".
>
> "You'll do as I tell you."

I had passed a few relaxing hours on the Thursday evening with my friends Lex Levey, Beau Ryan, John O'Neill and the parish priest, Jack Haseler at the Eastwood Presbytery, before driving up the mountains in my little blue VW. I had enjoyed myself and it wasn't a crime.

But Tommy was not happy. As our conversation progressed, he was stirring himself to fits of rage. Suddenly, gathering his strength and after a few agonizing moments of silence, staring fiery daggers, he spat at me –

> "You're a vulgar, rude creature."

That was enough. I rose from where I was sitting, switched off the heater and as I was leaving the room, I said:

> "You have no bloody right to speak to me like that, Monsignor."

My remark elicited a brief exchange:

> "I'm your superior. I demand your respect."

I held my ground.

> "I will be thirty in October. I have spent sixteen of those years in the seminary. I'm no longer a child. I have grown up in

> your institution and if I can't be treated as a loyal member of
> that institution, I want you to let me know and to tell me
> why."

I wonder – whom it was he thought he was dealing with? At least at that stage of my life, I hadn't yet participated in any protest march. I had walked piously in Eucharistic processions and stood silently in the midst of the toing-and-froings within the diocese. I was certainly no rebel. I had not interfered with altar-boys or caressed a worker in the local brothel. I hadn't even held hands with a member of the opposite sex. I belonged, body and soul, to his little world, though (to be honest) I was beginning to realize how tightly the bonds were drawn.

Other men of my age had finished their university course and were earning a living, paying their mortgage, raising a family. What gave this man the right to think he could push his way into my private world, without an invitation, and tell me when I had to be in bed? Anyway, there were acceptable ways of approaching other individuals, even very junior ones, ones you don't like – carefully, sensitively, cautiously. What gave Tommy the right to speak to me as he did? He was my superior, but his power over me was not boundless. He was not my master, or the chief of police. We were a Christian community of volunteers, bound together in mutual respect and love. He had to act properly and deal with me politely.

I did not realize that my boss was living in a country of hidden landmines and surrounded by faceless enemies. Almost mad with anger, he lunged for my jugular.

> "I have spoken to both the parish priests you have lived and
> worked with. I've spoken to Father Boland at Avalon and
> Father Madden of Cronulla. Each informed me you had been
> a failure in the parish. They were glad to get rid of you."

I was decked. I did not know what to say. I remember I made a pathetic attempt to inquire by what criteria they had judged me, but the old man just waved me aside with a dismissive gesture and a triumphant smile. He knew how to get the best out of a yearling priest. You have to ride him with spurs and crush his spirit.

I repeated what I had told him earlier, namely that I had found Father Boland a little difficult. He was an old-fashioned priest – distant, cold and military, a blue-eyed, balding cleric. We had lived together in a weatherboard presbytery, in a closeness which was uncomfortable for strangers, eating at the same table, listening to one another snoring through thin partitions. But we had never had a disagreement or an argument. I had treated him with respect. I thought he had been a kind and energetic pastor. But Tommy Veech was not interested. He had delivered his knock-out blow and he was not finished.

"I find your behaviour offensive. You ignore me and refuse to speak to me. I regard your aloofness as an insult to me."

I made some lame reply, but I had been winded. I had thought it was I who was being ignored. I had had the impression he did not want to speak to me, or for me to invade his space by addressing him. I was confused. I thought I knew what had been happening between us. Surely he was twisting the facts to catch me off balance.

Then, again without warning, he relaxed his ruddy face and softened his voice. His mood seemed to change in an instance – concerned and compassionate.

"Why aren't you happy here at Springwood?"

It was silly of me to be sucked into his web, but I replied that I had been pleased to be involved in the teaching work; that I enjoyed interacting with the staff; but that I felt cramped in such a narrow world. I told him that I felt I was being untrue to myself and my beliefs, adhering to a dull party-line, to a form of training when I was not convinced of its worth. In truth, I thought it was antiquated and destructive. I was, by now, prudent enough not to raise the problem of living in the same house with a man, who was disturbed and who saw it as his God-given role to contain and restrain me.

But the Monsignor had already delivered his body blow. Tears were filling my eyes. I was trying to choke back stop-start fits of sobbing. He had fallen silent. The anger and the viciousness had disappeared from his voice. He must have realised he had gone too far. Now, he grew solicitous. I was doing an excellent job in my classes. He had heard good reports. He believed he had always been kind to me, except on one occasion at dinner when he had turned on me with a mean and petty gesture. He put his arm around my shoulder as we walked up the polished staircase and parted as we disappeared into our own worlds.

That was not the end of this incident.

When I left him, stung by his accusations, with wounds still throbbing, I telephoned Father Boland and Father Madden. I apologised for having to embarrass them. When I told them briefly about the conversation I had had with the Monsignor both denied having had any contact with him at any time, much less about me. They both told me that they knew Monsignor Veech from old, that they considered him difficult and strange. Jack Madden from Cronulla laughed and said –

> "My dear (he used to call everyone "my dear"), you were only here six weeks or so. What would I know after such a short time? We didn't have any problem, did we? He's just making it up. Forget about it."

That was enough for me. Their responses had the ring of truth.

I smouldered for a few hours before I confronted the Monsignor again. His study upstairs, overlooking the quadrangle, was perfumed with the smell of tobacco. The walls were shelved high with old books – rusty with age – French books and books which symbolised a world closed to me. This was his world. Here he was safe. It was clear that my superior was an educated, refined, sophisticated man who was at home in the world created by his library, but who was functioning way out of his depth in the real world of the seminary system. The demands of his job were beyond him.

Monsignor Veech was not a leader. He was incapable of inspiring young men. He was a book-man who lived in the past – in North Africa of the third and fourth centuries, in Germany of the Reformation period, in Renaissance Italy or in the court of the Sun God in France. He was living in an era of rapid change when much was expected of people like him, but he could not perform and I now suspect that he knew it. My presence each day at his table, in his classrooms and corridors was a constant and bitter reminder of his incompetence. I did not realise it at the time. I thought he was dismissive and contemptuous of me, that he disliked me. I did not realise that he might have been threatened by me, frightened of what I represented, perhaps even jealous of someone who appeared to radiate a level of confidence he himself could not achieve.

As I entered, the Monsignor sprang from his leather chair and began to apologise.

"I'm sorry", he said. "I apologise for what I said to you earlier on. I lost control and said some hurtful things to you."

"That's okay. They were hurtful and untrue, but I accept your apology. I want you to know I have rung Father Boland and Father Madden and discussed the matter with both of them."

Monsignor became agitated again. He picked up an ink-well, as if to throw it at me. His face had turned to a dull shade of purple.

"They both deny they ever said what you reported to me. They told me they have not spoken to you."

I had taken him by surprise. He had not expected me to verify his allegations. I simply added:

"I just want you to know Monsignor, if you treat me like that again, if you ever say such things to me again, I'll punch you in the bloody face".

I turned on my heels and left his room.

chapter nine

1969
A CRUSHING BLOW

man is a deciduous species
Or is it that death is only a hibernation
from which we never awake?
Wimmera by Homer Rieth.

My sister, Maureen, was propped up in bed when I arrived – soft pillows framing her weary body; tufts of dark brown hair escaping from beneath the white skull cap, which covered her head and which nuns wore when they were in hospital; alabaster, chill-white skin, and rosary beads untold in her fingers. The fight was almost lost.

With a heart choked with tears and a sadness that ached in my body, I unscrewed my phial of oil, which had been gifted to me in a cushioned box as a memorial of my ordination, and I set about anointing my sister. I mumbled the words of blessing and forgiveness, of cleansing and strengthening and as I smeared the silken oil on her forehead, I looked again into the soft, sunken eyes of my dear and dying sibling. I greased her tiny, feminine hands and noticed how delicately she had filed and lacquered her nails. With the distraction of words, I folded back the bedclothes and observed beneath the long, white linen bed-robe which my sister was wearing, a body worn out by pain, wrestling for breath, consumed by the curse of cancer. With words full of tears, I anointed her lily white feet. It was a comfort to be useful in the hour of such darkness.

Some days before her death, I had visited my sister and sheepishly enquired if I could take a few final photographs. I feared she might have been taken aback, perhaps panicked, by such an intrusive request – maybe embarrassed, or even a little angry that her brother wanted to record an image of her when she was not looking "at her best". But she had made no protest. She had struggled to prop herself up on the pillows, straightened her veil, arranged a fringe of hair over her forehead (even to the end, she could be a little vain), and tried to smile as I snapped five or six photographs, blinding her each time with the flashlight.

Of course, she had known what was in my mind. I would need to have, close at hand, something to remind me of her feminine beauty as indifferent years faded her image in my mind. My memory would be as brittle as crystal and with time, it would shatter into little shards of glass. Without some record, I would be struggling to remember my sister's face, to recall her ethereal beauty. She had known what I needed and true to form, she had not denied her brother, though her smile into the camera lens had been weary and already far away.

My hospital visits had become more frequent. My little blue VW was exhausted from puffing up and down the highway between Springwood and Crows Nest. Maureen had been growing weaker and weaker as she sank deeper into the hospital pillows, growing pale, almost transparent. Sometimes, when I arrived she would be asleep, sometimes sucking oxygen into her lungs from a heavy iron bottle. I had watched black bands form around her eyes and noticed her voice becoming thinner. She would drift off into a vague, floating sleep while I was holding her hand, sitting by her bed, reading sweet passages from the Bible. We had spoken, as brother and sister, of the life we had shared as children; of attending Mass each morning, walking in the dark of winter or in the first light of summer to St Joseph's church, praying together; of the God we had served and loved, the God who we were taught to believe was prodigal, soft at heart and full of mercy. We had talked of life and of death. What was on the other side? Did I believe in heaven? Was she frightened? How was I going to survive on my own?

For the last few weeks, after wandering distractedly through my lecture commitments at Springwood, I had spent every free moment, sometimes late into the night, in a shadowy, antiseptic room, at my sister's bedside, at the Mater Hospital. Her sister nuns had popped in and out and fussed about a bit. Bishop Muldoon from Mosman had appeared to wave about his blessings. Her treating doctor, Noel Newton, had materialised with a retinue of registrars and sisters to minister as carefully to my sister as he would have done to his own daughter. She had been well cared for.

But death had been there in the room, hovering, ready to strike. Friends had come and gone as I watched Maureen drawing on her limited resources to welcome those she loved, to smile and envelope us all in a cloud of peace. She had tried to banish all gloom and sadness from her room. I had watched a ripple of a smile pass over her ivory face. To her last breath, she was trying to comfort us, to assure us that all would be well, that the Lord could be trusted, that life had been good and that she was not falling into a bottomless pit of nothingness.

I had been anxious to believe that my dear sister was going home to heaven, to be cuddled and caressed by the tender craftsman who had modelled her from clay. I did not want to rebel against the dead hand of my God. I did not want to see myself cursing bitterly or clinging to idle, useless dreams. As the end had drawn near, her smiles seemed to stick on her ghostly face. The love of my life was floating away, behind an impenetrable veil.

Though much of the distress of those last days has finally been blotted from my memory, as I remember, I was not present when my sister died. She passed away as I was driving furiously from my mountain fortress at Springwood to visit her, perhaps for the last time.

After her death, her sisters had dressed her in her black religious habit, eyes closed, face creamed, before I was permitted to enter her room. I stood frozen to the spot in that shadowy space, half looking at my sister's lifeless body, realising that she was gone and that I was left, and that I had to survive somehow. I looked, but I saw no one.

My dear sister had disappeared without trace. Her soft female body remained rigid in a hospital room as functionaries arranged funereal flowers and planned a casket and a fleet of limousines, a church, a ceremony and a dark hole in the ground at the northern suburbs cemetery among her departed sisters.

I had watched her die in pain, fighting for her breath, moistening her mouth with dribbles of water, while I had held her hand, sat with her for hours, anxiously watching her, wondering whether she was frightened to face death alone. Towards the end, she had drifted in and out of consciousness. A clammy smell of death had pervaded her shaded room and then, against my wishes, all of a sudden, the sister who had given warmth and light to my life had drifted away forever. I was cold and alone. She was only thirty-two. It was June 1969 and come July I would have been a priest for seven years.

The Geraghty family was not involved in the arrangements except as mourners and me, as the lead celebrant of the thanksgiving Mass and funeral rites. Maureen had been taken from us years before. For fifteen years, she had belonged to the convent at North Sydney. Since her days of teenage blossoming, while she was in the process of changing from a girl into a young woman, she had been a member of the religious "family" of Mercy nuns. She had been assumed, body and soul, into a harsh system of unquestioning obedience, able to be moved from place to place at the whim of the powerful Reverent Mother whom the nuns had christened *Big Philou*. And her wasted body now belonged to the convent.

Nuns in black had summoned the funeral directors, ordered the sleek, shiny limousines, selected the mahogany casket with silver handles and a heavy cross, placed the notices in the newspapers and informed Maureen's mother and father, her two brothers and her sister when and where the obsequies would occur. Even in death, she was not ours to bury. She had been handed over to the convent at a tender age, and then contacted, visited, written to, telephoned, enquired after only with the permission of her superiors. Even in death, Maureen was not part of the humble, working class home and hearth of her natural family. Her parents had surrendered her to God and to Mother Philomena.

At St Mary's Jesuit church in North Sydney, full to overflowing, we gathered in song and prayer to celebrate a chaste life of energy and generosity. We assembled to honour my sister and to pay tribute to the simplicity and strength of a brief life. My colleagues from Springwood were with me on the altar. The young girls who had entered the convent about the same time as Maureen were kneeling in the front pews –

Robin Gillies, Margaret Shakeshaft, Molly Seedsman, Ellen Cahill, Rhonda Bart, Jacinta Dolan, Jacqui Ford, Janet Quade and others. They had all been part of her struggle. They had lost a member of the team. Though my throat was paralysed with loss and self pity, my chest swelled with pride to remember the little greatness of my sister.

From her teen years, she had harboured a hot hatred of duplicity and dishonesty. She had loathed all double-dealing, shame and hypocrisy. She had spoken her mind, even to her fearsome superiors, with reverence and yet with disarming honesty. She had shown love and friendship, true respect, especially to the least (perhaps not to the greatest) among us. Those around her, those in authority and with power, had never been in any doubt about her feelings or her thoughts. Her way of life and her spontaneous remarks had sometimes delivered a harsh critique of the values and the attitudes of those in charge. But her greatest gift had been her willingness to show concern for others. She had driven the streets of Sydney to visit her friends, to bring her gentleness and laughter to people in need. Her love for her sisters and brothers had not been cerebral and studied. Her care for others had been warm and feminine, her charm irresistible.

With puffs of perfumed incense, I enveloped the bulky coffin which contained the empty body of my sister. In death she was covered in greater earthly splendour than she had enjoyed in life. I sprinkled the highly polished timber with blessed water to drive away the evil spirits and then I led a long procession of mourners down the aisle out of the church, to the fleet of W.N. Bull limousines which were waiting outside to glide down the highway to the cemetery.

With pushing and silent shouldering, the flood of mourners flowed out into the street and hovered around as each waited his or her turn to shake my father's dry and freckled hand; to hug my mother's aching body; to talk with old friends in hushed whispers about my sister, about how well her brother was coping, about the tragic end to a life full of energy and optimism, about office affairs, the latest defeat of the North Sydney Bears, the weather, the memory of events past. What else can wandering human beings do when confronted by death?

At the northern suburbs cemetery, with the family, some of her nun and priest friends, I planted my sister's body in the ground. The ritual prayers, the holy water, the rosary beads, wreaths and bunches of flowers, focused on the hole in the clay ground where her lifeless body would rest, surrounded with the soiled coffins and dry bones of the departed Sisters of Mercy from North Sydney. They had a plot of earth in the cemetery which was edged with frozen dark marble, where the remains of their dead sisters were parked until the final resurrection. The community grave-site is within sight of the place where my mother and father rest side-by-side, where Colleen, my sister, was later buried on the other side of the grass corridor between graves, and where my brother Sean now lies a little distance away.

Maureen's remains were not lowered into a Geraghty grave with her family name inscribed on a family tombstone, where she would await the arrival of her parents, of her brothers and sister. When it would eventually be inscribed, her simple tombstone would read "Sister Christine Mary – 1969" and her bones would forever belong to the congregation. The funeral plaque failed to record a family name, or my sister's date of birth. There was no reference to the names her parents had given her at birth – "Maureen Yvonne". She was to be forever identified by the name the convent had handed down to her from on high. No casual passer-by would be able to calculate her age, or observe that she was a sister and a daughter in the Geraghty family. No simple, hopeful scriptural passage, no wish for a life with the Lord, no prayer. No family name, no husband, no children.

I was angry. With all the best intentions, Maureen had been stolen from our family, as I too had been as a young boy. I did not know how my parents had felt – the subject had never been discussed. The institution had enticed her from us, her family, removed her clothes, cut off her beautiful hair, covered her nubile body in a black serge habit, which had hidden even her ankles, locked her in a convent and changed her identity. She had become a member of a team of vestal virgins who would never appear without a black veil to cover their head and a long black habit to hide their feminine form. They could be moved from here to there, ordered and expected to obey. Like all of them, she had sacrificed her personality, her individuality, for some noble cause, for God, for Jesus – and of course for the steely institution.

She had left the world – she had been prised away from her family and friends, to live a life of poverty, of obedience and heavenly virginity. Beauty hidden, spontaneity crushed, compassion controlled, joyfulness disciplined and an occasional family visit, but only with permission. In life and in death, and though we had loved her dearly, in the public arena she had been a lowly ecclesiastical functionary in a vast, anonymous system.

I tumbled a few sods of clay in on top of the casket, shuddered to hear the thud of death, and watched the covering of the grave as though a heavy door was closing on my life, locking me out. I walked away.

I was thirty and ill-prepared for such an intimate and intense experience as the death of a loved one. She was the girl I had loved. She had been the one with whom I had shared my life. We had played together as babies and prayed together as children. Our hearts had beaten as one.

But I had developed a strong interior system of control. I had grown into a cerebral being, a human construct, a fully trained priest. With marked success, I had passed through the Church system of formation and I was functioning smoothly as a junior officer in the clerical army. I was teaching theology and a bit of sociology in my old junior seminary in the mountains. But I was not prepared to deal with the agony of an endless separation, with the loneliness which rose from the grave. I had not developed the living skills necessary to cope with rupture, with conflict, divorce, rejection, or death. I did not have the comfort of an intimate friend, the softness of a family, the warmth of tears shed in the arms of a lover.

After the funeral, I returned to the isolation of the mountain seminary and appeared to get on with my regulated life. I steeled my soul, gritted my teeth and smothered myself in my work. I had stared into the face of death herself. I had looked into her dry sockets, I had watched the light go out in my sister's eyes, her smile vanish from her face, I had seen the breath leave her body, I had watched her warm flesh turn cold, the soft body harden. This had been a turning point in my life.

Friends and colleagues registered their sympathy and expressed their admiration for my dear sister. Within the limitations of their youthfulness and confined by the formalities of our iron system, some of the students in the seminary attempted to support me through my grief. My confrères in the institution and my brothers in the ministry – from the frigid man in charge, down through the cassocked ranks of senior clerics to one ordained classmate on the staff – were distant. I had been trained well to cover and control my grief and we had all been through the same formation process. They too had been drilled not to snuggle up to anyone, male or female, not to become part of anyone else's personal life, if only for a passing moment. Our training had leached the colours of human affection from our souls and I was alone with my loss.

I fell into a sticky pit of sadness and self pity. It was as if someone had savagely extinguished the source of my energy and drained the fount of my joy and happiness. Though I used to recite my Breviary each day, celebrate the Eucharist, deliver lectures on liturgy and sociology, sometimes play tennis, I wandered through the dry bushland grounds of the seminary with a dead rat in my heart. What was the use of this crazy routine and training? What was the seminary, the priesthood, my little life all about? What was I doing there?

I hung on in the midst of shadows, with memories which caused pain, questioning, but not caring, unable to find any strength or comfort in the tired formulas I had trotted out so often, so easily, for others who had also faced the horror of death.

The world of others around me continued on its course. The trains ran; letters were posted and delivered; babies were born; people made love; the newspapers were printed; races were run and the same television programs appeared at the same time each night. But for me, the wind did not blow; the flowers did not bloom, or the waves roll, or the rain fall; leaves did not rustle and fall gently to the ground; birds no longer flew across the grey sky. A private earthquake had opened up the ground on which I was standing and my world had disappeared into a gapping pit. No joy in living, no love of work, no happiness in learning, or teaching, or listening and caring. I was afflicted by an aching emptiness.

I had visited my sister's death chamber after she had gone and snatched her rosary beads from among her paltry possessions. I knew the possessions of the dead belonged to the bosomy Mother Superior and the trustees of the Order, but I would not be bound by Maureen's vow of poverty. I thought I had a right to something of my sister's. I also stole the tiny, silver cross and chain she had worn around her neck throughout her life as a nun.

For more than thirty years, though we had been apart for much of that time, Maureen and I had been constant companions. She had been my soulmate who had accepted and loved me. I had been intensely proud of her. In our childhood we had developed a special sibling bond. I had been touched by her boundless energy, by her sense of fun, her rebellious spirit, her vague, ethereal smile, the warmth of her personality and the depth of her faith. Once she was gone, I could not speak of her to anyone. I could not breathe her name, even to strangers. I lived with tears welling behind my eyes. For almost twenty-five years, I drew a shroud of silence over her memory. I couldn't bear to look at the photographs I had taken. I shared them with no one. My mother and father, my sister Colleen and my brother Sean, all died without seeing the images I had recorded of my sister dying.

For many years after her death, I could not think of my sister without warm tears in my eyes, without a shortening of my breath. But drawing on that tight discipline I had learnt from my youth, I would not allow myself the indulgence of dwelling on her. By imposing a strict custody on my mind, I tried to block the thought of her from my life. Yet even now, so long afterwards, while I am walking a street or looking in a window, without warning, I see a face which reminds me of her. Frequently, I see a nose in the crowd, or a set of sparkling, daredevil eyes, a broad Irish face, or a pair of stocky legs in dark stockings which will call up her presence. These precious epiphanies were private. I told no one of them. These dreamlike apparitions continued to disturb me for twenty-five years at least and continue, but more gently, more bearably, now that I have two boys and a dear companion.

Slowly, diffidently, I was forced to confront the reality of the loss of my sister, though I could see no way through this desert waste. I assumed that the ache of separation would last forever. I was wrong, but I didn't know it.

chapter ten

1972
LEARNING ON THE JOB

In 1975, Father Vincent Kiss was sentenced in Port Vila on five counts of gross indecency. He received a suspended sentence of imprisonment and was immediately deported.

In 1993, he came before the County Court in Melbourne on six counts of theft by deception. The judge sent him to prison for a minimum period of six years.

Then, after he emerged from his Victorian gaol, the police charged Vince with offences in New South Wales. In September 2002, Judge Hock convicted him in the District Court on thirteen counts, including multiple acts of indecent assault and several acts of buggery on under-age boys. She sentenced him to a total period of imprisonment of ten and a half years, and to a non-parole period of seven years. His entitlement to apply for release on parole commenced on 5 September 2009.

I knew Vincent Kiss quite well. Though he was older than me, he had been a colourful member of a class some years behind me at Springwood. He was what we liked to refer to as a "late vocation" because after leaving school, he had spent some years in the world, working for a living with the Rural Bank before deciding to dedicate his life to the Lord's work in a country diocese.

After his ordination, Father Kiss had been high-profile and hyperactive – driving to Sydney, flying to Melbourne, dashing from one parish to another along country roads, charming classrooms of prepubescent boys, chatting to them in the playground, visiting youth clubs, laughing, teasing, entertaining, exuding energy, gaiety, always flamboyant and full of confidence. People admired and loved him. Life was a breeze. He was a handsome, charismatic young priest who enjoyed being the centre of attention in any gathering.

From time to time in the late 60's and early 70's, maybe once every second month or so, Father Vince would drive the highway from his country diocese to Springwood, or hurtle up the highway from Sydney where he had been leading a renewal seminar for nuns. He would arrive in a loud flurry, full of interesting clergy gossip, entertaining the staff over cups of tea in the common-room and sometimes armed with a little present for Monsignor Veech. Like many of us, like some of the parents of his seminarians, Tommy Veech was flattered by Vincent's attention. He knew how to pay court to our leader. He chatted him up, jollied him along, teasing him gently. No one on the staff had this gift, but he had the knack of dealing so easily with this difficult man. He was a natural performer. I remember his regal presence on the Springwood stage as the Mikado when we were students.

As the director of vocations, Father Kiss would naturally make contact with the students from his diocese when he visited us. He used to spend an hour or so entertaining "his boys" in the recreation hall and then, invariably, he would make an appearance in our common-room when the priests gathered after study, at about 9.30, for a cup of tea and a chat before night prayers and bed. At the end of the evening, he would bid us good night and jolly us off to bed.

Once the students had had a chance to observe and assess me as a member of staff, some of them used to come to my room in the evening for a talk. Some were seeking further reading material (though not many); some wanted to discuss matters raised in lectures (again, not many); others wanted to brood over their spiritual journey, on their vocation, over social stresses, perhaps problems with other members of staff, an ex-girlfriend, maybe with some classmates. I was young and ready to listen. I saw this as an important part of any priest's life and ministry and I had inherited a pair of good ears from my mother.

One evening I heard a faint knock on the heavy oak entrance to my study-boudoir. It was late and my visitor was obviously hesitant. Sitting uncomfortably in the half light, on a chair at the edge of my desk, he needed to talk to someone, to anyone he could trust, hopefully someone who might be able to understand, someone not too judgmental, someone who would be able to advise him, perhaps even to do something. I was the youngest and undoubtedly the one member of staff most out-of-place in the establishment. He had selected me with care.

Slowly, shamefully, my visitor began to hint at some secret business between himself and the cool Kiss. Apparently he and the vocations director had been really good friends for years – close friends since before my visitor's pubic hairs had began to sprout like tangled wires in his loins. His cheeks were wet as he blurted out, at random, unconnected pieces of his story. Long pauses. Sobbing. This was an encounter which demanded moral courage, trust and time. I watched him heaving and trembling as he spoke of trips to the Gold Coast or to Sydney as a young teenager, fast cars which he was encouraged to drive unlicensed, luxury hotels, steam-baths. Father Kiss had told him how much he loved him, how his whole life and ministry depended on their special friendship. God understood. They were not doing anything wrong. The doctor had told him he had cancer and that his life was almost at an end. Their time together was precious. It was all that kept him going.

Rigid with guilt, my visitor was forcing himself to reveal a shameful secret, trusting me, relying on me to listen. He wanted me to take his hand and guide him out of the black bog into a land of peace and freedom. It had not dawned on him that I was such a baby in the woods, thrashing around in the thicket of twisted human passions.

Many things were left unsaid that night. My visitor was too embarrassed, perhaps confused, and I was unwilling to probe for fear my mind would be clouded by unwelcomed shadows. I knew it was wrong to be too inquisitive about such matters. I knew I had to be careful to avoid images and illusions which might pollute the mind and inflame unnatural urges. It was only later that details of the diabolical activities of the director of vocations appeared like phantom figures out of the darkness.

Truth to tell, I did not really grasp the full import of what my visitor was saying. I realized there was some sexual bond between him and

Father Vince, and that their relationship was seriously twisted. We were talking mortal sin.

But I had no picture in a head full of piety and devotions to envisage what this young seminarian was really telling me. His story was beyond my power to imagine. I knew nothing of the world of eroticism, of pornography, or predatory sexual behaviour. I had never visited a brothel or turned the handle of a pornograph. At that stage of my life, though I was already thirty-three or so, I could not envisage how heterosexual couples conducted their intimate activities. I knew in theory what went where (though my knowledge of the extent of those physical manoeuvres was very limited), but how anyone initiated this coupling, or positioned himself, or herself, how they achieved a satisfactory outcome was outside the boundaries of my imagination. Prurient interest in sex had been strictly discouraged – a mortal no-no. I did not know exactly what homosexuality was. I had no idea what gay men did to one another in the privacy of their home or their club. I had observed, from a distance, the effeminate behaviour of some of the seminarians and priests – the mincing gait, their fascination with ornate vestments and their giddy, giggling outbursts when they were together. Hard as it may be now to believe, embarrassing as it is for me to admit, as I remember, that was as far as my understanding of homosexuality went. I equated it with effeminate affectations.

Father Kiss was in big demand to conduct retreats for religious sisters or youth groups at Point Piper in Sydney. After a day of talks and conferences, he would jump in his sporty Ford Falcon and drive up the mountains to meet his young friend (my visitor) near the gates of St Columba's. When he was supposed to be asleep in bed, on the invitation of the vocations director of his diocese and under his spell, he would sneak down the drive under the shadow of the gum trees, jump into his patron's car and spend a few hours in a local motel room, drinking and exercising. Then, after hearing his young friend's confession and raising his indulgent hand to forgive his sins, Father Vince would return him to the college gates around four in the morning and drive back down the mountain to say Mass, preside at group sessions and continue to offer his spiritual nourishment to those who were trying to live a life of Christian virtue. Tormented on a lonely rack of shame, my troubled visitor would appear with the other boys in the chapel at 6.30 for morning prayers.

On other occasions Father Kiss would arrive, radiating his showy charm, to visit the students whom he had gathered for the Lord, to entertain the staff, especially his friend the Monsignor – and, of course, to spend time with his other friend late at night, after we had all disappeared to bed. The motel room had been booked and our seminarian would be back in his narrow bed before he was expected in chapel for Mass.

The bare facts revealed on that evening in 1972 horrified me. This was uncharted territory. I could not begin to imagine what my colleague and companion from seminary days had been doing with one of our students. Apart from anything else, it was a capital offence for a student to be out of the college when he should have been in bed complying with the rule of a Solemn Silence from night prayers until after chapel the next morning. For that misdemeanour alone he could have been sent home. I did not know what to do, but I knew I had to do something.

The following few weeks was like living with Alice in her *terra mirabilis*. The staff members would gather in the common-room – the Monsignor, the dean of discipline, the senior lecturers who taught philosophy and biblical studies, the bursar and me. We would gather to review and discuss the students, to assess the progress of various individuals and to pass one after the other through the radar. I knew not to say much. The boss had let me know where I stood. I was still learning the trade.

No one contributed very much anyway. The others permitted themselves to say what they thought the Monsignor might be thinking. One student might be unsatisfactory because he tended to walk with an arrogant gait which might be considered inappropriate in a member of the clergy. Another had been walking around the grounds with his hands in the pockets of his cassock. The authorities couldn't say whether he was telling his rosary beads or massaging his balls. It was against the rules to have your hands in your own pockets and a sin to have a hand in someone else's pocket. A third had been late for morning prayers – twice. Someone else had broken the Solemn Silence by whispering to his neighbour after night prayers – while I had information that another student was leaving the compound late at night to meet up with his spiritual mentor somewhere in the village. On and on we went, passing various seminarians in review. Unbeknown to the others I had to sit in silence on a ticking bomb which could have blown the institution off the mountain. My secret had to be kept, at least for the moment. My night visitor had spoken to me in confidence, but I was wondering what other scandals might be bubbling under the cover of hymns and incense.

I later came to hear that while I was working in the college, one of the students had made a messy attempt to take his own life and that he may have been involved in a love affair with another seminarian. It was only a rumour, but knowing what I know now, such a scenario would not surprise me. Anyway, it appeared the unhappy episode had been covered up, and the routine of the house remained undisturbed.

In the late 60's, again late at night, an earlier encounter had taken place in my study when one of the students, Paul, had stepped out of the shadows and shared with me how he had found his way into the seminary. He had been a snowy haired, handsome altar-boy serving Masses at a country cathedral when the Dean had taken a shine to him. He had encouraged him to answer God's call to the altar and to pursue a life of special holiness in the priesthood. In the meantime, the Dean required Paul to supply him with the personal services which any attractive little boy could offer to a predatory paedophile. Paul did not persevere in his calling. Shortly after our conversation, he left our enclosure on the mountain (at that stage I was beginning to feel I was gaining a reputation for encouraging our apprentice-priests to turn away from their calling. Perhaps I was). Paul packed his belongings and caught the train back to the city. He had made his escape from the clutches of a troubled member of the clergy and from the sexual tensions of a celibate life.

On another occasion, a deserted wife and mother of three drove into the college looking for someone to speak to. By chance she ran into the junior member of staff and unloaded her burden on me. She told me that one of the local priests – someone who often visited us, who heard the students confessions and who was in charge of a parish on the lower Blue Mountains – was visiting her home regularly and demanding special favours. She had come seeking understanding and advice. But what was I expected to do? What advice could I have given her? Was it my duty to confront this man of God? – he was seriously more senior than me. Expose him? Dob him into the Cathedral? I didn't know what to do and wondered whether any of the other staff members were privy to such secrets. We never discussed these serious, deeply personal matters, even in general terms. We never talked about ourselves, our needs, our problems or our lives together. Each of us was a tiny island in a vast unexplored ocean. We kept each other out there, at arm's length, at a safe distance. Maybe the rector or the senior staff knew more of what was happening in their establishment, but I have my doubts.

Despite my failure to explore the intimate details of Father Kiss's "missionary" activities, from the little I was told, I knew in my bones that what he had been doing constituted a grave sin. Years passed before I would click on the "crime and punishment" tab of my internal computer. At that stage, the criminal law was well outside my clerical purview. My points of reference were heaven and hell, virtue and sin, especially sins of the flesh. One of my ingrained and principal concerns was loyalty to the institution founded by Jesus and his Apostles. Its reputation had to be protected – at all costs.

The Vince Kiss transactions were one of those fleshy sins. Every act or thought against the sixth, or sex, commandment was serious – adultery, bestiality, homosexuality, and even solitary acts of masturbation. Entertaining impure thoughts was gravely wrong – and kissing passionately, as well as anything other than accidental touching of someone else's unmentionables. These were always mortal sins, deadly offences, punishable in hell if you died without purging these foul deeds. If victimless misdemeanours could be so serious, what could one say about Father Vincent's night-time activities?

Whenever he stayed with us overnight, he used to celebrate Mass with us in the morning. I am ashamed to retrace the twisted path of my thinking as it twirled around over thirty years ago. I assumed at the time that because he was celebrating the mysteries with us, he had approached a confessor first thing in the morning, before Mass, and sought absolution. Otherwise he was condemned to an eternal double jeopardy – a sex sin and a sacrilegious celebration of Mass and communion. In order to receive a valid forgiveness, he had to sincerely express a determination not to sin again. He must have had a "firm purpose of amendment", otherwise his expressions of sorrow would have been a sham. Since he was "saying" Mass with us, I assumed our guest was sincerely sorry; that this behaviour had been a sudden lapse, an aberration; and that he was back on the straight and narrow. I was wrong – but how wrong would come to light later.

In my wildest imagination, I did not conceive of the possibility that Father Vince was hearing my visitor's confession after their secret encounters, forgiving the sins he himself had committed with him, forgiving his friend in the name of God and of holy Mother Church, and thereby incurring the curse of an *ipsissimo facto* excommunication.

If my visitor had told me about the confessions, I would have known immediately of Vince's canonical status. I knew all there was to know about excommunications – nothing about crimes, or about homosexuality, or about paedophilia, but everything about excommunications, about their various types and categories.

I had spent months at Manly in Moral Theology classes listening to Monsignor Jimmy Madden lecturing in Latin. I had taken detailed notes. I had laboured over this 'fascinating' topic, learning by heart what offences attracted which category of excommunication. There were five heinous offences which incurred the worst of all excommunications, the ban which could be lifted only by recourse to the Vatican. When a priest absolved the sins of his accomplice, his exclusion from the community of believers immediately kicked in and to be reconciled, he had to approach the Holy See. No one else had the power to bring him back into the fold, or to bury his body in consecrated ground.

But none of us at Springwood knew at the time what our colleague was doing. Had we known, had I known, I would have had to ban him from celebrating the sacred mysteries with us, from praying with us, as well as preying on one of us.

Of course, what I should have done was go straight to the village police station at Springwood and report the criminal offences. But my visitor told me later that had I proposed that course, he would never have told me his story.

In truth, I didn't know what to do. I was way out of my depth. I didn't think of the police, of criminal offences, trials and possible gaol sentences. That was to come.

I realised that these foul priestly deeds had to be hushed up. The reputation of the Church and of the priesthood was at stake. I suspected that this charismatic character who had gone through the system with me was some seriously sick priest, but it did not enter my head that he was also a criminal. I was not living in the wide, open, secular world of New South Wales. I had only ever functioned in the ecclesiastical world – the parish, the Catholic school system, the seminary, the priesthood.

I am ashamed to confess that I did not seek my visitor's permission to go straight to the rector and to the police, to expose the deceitful hypocrisy of one of my brothers and to blow his clammy relationship with a number of the young, vulnerable men of his country town out of the water. I should have marched in on Tommy Veech and given him the shock of his clerical life. I should have visited the police and had Father Kiss arrested and charged, as he was in March 2002, with numerous indecent assaults and acts of buggery on other boys – some of them attacked and polluted at a time *after* my counselling conference in the seminary.

When I advised my visitor to confront his tormentor bluntly, full-frontal, to surgically remove him from his young life, and told him that there was life after Kiss, he did exactly as advised. Some months later, he found the uneven track out of the seminary. I am proud to report that I assisted him to go in search of a life, any life, a real life, in the sun. He left with a sense of profound relief, and no permanent sense of failure. He was free.

I now know that my response to my visitor's predicament had been breathtakingly inadequate. I had failed to comprehend and deal with this dirty wickedness as any reasonable adult should have. I should add, knowing now full well how incomprehensible and abhorrent it is for any reasonable person outside the ecclesiastical world, that I understand how it happened here in Australia, in the United States and throughout the world, that cardinals, bishops, senior priests, even a Pope, covered up the sexual scandals of some of the clergy. They moved them from parish to parish, hid their criminal deeds from the civil authorities, protected the culprits and hoped, prayed that the victims would simply go away. It shames me to admit this profound vacuum which once existed in my humanity, in my Christian spirituality.

It is now apparent that a deadly virus has attacked the very fabric of the institution. The Catholic Church had built its modern image and reputation on the glories of its celibate clergy, the vow of chastity freely undertaken by its religious men and women, on its preaching of the virtue of purity and on its hard stand on everything to do with sex outside of marriage – even the mortal consequences of impure thoughts and masturbation.

Now it had been revealed – underage boys, little girls, homosexual relationships, one-night stands, illicit affairs – and cover-ups, protection from on high, pretence, silences, hypocrisy. These matters cannot be cured by ceremonial apologies, however sincere or abject. The cancer was too deeply imbedded. In an institution which has fostered devotion to the Virgin Mary, which has never explored the sexuality of Jesus or his mother, of St Joseph or any of the Apostles (at least some of whom were married), in an institution which declared infallibly the doctrine of the Immaculate Conception, which declares in its faith statements the virginal conception and birth of its founder, an organization which has encouraged shrines to the Virgin to be set up in its churches, in streets, in market-places, bus stations, taxis, buses and family homes – the earthquake caused by the rumble of scandalous revelations has registered at least 8 on the Richter Scale and has produced havoc and devastation among the faithful. The damage will not be remedied for centuries.

It was inevitable that the system would come unstuck. As much as we pretended that priests were above the common herd, that we were different, that we were all, as a group, unusually holy, that we were in the world, working *in* the world, ministering unselfishly to others, but that we were not *of* the world – the truth has always been that we were mere mortals, just human beings. Many of us were generous and committed to doing good. Some few were really holy, but they were truly the exception and often a real pain in the arse. Others were weak and inadequate – some really crazy; some a danger on the loose and some few were truly evil. It does no good to the Church or to the priests to pretend otherwise.

When the pedestal toppled, the true goodness – not the pretend sanctimonious, barbie-doll holiness – the true human weaknesses and sometimes the searing wickedness of aspects of the institution and its officers, were there for the world to see. It was a surprise to all of us (especially to the multitude of believers, to the faithful religious women who had spent their lives teaching in schools and nursing in hospitals and to many of the labouring clergy) just how widespread the problem was – just how deeply it had penetrated into the fabric of the institution.

chapter eleven

1972
WITH A SIGH OF RELIEF

On my arrival at Springwood at the beginning of the academic year in 1967, I had received no welcome from the members of the staff or the rector, or from the students. No muffled clap, no glasses raised, no scones and jam, no speeches, not even a warm handshake or a pat on the back. That was normal. No fuss. Just get on with it. I had arrived, found my room, unpacked my few books and clothes in my allotted study-cum-bedroom on the second floor of the old sandstone building, and started my new life as a priest working in the seminary system.

When I was leaving my mountain hide-away in about late July 1972, I wasn't going to wait to see if my confrères would farewell me. I decided to arrange my own celebration.

I chose a Sunday – one on which I was programmed to celebrate the solemn, community, high Eucharist in the chapel – and I posted invitations, far and wide, to my friends and family, to attend at 10 a.m, with picnic baskets, cooled beer and wine and children. My departure was a good excuse for a party.

Friends came from everywhere. Friends out of my past and friends out of the life I had lived away from the seminary at Springwood. With my mother and father, my brother Sean and my sister Colleen, their partners and children, my friends mingled in the college chapel among a hundred and eighty or more students in black cassocks and pretty, white lace surplices and together we let loose a loud, happy Mass.

Monsignor Veech was in residence as usual and concelebrated the Mass with me. He seemed a little petulant, perhaps even furious because, although I had sought permission to have a few friends and family visit the college and celebrate Mass with me before my departure, he had had no warning of the scale of the exercise I had planned. I had taken him by surprise but he said nothing – not a word of comment, or criticism, certainly no word of appreciation or contentment that the day had been such a success. This Sunday "nonsense" would have been seen as just "Geraghty on an ego trip, big noting himself", and there would have been an element of truth in his observation. Human motivation is never angelically pure. I understand that later, in my absence, Boo came to refer to my farewell as "the Geraghty day".

The chapel stirred with the undisciplined murmur of intruders and was filled to the rafters with sacred songs tortured by family and friends singing with unaccustomed gusto. The students seemed pleased to be part of a happening overflowing with joy, with genuine good wishes, and happy to welcome visitors in such numbers into their compound. I imagine they were also keen to observe how the boss was taking the intrusion.

After the liturgical celebration in the chapel, my guests drove onto what we used to call "the top-field" – a cleared, paspalum grassed and stony paddock where I had played cricket in my young days. It was an area several hundred metres from the college building, with rustic picnic tables scattered around the fringe of the field, some hidden in the bush, just off the track.

My guests set up picnic centres, spread out blankets and tablecloths, opened beer cans, popped corks and began mingling with each other as though they shared something in common. The children screamed and shouted, played cricket, threw balls, teased one another and disappeared down bush tracks. A day I will never forget. When we get together, a number of my old students often remind me of that Sunday when my friends invaded Tommy's fiefdom.

Then, to my astonishment, a few words of farewell were spoken one evening in the refectory, after the meal. The Monsignor, in a moment of generosity, invited me to address the students on the eve of my departure. In the five years I had been among them, I had grown older and wiser. Despite our unsatisfactory and unhappy relationship and despite the daily stressors of the system, I could not say that my life among them had been totally wasted, that there had not been good times and some enriching experiences. I would come to value the opportunity I had been given to expand my mind, to nourish my spirit in silence, to learn new skills, to live in the midst of discord and survive, to cope with the loss of my sister Maureen, to share my life with a group of generous young men and to grow to some level of maturity.

The rector could not bring himself to draft a few bland words of well-wishing, so he called on Dr John Walsh, one of the senior priests on the staff, to say a few words on behalf of the community. I remember him addressing me in a warm and friendly tone. I recall with gratitude the sincerity and honesty with which he spoke. He told the students, and me, that they had all known that Dr Geraghty had not warmed to the training policy in the institution. I had made no secret of this to him and to the other members of the staff. It was clear that I had felt uncomfortable with the tone and the direction of their formation program. But, he said, to my credit, I had not sought to undermine the work that the other priests were trying to do in the seminary. He observed I had been loyal to my confrères and for that, he thanked me. I hope the Monsignor was listening. At that stage of my life at least, there had been no need of suspicion or fear that a terrorist was in their midst.

I was flattered to hear John Walsh's words and not a little stunned. He had spoken so openly in the presence of the students (something rarely, if ever, done), and he had given voice to the conflict which had eaten into my soul during my time among them.

I packed my belongings into my VW, drove down the long, sealed driveway, out through the stone gates, and never returned. It was high time to begin my escape.

As I drove away, I am sure the Monsignor must have stood on the steps of the college and breathed a deep sigh of relief. I too was breathing easier, happy to see the back of the likes of Tommy Veech and his grey world. I was on my way to Paris, to study the history and theology of liturgical worship and I would not be back until October '74.

For a number of years I had been scheming to escape from Springwood and spend some time overseas. Originally I had planned to study sociology in America, preferably at Syracuse University or Berkley, but I couldn't elicit a flicker of interest in that direction from Cardinal Gilroy and I needed his permission and financial support. The President of the Theological Faculty, Paddy Murphy, was looking for someone to lecture in Liturgical Studies and Sacramental Theology since the liturgy had recently emerged from the Second Vatican Council as a new and exciting area of theological inquiry. Somehow I persuaded both the Faculty and Cardinal Freeman (who had by then taken over from Cardinal Gilroy) to let me go to Paris to study with the French Dominicans rather than to central headquarters in Rome.

Doctor Grove Johnson had recently spent a year or so on study leave in Paris and was prepared to recommend me to the parish priest in the left-wing, working-class parish of *La Garenne-Colombes* where he had lived. Board and lodging in exchange for working in the parish, with the added bonus of daily contact with ordinary French people. Those plans looked much better on paper than they proved to be in reality. For someone who could not speak the language, my life would prove too tough, too lonely out there in the suburbs of Paris, at the end of a long train ride from the centre.

Neil Brown and I had planned to travel together. We had been class-mates since 1956. The Brown and Geraghty families, our proud parents, our brothers and sisters, as well as a few close friends, stood around in the overseas terminal at Mascot, hovering, chattering, pacing, filling in time. After Neil and I had booked our modest luggage through, we said our restrained celibate farewells, heart pumping in expectation, cold handshakes for the men and uncomfortable kisses for the womenfolk, we disappeared behind the grey-frosted glass on our way to a new world.

We were sitting on the tarmac waiting to become air-borne when Neil turned to me and without a word of explanation, quoted the prayer of a mother from *A Portrait of the Artist as a Young Man* –

> "She prays now, she says, that I may learn in my own life and
> away from home and friends what the heart is and what it
> feels. Amen. So be it. Welcome, O life! I go to encounter for

the millionth time the reality of experience and to forge in the smithy of my soul the uncreated conscience of my race".

He had learnt it by heart especially for the occasion.

In July 1972, I flew out of Sydney with my lifelong friend – a maiden voyage, an adventure of a lifetime for both of us. He was on his way to Rome, me to Paris. We were both on the verge of a new life.

1972-74
SOUS LE CIEL DE PARIS

If you are lucky enough to have lived
In Paris as a young man, then wherever you
Go for the rest of your life, it stays with
You, for Paris is a moveable feast.
Hemingway, 1950.

Paris was full of extravagant possibilities and excitement. The vast metro system, the psychotic traffic, the many hubs of human activity in motion day and night, boulevards of beauty, Notre Dame, the Eiffel Tower, parks, museums, galleries, the River Seine winding its way quietly under bridges, carrying barges full of coal or rubble, timber or tourists, up and down the locks – everything was new to me.

Within days of my arrival, I began to feel my way round in the city. I came to know her churches, boulevards, streets and her changing moods. For the first time in my life I wandered aimlessly, looking in windows, watching people, fascinated by the high fashion in the shops and the elegance of the buildings and the men and women on the sidewalks.

I relished the freedom of a nobody wandering in mufti along *Boulevard Saint Germain*, observing pretty faces in the street and smiling at the old Arab roasting his nuts on a large copper kettle. I explored the narrow streets behind the church of *St Germain des Près*, passing the fishmonger on *Rue de Buci* with his fresh fleshy oysters arranged in rows on the footpath. I strolled along the snaking alleyways chocked with cars parked higgledy-piggledy, among the aggressive pedestrians on *Rue St André des Arts*, stepping over dog poo. I would drop into the theatre where the Marx Brothers were playing twenty-four-seven or have an occasional, expensive, coffee at *Café des Deux Maggots*.

Books had been a lifelong fascination for me so the bookshops around *Place St Sulpice* drew me in like a magnet. I began to spend afternoons on tall ladders in second-hand bookshops searching out treasure and to spend many an enjoyable hour in *La Procure*, one of the world's largest theological and religious bookshops.

In all her guises, Paris was beautiful, fascinating, elegant and exhausting.

Neil Brown stayed with me for a month or so, exploring the wonders of Paris before leaving to begin his doctoral studies in Rome. While he was with me I moved in with the priests working in the parish of *La Garenne Colombes,* on the outskirts of Paris. It soon became obvious however, that the arrangements I had made in Sydney were not going to work out. The priests on staff were expecting me to labour as a full-time assistant, in a parish which covered a large area with many working-class families and a multitude of social problems. I couldn't speak the language sufficiently at that stage and besides, the place was way out in the suburban wilderness – several hours by public transport from the institute where I was studying. I was isolated and out of my comfort-zone.

While I was out there in the parish on the fringe of the metropolis, one of the junior priests invited me to go with him on a renewal seminar organised by the local clergy. We were about twenty participants and a theologian from Bordeaux, who had agreed to facilitate the discussion.

I went along for the ride without any idea as to where I was going, or what was in front of me. The next few days were a surprise and a window into the world of the French clergy. I was not accustomed to such unabashed seriousness among the ranks of the clergy. I could have understood a three-day golf tournament, even a pious three-day retreat, but I was not prepared for the level of intensity, the depth of discussion, the reverence with which the participants spoke and their obvious scholarship. It was humbling for a priest trained in the good old Irish tradition at St Patrick's.

Before the seminar, the participants had submitted questions and observations to their expert from Bordeaux and he was expected to address their areas of concern. I listened attentively as he reflected on the possibility of a new church, different ecclesial structures and different orders or roles for the laity. He spoke about the possible retirement of the, then, Pope, who appeared to be tormented by doubts, wounded by his decision on the contraceptive pill and exhausted by the burden of office and he discussed the theological and pastoral implications of his retirement. He also addressed some of France's contemporary social problems and how he saw Christian beliefs and principles as interacting with society and the modern community. He shared his ideas about the enculturation of Christianity to the modern, Western, world and about the notion of redemption as an experience of freedom. A different world was opening up before me so soon after leaving Australia. These priests did not conform to the prototype that was on show in Sydney.

I only had to sit for an hour or so in the seminar group, or in any café in Paris, or spend an evening watching television, to realise that the French were great talkers. Ideas seemed to fascinate them. They talked rapidly and over one another, arguing, huffing and puffing, discussing politics, philosophy, art, movies, fashions, sex, literature, social questions and religion. I sat for long periods at the meal table, listening while the clergy discussed edgy, personal questions about their vocation, celibacy, their Church; reflecting excitedly on fundamental, theoretical, philosophical, ideological issues and they never appeared to achieve consensus or agree on practical conclusions. I was in foreign territory and with only a limping familiarity with the language, my head was as thick as porridge.

During the evening concelebration of the Eucharist, all twenty of us sat around a simple table, the Vicar-General presiding in mufti, as we broke bread together and passed the cup of blessing to each other. An enriching experience, apparently unremarkable for anyone other than the stranger. I had come from another planet, from a society in which the Eucharist was celebrated with an overload of formality and uniformity, with ritualised solemnity, but without much personal expression of faith or close communion. I was still defrosting, so I was a little uncomfortable but I was also excited to be part of other, richer, possibilities.

On a Monday towards the end of October, without proffering any satisfactory explanation to the parish clergy, sheepishly I crept out of their presbytery and moved into the *Fraternité Sacerdotale* in the heart of Paris. It was within walking distance of *Notre Dame, Les Invalides, Musée Rodin, La Tour Eiffel,* and the Seine.

This Babylonian *Fraternité* was a haven in the heart of Paris where clergy from all parts of the world could find a heated room to sleep, a community television to watch, a place where we could celebrate Mass privately or in groups, eat together in the refectory and be looked after, as was our custom, by nuns and lay brothers.

The *Fraternité* was a palatial residence hidden away behind high walls in one of the chic centres of Paris. It was next-door to the city residence of the French Prime Minister and up the street from the *Hotel Lutetia,* where the Gestapo had had their Parisian headquarters during the war. Two rows of giant French windows opened up onto the interior of the stately home. On the ground floor of the main building (which was reputed to have served as the Paris residence of Cardinal Richelieu), was a maze of connecting rooms with imperial gold-leafed doors and windows, bucolic scenes hand-painted on the ceilings and which once upon a time had served as ballrooms and dining salons. Elegant off-the-shoulder dresses displaying soft flesh, salacious curves, sparkling diamonds and powdered wigs, had danced and strutted about in the mirrors set into the walls.

At the rear of the main building, through the stately French doors and down the curved stairway of the balcony, was a sunken, geometrically designed garden about the size of a football-field where miniature, dark green hedges traced patterns on the edges of blue and rose metal paths. A fountain in the centre was home to families of goldfish and a group of dancing nymphs, which were clothed throughout the winter months in ice and snow – icicles hanging from elbows, chins, bosoms and private parts. Against the rear stone wall, at the bottom of the garden, stood a modern, two-story residence, in which I had a room looking out through another French window onto the fountain and its surrounds.

A short stroll down the street brought me to *Rue du Bac* with the *Bon Marché* on one side and a row of boutique shops opposite, which hid the mother-house of the Sisters of Charity. I used to shepherd my pious visitors to the chapel of *The Miraculous Medal* where the bloodless heart of St Vincent de Paul was mounted on high in a monstrance. A tourist could find the rest of his body further on, in a dusty, shadowy church on *Rue de Sèvres*, where a blackened, wizened body in priestly vestments rested peacefully inside a glass case, motionless on a soiled cloth with frayed edges.

Also in *Rue de Sèvres,* was the Jesuit church where Gelineau SJ used to present the most joyful, energetic Sunday celebration. Drums, tambourines, trumpets, gentle and meditative psalmody, designer vestments, stately processions – the ten o'clock Mass on Sundays at *St Ignace* was a most prayerful experience.

St Ignace presented a different picture of Christianity to the reactionary, devotional, clergy who serviced the chapel of *The Miraculous Medal*. These expressions of Catholic faith in France were within shouting distance of one another and together, they seemed to characterise the ethos, the politics, the ecclesiastical life of Paris and of France, where one could witness everything from extreme, right-wing fascism to anarchy and rebellion. The Catholic Church in France came in all sizes and colours, but without the threat of supervision and control by the temple police, so warmly embraced in Australia.

I was to learn that Paris was a city of extremes, extravagances and excesses; super rich, yet with grinding poverty; saccharine piety and brazen pornography; *La Belle Epoque*, Rodin, Picasso, Cocteau, Proust; imperial receptions, state occasions, processions and parades. On one side of the spectrum were Catholics whose reactionary conservatism would confound the most tolerant. Mixed together were aggressive fascists goose-stepping in the streets, monarchists covered in medals, out of touch rat-bags of every persuasion, and in the same city – anarchists, revolutionaries, poets, ideological unionists, smoldering workers, liberal theologians and members of the Communist Party.

The steamy, throbbing, *Quatier Latin* was within walking distance of where I was living and I would often stroll down into its winding streets with other students, especially late at night after study for a cup of coffee and to taste and smell the atmosphere. I would pass by bookshops and art dealers, exquisitely decorated boutiques, antique shops, people walking dogs, playing with monkeys, laughing and talking loudly, broad streets, cafes, people from all parts of the globe, immigrants from India, Arabs in their turbans and white robes, black Africans speaking French and a wide choice of cuisines.

The *Fraternité* was so conveniently placed – and only a ten-minute walk from the *Institut Catholique* where I was studying. I was keen to make the best of what was on offer there, aware that I was costing the diocese good money. I was ready to study and anxious to learn.

I was not at the *Fraternité* long before I became conscious that other clerics staying in the house were spending money, diocesan money, as if they were living in a world of millionaires – expensive restaurants, stylish clothes, luxury holidays, for some, anything but what they had come to Paris to do.

On reflection I might have been mistaken in my assessment of these priests eating at the same table with me, celebrating Mass each day together. I thought they were students, but maybe they were not there to study. Perhaps they wanted to be anonymous in Paris to resolve their personal problems or maybe study was an excuse for them to untangle their brains, to extricate themselves from an unhealthy relationship or to escape the pressures of pastoral work and commitment back home. I was an outsider looking in on other people's lives. Father Rupert, for example, was probably not in Paris to study history. He was spending too much time away from his desk, smoking, idle chatter, drinking endless cups of coffee and obviously bored. Father Francis Xavier may not have been among us to study patrology and research a thesis. He was always out and about, not reading the course material, skipping the regular lectures, talking about his thesis but never researching, never completing. Together, these two north Americans would talk constantly about the demands of their work, but hardly focusing any serious attention in that direction. Life was too good.

The *Fraternité* was a French-Canadian establishment mainly for French-Canadian clerics, some of whom were enrolled in fluffy, pastoral-type courses, others sent abroad to work themselves out and probably to ease their way out of the service. Some seemed to be engaged on a highly dubious and secretive Parisian life, on holidays from their calling. One cleric who was a friend of Cardinal Danielou and whose parents were obviously filthy rich, moved out of *Rue de Babylone* into his own digs in the seventeenth arrondissement and engaged the services of a black, handsome, live-in, man-servant.

In November, when the university students back home were sun-baking on the beaches of Sydney, I attended an ordination ceremony at the parish church of *St Severin*. As I walked from the Fra*ternité* in *Rue de Babylone* down into the Latin Quarter, flakes of snow floated down from heaven covering the shoulders of my overcoat and settling gently on the grey streets. I was far from my home base, in a magical world.

St Severin used to attract a regular community of believers throbbing with renewal in the heart of the Latin Quarter (close to the oldest university in Paris where Abelard and Thomas Aquinas used to teach, near institutes of higher learning such as the *Beaux Arts*, with students from all parts of the world, in scungy clothes, wandering aimlessly day and night). The building was hidden among Greek, Chinese and North African restaurants pressed up against one another, in narrow streets where a mixture of cooking aromas wafted over piles of rubbish. Students and tourists wandered in the laneways, looking at pigs roasting on spits in shop windows, Lebanese or Turkish cakes, film theatres, bookshops, little art boutiques, and *St Severin* with buildings huddled against its walls as if for warmth.

The ordination music prepared for the occasion was magnificent. The leader practised us painstakingly before the celebration and led us discreetly throughout the ceremony. I was full of admiration at his mellow, unobtrusive voice. The overflowing congregation sang lustily and the penetrating sound of a trumpet and an organ, played in an echoing building, was spine-tingling, stark and haunting, as the music sounded round the recesses of the sacred space – liturgy at its best.

One of the auxiliary bishops of the Archdiocese was presiding. He spoke openly and favourably, about married clergy, the ordination of women, the senate of Bishops and about the priesthood in general. This was 1972, and nearly forty years later, no ecclesiastical leader in Australia has addressed these explosive topics. Like a trembling dictator, the Polish Pope had decided these urgent questions were off-limits. One would think he was controlling an army, or a Soviet department, or an unruly classroom of primary school children, rather than shepherding a gathering of believers. There was to come a time when a country bishop in Queensland would be forced to resign his post for raising the same issues.

Once I had settled into my courses at the *Institut Catholique*, I began to attend a number of regular seminars. Boris Brobimskoy, a bearded Russian Orthodox scholar, led a weekly study session on St Augustine's sacramental theology; a French Franciscan led a Saturday morning, two hour, packed to the rafters, lecture on religious myths and symbols; and a Jesuit scholar, Pierre Kannengeizer, who had succeeded to the academic position held for years by another Jesuit, Jean Danielou, ran a weekly lecture in patristic studies. My membership in this last seminar brought an unexpected bonus.

On 9 November 1972, Jean Guénolé Marie Cardinal Danielou SJ had become a member of an exclusive club of French scholars founded in 1635 by Cardinal Richelieu – the *Academie Française*. His club was restricted to only forty members, so to be chosen as one of the "Immortals" was considered a supernatural honour – more exclusive than the College of Cardinals.

Kannengeizer invited his seminar students to attend a reception, held to honour the newly elected member of the *Academie*. The function was to be held in an exclusive hotel – several chandeliers in each room glowing out through the magnificent French windows into the darkness beyond and onto the carriage-way entrance. Like the *Fraternité* and many of the palatial residences in Paris, the building was discreetly hidden behind a stone-wall barrier. I thought myself too junior, too unimportant to attend, but curiosity and my sense of adventure eventually overcame my humility.

Kannengeizer had arranged for each of us to receive a formal invitation and we dressed as well as we could for the occasion. On my arrival, I stood waiting at attention in the vestibule. When I was finally called upon to make my entry, the Master of Ceremonies for the evening, a corpulent man with a flourish of white hair covering his skull, dressed in tails, with booming voice, a heavy silver chain around his neck and the medallion resting heavy on his chest, proclaimed to the assembled dignitaries; "Père Geraghty, Sydney, Australie". Suddenly I had become an important personage but only for a few seconds. The seminar group stayed close to one another while the others mingled. French champagne and cocktails preceded a program of long, scholarly, agitated speeches, peppered with extravagant adjectives and gestures.

The Cardinal, dressed in his black suit, was working the room with Vatican finesse – a pectoral cross and gold chain shining on his bright red stock, red socks disappearing into his patent leather shoes. His vow of poverty was invisible for the night.

My companion at the reception was an American priest from the Bronx who, mixing in a crowd with quasi-royalty and hangers-on, found himself juggling two glasses of champagne, one in each hand, and a cigarette in his mouth. In a moment of international confusion, he managed to slop half a glass of champagne on the guest of honour who was moving quickly through the crowd, smiling at everyone.

In his acceptance speech, the Cardinal delivered a diatribe addressed to those among us who had neglected to study Latin and Greek to an elevated standard, with a special blast for those who considered such study was passé in the modern Church. Like the preacher who savages his Sunday congregation about those who fail to attend to their Sunday obligation, he was preaching to the converted.

Cardinal Danielou had become a controversial character in the Church, and among the French, and he was soon to become notorious. In a former life, he had been one of the leaders of the New Church in Europe, a member of the avant-garde and an important character at the Second Vatican Council. However, by 1972, he had shed his winter skin to become a reactionary conservative and a high priest in the ecclesiastical bureaucracy.

Suddenly, towards the end of my stay in Paris, Danielou was dead, and the whole of France took a gulp of horror. The French daily papers were reporting the news across the front pages – *Le Figaro* and *Le Monde* were pretending to maintain a sober, superior objectivity, while the scurrilous *Le Canard Enchaîné* was relishing the moment. The high Church dignitaries were fluffing around like headless chooks, trying to hose down a potential scandal.

The Cardinal had dropped dead suddenly from a ruptured aneurysm while visiting someone in the seventeenth arrondissement – one of the less salubrious quarters of Paris, famous for its prostitutes and strip-tease artists. Rumours were circulating. He had died in the street, in a number of different streets (no one could be sure), on the stairs, on the sixth floor of a building (which, like most Parisian buildings, was not serviced by an elevator). God had summoned his servant while he was in the apartment of a certain Madame Santoni, perhaps even in her bed. No one knew her first name but the papers were calling her *Mimi*. Some were saying he had expired in her arms, *in fragrante delicto*. So much for Latin and Greek! Mimi Santoni had been a friend in need, a cabaret dancer, a strip-tease artiste, a prostitute. She was not talking. The members of the clergy were unavailable. The press was on fire.

After a few days, when the monsignors and bishops had had a chance to visit the scene and speak privately with the lady in question, the official Church story began to emerge. The Cardinal had acted as the unofficial chaplain to the demimonde of Paris. He had been visiting a damsel in distress to give her the money she needed to stand bail for her lover. He had collapsed climbing the stairs on a corporal work of mercy. He had been merely following the evangelical dictates of Jesus. *The Affaire Dani* was a beat-up.

But the horse had bolted. The Parisian journalists were far from convinced. Why had it taken so long for the Church officials to come up with their story? How friendly had the Cardinal been with this shady lady? What had been the real cause of his sudden *crise de coeur*? Where had the different versions of events come from? What had the Cardinal been doing in that apartment? Hearing her confession? What had he been doing when the angel had tapped him on the shoulder? The imagination of the nation was going wild. Those who should have known had been reluctant to speak for days, for weeks. The people of Paris were left in doubt, to guess, to speculate, to presume the best, to hope for the worst.

Danielou would not have been the first of the rich and famous to stray from the path of righteousness. Over the centuries there has been a tradition for royalty, for Popes and prelates, and presidents, to savour the aphrodisiac of power, to dress themselves in the garments of virtue, to lie and cheat, accept petty bribes, to pretend to be chaste, to preach purity, while all the time unbuttoning their shirt or their soutane to taste the delights the Lord has blessed men with. What did Danielou do when he was not writing books, or giving scholarly lectures? When he was not dressed in flashing red, celebrating in Renaissance ceremonial style? No one knew for sure, but some thought they had a pretty good idea.

In May 1974, as a little priest from Australia, I attended the Cardinal's funeral. I was agog with the stories swirling about the corpse. The only cardinal I knew was the Archbishop of Sydney, Cardinal Norman Gilroy, who may have known a little Latin but who had forgotten any Greek he had learnt. He was not a scholar of international repute, or a member of the *Academie Française* – more like an accounts clerk, but well-behaved. I had simply assumed that all cardinals were like him.

The eulogy did not mention the circumstances of Danielou's passing. We buried him from the parish church in the Latin Quarter, *St Sulpice*. I stood in this immense building, crushed in the crowd at the back, surrounded by dignitaries who may have known the truth and the simple faithful who hoped the rumours were false. Together we listened to the distant strain of Gregorian chant and to the fruity tributes offered to the dead Eminence. We prayed for his soul in this heavy church, supported by stone and marble columns, whose shady, dusty side-altars were in desperate need of a scrub, and hoping to meet the Cardinal in heaven.

During the two-year, four-semester, liturgical course I was following, Père Yves Congar came to our Institute. He had agreed to a two-hour session with us, to answer any questions we might like to ask him – on the liturgy, the Church, the development of doctrine, ecclesiastical authority, the episcopacy, the priesthood, St Thomas Aquinas, the early Christian writers – on any of his favourite topics. He came as the confrère of our director, Jean-Marie Gy, as a friend, a fellow searcher and a member of the community of Dominicans at St Jacques with Dalmais and the priest-worker warrior Marie-Dominique Chenu.

Carefully supported by his friend Gy, Congar struggled into our lecture-room on steel crutches – old, frail, and pale from a lifetime in the libraries of Europe. He had published more than one thousand, two hundred scholarly articles and books, some more than a thousand pages, with heavy, detailed footnotes. Scholars were already writing heavy tomes on his contribution to theology and to the life of the modern Church. We had awaited his appearance with thrilling anticipation. I sensed an aura of brilliance and dedication surrounding this man who had become, in all humility, one of the most influential theologians of the twentieth century. One of his major works, published in 1953, *Towards a Theology of the Laity*, had caused a seismic disturbance in Catholic thinking on the structure, organisation, character of the institutional Church and had challenged the clerical, centralized, authoritarian monopoly of the Roman bureaucracy. It was said that before announcing his reforming council in Rome, John XXIII had read *True and False Reform in the Church,* published by Congar in 1950.

But Congar's success had come towards the end of his life, after years of dealing with faceless bullies on his own side. He had fought many battles with blind Roman bureaucrats, before eventually becoming a focus of influence at the Second Vatican Council where he had lectured, informed, enlightened and persuaded the bishops of the world.

During the Second World War, Congar had served as a medical orderly in the French army. When he was taken prisoner he had been interned in the notorious Colditz prison camp for "dangerous officers", where he had given lectures to the other prisoners and learnt to speak Russian fluently. After the war he had been involved in the worker-priest movement with his close friend Chenu and together they had come under Vatican scrutiny. In the early 50s, he and other Catholic scholars (Teilhard de Chardin, de Lubac, Chenu) had been the subjects of religious denunciations, warnings, rumours, libels and Roman decisions restricting their work and influence. Later he was to show the same contempt for the busy-bodies of the Vatican, as he had earlier shown for the *Boches* who had invaded his homeland. In 1954 the Master of the Dominicans in Rome, on directions from the Vatican, had expelled him and others from their teaching posts at the Dominican study centre, *Le Saulchoir,* near Paris. His years of exile had begun – at the *École Biblique* in Jerusalem (1954), Rome (1955) and Cambridge (1956). He had been banned from speaking in public or publishing his writings. Faceless Vatican bureaucrats had treated him appallingly.

Then in 1960, to his great surprise, Good Pope John had made him a consultant to the theological commission charged with preparing Rome and the world for a council of bishops. Congar had come in from the cold, covered with scars. In his journal he had recorded that in Cambridge he had "cried and sobbed in (his) solitude without end" and he had spoken of being tempted, in the depth of depression, to end his life. But he had gone on to become an official consultant to the bishops at the Second Vatican Council and one of the principal authors of the central ideas and the final statements emanating from the Council – statements on the egalitarian notion of the Church as the People of God, revelation, the Church in the modern world, the celebration of the liturgy, and ecumenism. Towards the end of his life, he was standing tall at the centre of ecclesiastical power.

Congar appeared among us in his white Dominican habit – crushed, soiled, as a bachelor who lived alone in a monk's cell or in a library choked with books. Like a proper monk, he was bald to the middle of his crown, with scattered, mousy hair beyond the inner circle. This elderly man with bright, flashing eyes, was hard-headed, shrewd, prickly and uncompromising. Over the years he had earned a reputation for speaking his mind in tough, unambiguous language – a plain, blunt Frenchman from the Ardennes. He had spent his life searching and researching in the service of the Church, suffering for his faith. His was not a narrow, bigoted vision of Christ or his Church. His tireless familiarity with historical figures and events had given him a rich, colourful and variegated vision of the Church in all its guises, different outfits, periods of depression and of high achievements – battle scars, unhealed sores, warts and all. But he showed no patience for the thought-police of the Vatican "who (were) disarming in their goodness and piety".

This frail figure in his Dominican uniform showed few of the features I was expecting to find in an intellectual giant. He was physically disabled and in pain, completely devoid of arrogance and hubris, attentive to his questioners, humble, somewhat reticent, unhurried, searching carefully for an accurate expression of some insight or opinion and without the gift of infallibility.

My life had been blessed by this man. Since my seminary days, I had read a number of mind-bending publications under his name. His honesty, his courage, his exacting scientific, historical methodology, his originality and that of his contemporaries, had inspired their younger confrères – men like Dalmais and Gy. I had been studying almost all of my life, but Paris was my first encounter with scholarly men who were not paralysed with the fear of knowing, with the need for permission to question, who welcomed questions and other points of view.

I had had an earlier, brief contact with this man. In the darkness of my search for a doctoral topic in 1963, I had written to him, in English, to seek his advice. I told him that I had been fascinated with the Pauline images of the Cosmic Christ, in his letters to the Ephesians and Colossians and with the poetic creational vision of Teilhard de Chardin. He had answered in his own handwriting, in French, and pointed me in the direction of St Irenaeus. I had followed his nudge and after more than two hard years of lonely research, I had gained my doctorate on the topic Congar had recommended. A young student on the other side of the world was, and remains in his old age, grateful for the humility and enthusiasm of this great scholar. Now, towards the end of his life, I had the privilege of a two-hour encounter with the man – a memorable experience.

Sunday by Sunday, I attended different liturgical celebrations in various parts of the city. Every few months, for example, I used to travel by Metro to *Alexander Nevsky Cathedral* near the *Étoile* to spend three or four hours celebrating the Russian Liturgy – feeling the vibrations of the deep-throated thunderous choir floating over me, watching the worshippers kissing icons, lighting candles, prostrating themselves flat on the mosaic floor or wandering outside for half an hour or so for a cup of coffee and a cigarette. They seemed to have no concept of remaining quietly in their pew and being present for the whole of the ceremony. Then at Easter-time, I visited the monastery of *St Serge* on the outskirts of Paris, to celebrate the Russian Easter in a more traditional way.

From time to time and for a change, I used to seek out the celebration in an underground chapel at *Montparnasse*, buried deep in the bowels of the earth, in the huge railway station and business-residential complex which dominated the Paris skyline. The chapel was jam-packed each Sunday. Contrary to the rules of Rome, the celebrant used to compose his own Eucharistic Prayers, Sunday by Sunday. St Bernard's was more revolting than any church congregation in Australia would have dared to be. The character of Christian ministry in the underground church, involving the laity and female religious, seemed to be in the process of radical change – not radical enough or quick enough perhaps to reflect *The Signs of the Times*, but ahead of Australia by many laps. Unfortunately, this healthy impetus for renewal was later strangled, principally by Pope John Paul II and the present Pope.

My regular Sunday celebration, however, was at *St Ignace* where Gelineau SJ had taken charge of the liturgy and where no effort was spared to give dramatic voice to man's faith-filled, joyful praise of God. The homilies nourished and challenged; the prayers expressed modern needs and yearnings; piercing trumpets and thumping drums echoed in the upper chambers of the building; and music and movement created a profound sense of mystery and celebration. Like experienced choreographers, those in charge would vary the rhythms and structures of the liturgy to reflect the seasonal moods – Easter, Pentecost, Lent, Christmas. Readings (scriptural, religious, secular) were arranged antiphonally and interspersed with periods of reflection and prayerful singing. Nowhere else did I experience the liturgical know-how and expertise of those involved in the Gelineau celebrations. I did later feel the thrill of loud, sometimes chaotic, congregational worship in Germany (at Paderborn) and in a Franciscan church in Amsterdam, but nowhere in Spain, Italy, Argentina, Australia or Ireland. The Christmas liturgy I attended years later in the Cathedral in Toulouse, when we were on holidays and visiting family, was pompous, studied, clerical and cold, like a dwarfed version of papal liturgies in St Peter's in Rome. *St Ignace* on Sundays in Paris was superb.

A wave of clerics from Australia kept arriving at regular intervals at the *Fraternité* expecting to be entertained. Some had their hearts set on visiting the shrine of the Miraculous Medal around the corner, or the basilica on the hill at Montmatre (which had been built to appease the wounds inflicted on the Sacred Heart of Jesus, by the excesses of the Second Empire and the Communist Paris commune of 1871). Others were more interested in the night-life in *Pigalle*.

Towards the end of my stay in Paris, William Brennan (known to his colleagues as "Billy") flew in from Rome. He was on his way to becoming the frigidly affable bishop of a country diocese, where he was destined to alienate many of the clergy and nuns, establish his own narrow seminary, order his few students back into soutanes and make them submit to the restrictions of scholasticism. As the years passed he would grow gaunter, almost to the stage of a disembodied spirit. When he visited me in Paris though, he was still comparatively young (if Billy was ever young) and I was welcoming a holy soul, hidden in a grey, emaciated body clothed in an oversized frock-suit.

At the same time, Father Edmund Campion (who early in his life became "Eddy") arrived from England with his friend, John Davoren (who never became a "Johnny" or a "Jack"), and both of them were disguised in mufti. John and Eddy had once been classmates, but towards the end of his course Paddy Murphy, the dean of discipline, had "clipped" Eddy (this was like scratching him from the list of runners or if he had been investing in the stock-exchange, giving him a haircut, or removing his name from the diptychs). Anyway, his ordination was delayed and Eddy had to drop back a year, so that the authorities could look at him more closely to assess his loyalty, his obedience, his humility and his suitability for priesthood. Eventually he was ordained, in 1961 – both of them just ahead of me in the seniority stakes.

At the time, John Davoren was in charge of the Catholic welfare bureaucracy in our diocese at home. He had studied at Sydney University and massaged his career path out of parish work into a desk job. (If you persevere, you will meet him again later in this story.)

Eddy Campion was like a bachelor-cleric out of *The Great Gatsby* – handsome, a full crop of curly, sandy hair, an Irish complexion, apparently at ease in any company – religious or secular, working class or elite – a happy mixture of the religious, the urbane and the larrikin. From his days in the seminary, Eddy had progressed through the system surrounded by an aura of secrecy and reserve, and had been a puzzle to the authorities. A member of the authors' and journalists' club, a Peace activist and protester, but he always presented in his clericals at clergy funerals and seemed ready to judge even the coldest, meanest cleric with gentle compassion. Perhaps there were just a few exceptions.

I had a few free days so together, the four of us, drove south-west of Paris, in my Peugeot, to enjoy the French country-side and to visit the Benedictine monks of Solesmes. It proved a memorable weekend.

At the Liturgical Institute in Paris, I had been well drilled on the influence the Benedictine monks of Solesmes and particularly Dom Prosper Louis Pascal Gueranger, the first abbot of that priory, had had on the blossoming liturgical movement of the twentieth century. From a prepubescent age, I had prayed the Latin psalms and parts of the old Mass in Gregorian chant and it was the Solesmes monks that had been the world-famous exponents of this form of high culture. Every Sunday at High Mass, often during the week at Requiem masses for deceased members of the clergy and on major feast days, at Springwood and later at Manly, I had sung from the heavy *Liber Usualis* published by the Benedictines of Solesmes. During my first year at Springwood in 1951, I had piously sewn into the binding of this weighty book a flutter of various coloured ribbons as markers. The Solesmes monks had, by repute, dominated the renewal of the Roman Liturgy since before the reign of Pius XII.

So, with enthusiasm and a sense of history, to say nothing of St Benedict and the medieval foundation of Cluny which had spread monasteries like hundreds and thousands all over the map of Europe, I welcomed the opportunity to accompany "my friends" on a pilgrimage to the very centre of the modern liturgical movement.

For centuries the Benedictines had had a reputation throughout the religious world for their hospitality. I had already savoured its sweet taste at *St Benoit-sur-Loire* and I was ready for more.

When we arrived at Solemnes and without the slightest doubt fluttering about in my mind, I led the "boys" to the gate of the monastery where we had planned to accept the monks' hospitality for the night. I was the unelected French speaker and intermediary, and spoke to the "hospitality" brother through the grill. I told him that we were four priests from Australia who had come to visit his monastery, that we would like to stay the night under his roof and concelebrate with the monks in the morning.

But I did not get past the "hospitality" brother's defence-line. A bored look, a shrug of the shoulders, empty, vacant eyes and a silent invitation to move on. He informed me in his clinical, clipped French that we should return the next morning if we wanted to concelebrate the Eucharist. No smile, no warm embrace, no kiss on both cheeks and no invitation. The monks, renowned for their angelic Gregorian chant, had "given us the shoulder" and let us go without a sou. My three companions seemed to share some amusement at my expense. While I had entertained this strange notion that our fellow Christians, joined to us in a common seal of ordination, like Masonic monks, would open their arms to us – the others had come expecting nothing. The grey Benedictine brother with his high cheek bones and thin lips, slid the shutter closed. The medieval compound remained locked for the night.

Back in the Peugeot, I drove my laughing companions to a Bed and Breakfast nearby – chandeliers in the downstairs lounge and dining rooms; large mirrors; parquetry floors; magnificent French windows opening out onto a garden of purple irises, daffodils and tulips, with rows and circles of miniature, tonsured hedges; a fountain in the centre of the front driveway and French-speaking ducks gliding on the pond. At the dinner table that evening we had the choice of *entrecôtes grillés au beurre d'anchois* or *boeuf bourguignon* (my favourite), followed by *crème vanille en petits pots*, *gateaux aux pruneaux* or *tarte aux pommes*, a generous cheese platter, wines of the district, a cigar and a finishing gulp of Benedictine which tended to stick in my throat. The "hospitality" brother from the local monastery, even at the top of his form, could not have excelled this establishment for its atmosphere and class. His cold insouciance had proved a blessing. (Similar "favours" have descended on me throughout my life and knocked me over with grace.)

The following day, the four of us returned to the monastery to celebrate the Sunday Eucharist with the monks. Eddy and John were not too keen to exercise their priestly orders so they simply joined the congregation, silent in the body of the church. Bill and I, being pious nerds, went to the sacristy and found thirty or more monks gathered, each enclosed in his own tiny world and vesting for the Eucharist, white chasubles, white albs, the rustle of starched linen, the cincture of chastity tied tightly around the loins. Not one of the assembled brothers lifted his eyes or turned to greet the strangers. Not a word of welcome. It was cold outside, and freezing in the sacristy.

The Eucharist was celebrated in Latin, of course, and to a standard of precision and perfection beyond the reach of any parish or ordinary mortal. The Gregorian was chanted without a tremor, without the least hesitation, every note measured with its exact emphasis and length, each note pure and angelic. This was the music of heaven – slow, gentle, simple and haunting, as it drifted down into the church and up into the bell-tower.

When we came to the stage of offering each other the Kiss of Peace, I turned to my brother-priest on my right to wish him the blessing of peace. "Pax tecum", I said. He answered me, in French; "Vous vous êtes tourné dans le mauvais sens" (I was turning the wrong way) and he did not even use the familiar "tu" form which was generally used among friends. Anger rose steadily in my stomach, bubbling and churning. These were the religious men whose predecessors had led the liturgical movement, who had performed the ritual to perfection, like angels, but who had no feel for what they were celebrating, no idea of the mysteries beneath the surface. They needed a good kick in the monastic arse. I followed the rubrics, turned the other way (but not the other cheek) and, in anger, wished a dried-up monk the gift of peace. Again, my companions were highly amused by the behavior of the monks and by my reaction. The trip into the country-side had been worthwhile.

Off they went across Europe, Bill Brennan back down to Rome, John Davoren and Eddy Campion on their way to Sweden before the two of them returned to me in Paris, with one day to spare before they took the train to Spain.

That very day I had walked to the Dominican monastery of *Saint Jacques* where the director of the Institute, Gy O.P., was a member of the community. I had gone there to deliver my memoir for assessment, so I had another few days free before beginning a reading program in preparation for my final, rather informal, examinations. The three of us (Eddy, John and myself) walked to an exclusive little restaurant I had discovered hidden away on the *Ile St Louis*. From time to time I would take friends there to experience the musty atmosphere of a strange world created by characters from *La Belle Époque*.

The restaurant was run by an odd elderly couple. The wife fussed and chatted while she cooked for us behind a silk screen and her husband sat in the corner on a cushion, his back against the panelled wall, chewing on a pipe and occasionally contributing to the conversations of the guests. The rickety double front-door of frosted glass was always locked – to keep customers out – the tourists, the riffraff and the homosexuals who frequented the *Quatier*. The pokey interior was decorated with dusty, faded plastic flowers, sepia photographs, antique furnishings and an upright piano which had stood un-tuned for many years. The owners had a policeman's whistle on top of the piano, which they blew from time to time to entertain their exclusive guests and which, they said, was kept handy to summon the police in case of an attack.

The restaurant was "open" from midday till three in the afternoon and offered a menu which never varied. Anytime we attended, my friends and I were their only customers. Each table had a reserved notice on it in case a cagey and hungry intruder might penetrate the closed door and prove unacceptable.

During my first year in Paris, I had sometimes passed the restaurant, looked in through the windows, through the tattered lace curtains and noticed the reserved signs on all the tables. I had assumed that the proprietors were catering for an exclusive clientele, but I had never seen anyone sitting at table in their establishment.

One day I had knocked on the door, but the elderly lady had waved me away. I knocked again, another impatient wave of the hand. I persisted. She opened the door and questioned me through a narrow opening. Who was I? What did I want? Where did I come from? I told her I was an Australian, a student in Paris. She looked me up and down and questioned me further. What did I do? I was a Catholic priest. She opened the door wide and invited me in. Where can I sit? She told me I could choose any table I liked and, when I looked puzzled, she told me that the reserved signs were on the tables to keep unwelcomed customers away. She had thought when she saw me that I was a homosexual, or a tourist. The *Ile St Louis* was full of "them" and she did not want anyone like that in her restaurant.

As I came to know these proprietors, I learnt that she was originally from Brittany, excessively superstitious, she voted socialist and attended silent Masses. He husband voted conservative, occasionally went to Mass but only to a Latin Gregorian Mass. He had been a merchant seaman before the war and had visited Sydney. He loved to repeat over and over again, the gurgling sound – "Woolloomooloo". Whenever he saw me, he would play with these sounds, rounding his old French lips and exaggerating the "O's". The lady boasted that she had the President's wife Madame Pompidou, as a client, and other exclusive silver-tails who lived on the island, but she spent most of her time walking through the narrow streets, feeding stray cats. Whenever I attended her restaurant, she provided the floor-show and her husband the commentary.

Eddy and John joined in the fun. We ate and drank and laughed until well beyond the time for closing. Then off we went, on foot, to the cemetery of *Père Lachaise*. After a few glasses of wine, Eddy wanted to visit the place where Eloise and Abelard lay together, the graves of Victor Hugo, Molière, Proust, Balzac, Edith Piaff, and the tomb of Oscar Wilde where the Archangel who stood watch over him had been cruelly castrated. I was happy to have the company.

For fear of embarrassing both of them, I hesitate to record that before they caught the train for Spain, each left a generous envelope on my desk. They excused this misdemeanor by claiming that they were keen to support students studying overseas. As a student on the edge, I blessed them then – and bless both of them again now.

chapter thirteen

1974

A LUCKY SECOND CHANCE

As I drove away from Paris in the summer of 1974 heading for Germany, I had not the faintest tinkling as to what lay ahead. I assumed that I would learn a little German at the Goethe Institute so I could feel my way through some scholarly articles about liturgical worship or the theology of sacraments. The Germans, like the French, were at the cutting edge of those areas of theology which interested me. I assumed that after the six-week course I would fly home to Sydney, slide back into a minor clerical position and take up an appointment teaching theology to students for the priesthood. I was mistaken.

I had spent almost two years living and studying in France and I had fallen in love with her – her proud culture, her elegant buildings and boulevards, her fascinating history, her Gallican style of doing Church, her cathedrals, her liturgy and her tender spirituality. My little Sydney world had expanded beyond imagining. My mind, my values, my faith had exploded like fireworks on the Sydney Harbour Bridge on New Year's Eve. As I had wandered the streets and boulevards of Paris, the fashions on show in the shop-windows, the styles of the ladies, the beauty of the buildings and the richness of the nation's history (religious, commercial, artistic, scientific or military) had fascinated me. The city of *La Belle Epoque* had filled me with awe and reverence. In Paris I had discovered it was possible to be a Christian and to journey in search of fresh insights, to enjoy a life of faith while walking in a forest of doubts. I did not have to base my life of faith on closed-minded assumptions and unexamined prejudices, in a world where sex was the only sin and obedience the only virtue.

Gradually, I had come to understand that there have been many legitimate traditions within the Christian movement; that the life of the Christian community through the centuries has passed from crisis to crisis, from age to age, through many stages, searching, erring, squabbling, reflecting and praying. Christian people have not always believed that the Pope was infallible, or that forgiveness depended on a punctilious recitation of sins in the darkness of a confessional, or that there are two natures in the one person of Jesus and two wills, or that the Eucharist can be "explained" only by the ungainly philosophical notion of "transubstantiation", much less that the mother of Jesus was a virgin, or that Jesus was immaculately conceived and born free of original sin. Jesus had not been a teacher of dogmas or a petty canon lawyer. In fact he seemed to have been rather contemptuous of the arcane knowledge of lawyers and religious leaders and of their legalistic mentality.

In taking distance from my tribe in Sydney, and while I had been conscientiously engaged in my studies in Paris, the tight foundation garments designed for me in Sydney had burst at the seams and I was free to breathe deeply. I knew that this newfound freedom would cause me heartache, but it might also prove a problem for others. I had not studded my Roman collar since I had escaped with Neil Brown, on a Qantas flight out of Sydney. I was thrilled to have lived and prospered, if only for a brief period, in a colony of genuine Christian scholars who had been responsible, among many others, for the success of the Second Vatican Council.

As I drove north from Paris, towards Triers, into Germany, wondering what I would be doing when I returned to Sydney, I was suffering twitches of uncertainty. I had trained in Paris to be an 'expert' in the field of liturgical studies. My Archdiocese had invested a substantial amount in my education, though I did not then appreciate that that expense would become a petty accusation, levied against me by my Archbishop in days to come. What could I do with the liturgy – in the seminary, in the parishes? What would I be allowed to do? How would I fit back in and remain free to make a contribution? Ghosts of misgivings were hovering over my speeding car.

In Paris, I had learnt to celebrate the community's liturgy, happily, meditatively, but without obsessing over petty rubrics like Monsignor Madden had taught us to do at Manly. The need to trace compulsive circles and crosses in the air, to make rushed genuflections, the need for the exaggerated articulation of magical words, had all evaporated. I hadn't celebrated the mysteries with such obsessive, ritual precision for at least two years.

After a brief stay in Germany to soak up a little of the language, I would be on my way back to Australia – returning to old haunts, to old friends and colleagues. But at the back of my mind were some painful memories. Would I be able to tolerate the old fights, to smile at the old faces, to survive where nothing had changed, where the leaden leaders and many of the clergy had set their hearts in stone against the twentieth century?

I was leaving the thrill of Paris and journeying back in time, to the Roman Church of the nineteenth century. I was conscious that I would be expected to justify the time and expense of my studies, to pull a few religious rabbits out of my biretta, to do something for the liturgical life of Sydney, to teach the future religious ministers to celebrate the mysteries, but without teaching them too much, without inviting them to gaze over the horizon.

I was on my way to a tiny dot on the map in the German mountains east of Cologne – white two-storey homes, verandahs and windowsills decorated with colourful garden pots overflowing with red geraniums – to a village surrounded by farms and pine forests. The Goethe Institute had arranged digs for its students in Brilon. I would have a narrow bed in a loft and a shower with hot water in the afternoon, after five. The neat and polished house would be occupied by a chubby frau who would refrain from uttering one word in German (or in any other tongue) in my presence. Contrary to the publicity in the brochure, she would prove no help to me with the basics of her language.

I stayed in Brilon for six weeks. For one last time the isolated village was alive with students from around the world – Spain, Portugal, France, Turkey, Greece, Italy, Japan, Holland, Ireland and Australia – but the sole Australian was alone in this foreign place, trying to learn a little German from weary, bored teachers in a school which was about to be put out of its misery. This branch office of the Institute was in the throes of closing down. It was apparent that the gifted teachers had already left the district in search of more permanent work. Brilon was dying. I knew I had struck a dud, but I gritted my teeth.

During those weeks I swatted a few German nouns and verbs. Each day I ate breakfast in the canteen, and at lunchtime with the other students in the local café. In broken German, I ordered half a chicken and drank a large stein of beer. I exercised early in the morning, shopped in a little supermarket for basic necessities for my evening meals, I said Mass each day, late in the afternoon, in the local parish church and read a few novels in English before drifting off to sleep. It was a Spartan existence.

The German workers in their overalls and heavy work-boots, on their way to the factories and into the fields, used to shout encouragement, greeting me cheerfully as I ran past them early in the morning in my shorts and sandshoes – probably amused to witness the waste of a young man's earning power. Why was this stranger expending so much valuable energy? The workers were unable to imagine the sedentary life of a student. As a general rule, like most country people, they were not book-happy – or was this another one of my debilitating prejudices? Like my father, they were paid for sweat, paid by the hour for their muscle-aching activity.

My life had turned out differently. I sat – and wrote sometimes – never enough. I thought a little – and I read. Most of my day was spent alone in a room, at a desk, isolated, communing with a shadowy medieval figure on a page, sometimes in Latin, or with a scholar from another closed world. Even in Brilon I had to escape the rarified air of the intellectual life, if only for an hour or so. I was in my early thirties, with energy to burn. I had to put my body into motion and push the thin blood around my flabby, thinking carcass. To clear the brain and tame the savage beast, I forced myself out into the German countryside, pounding a pathway, stopping from time to time to stretch, to do a few press-ups or some press-downs on the all-weather exercise equipment which the local council had provided.

My evening meals in this remote village were somewhat monastic. Perhaps a little ham or German sausage, two boiled eggs, stale bread, apricot jam, some soapy cheese and a cup of instant coffee. I used to boil the eggs in a billy with an immersion heater and use the hot water to make disgusting coffee in a large plastic orange mug, which a mate had bought in an Italian village and which was decorated with elephant ears and octopus tentacles. There was no television to watch and no radio to listen to. It was like old times.

To alleviate my boredom, one weekend I drove to Cologne to visit its medieval cathedral, the modern museum exhibiting the relics of early Roman civilization on the northern bank of the Rhine, and to wander through the little streets round the principal square. I walked and walked through the pathways of the medieval city until my swollen feet felt as though they would throb off at the ankles. But I had grown weary of sightseeing, visiting museums, galleries and cathedrals on my own. I had no one with whom to share the experience of being alive in a foreign country, surrounded by monumental works and delicate relics fashioned by hands which had turned to dust thousands of years before. I had no one to nudge, to tease, no one to enrich my world, to draw my eye to something of interest, no one with whom to share some trivial observation. I was a celibate abroad and out of my comfort-zone.

Then in early August, I happened to meet a pretty French girl from Toulouse.

It was difficult, perhaps impossible, even for a celibate who had been drilled from early childhood to a supernatural level of control, not to notice the young woman who was a student learning German in one of the more advanced classes. She was stunning, in her early to mid twenties, with olive, silky skin. An ample bosom sculptured above a delicate waist, with flesh lines descending onto a paradise of ripe, juicy curves. As she drifted in and out of my field of vision, she was an apparition full of grace. She seemed to float in the crowd of students, unaware of the choir of foreign eyes observing her in motion.

I knew nothing of her except that I had heard her in the distance speaking softly, with a French accent – and she was beautiful. I did not know that her parents were originally from Spain; that she spoke Catalan, Castilian and English; that she had two brothers; that her father had fought with his six brothers on the side of the Republic against the friend of Pope Pius XII, the Catholic Generalissimo. I did not know that her father was fiercely anti-Catholic. For some weeks she was just a figure on the edge of my consciousness. I did not know that this glorious female had an intellectual and political life of her own. I did not even know her name, or that she was going to be the love of my life and the mother of my two boys.

I was far from home, free of the tight shackles of my priestly life and with no pastoral role to play in her world. The custody of my eyes was beginning to falter, but I did not feel compromised. I was set apart as a priest but I could still enjoy the beauties of creation, without stain. Watching beauty in motion was a simple gift from God for all men of flesh to enjoy.

I loved to watch her, albeit from a safe distance, as she mingled with others in the narrow streets of the village, in the crowded corridors of the Institute. Over the ensuing years, this lovely woman has continued to give me pleasure, observing her from the watch-tower within me, always at a distance, separate, as she works in the garden, walks on the promenade at Manly or Balmoral, at a party, in a crowd, as she knits, or carefully chooses beads for her necklace, or in bed as she sleeps. As the years passed and we lived together, sharing in the same space, working, holidaying, playing, I felt somehow complete, at home in my body, graced by her presence in my life. My unconscious wait for a life-companion had ended in a shower of blessings, but in Brilon she was only a passing attraction.

We were never formally introduced. One day towards the end of our intensive language course, I was seated at a green laminex table at the far end of the Goethe cafeteria. The hall was full of noise and bustle, with students on the move again, preparing for another day at the desks. It was breakfast time and I was busy with my cornflakes and coffee. There she was, making her way through a maze of tables and scattered chairs, passing chattering patrons, coming towards me with her tray of canteen offerings. She was late. All the table-places were occupied except where I was sitting. I was alone in the corner, at the end of the room. I watched her coming, drifting calmly on the current between the tables – a vision of gracefulness. I wondered whether we would sit together in silence, or would she be moved to talk to me. Who would break the seal and let the conversation flow? Softly, in French, she enquired if she could sit at the table or whether the empty places were reserved. My guardian angel was interfering in my private affairs.

She placed her tray on the table, sat down and began to arrange her tea and toast, her plates and utensils in front of her. She was paying me no further attention. She appeared in a zone of her own, oblivious to the presence of others in the large, restless assembly. Unlike me, always looking for company, she seemed content to be by herself. I felt uneasy – an awkward novice, full of inhibitions. I was verging on forty, but at that moment I could have been fifteen and covered in pimples. We couldn't just sit there in silence. I had to say something. I had to trust my arm and draw on the brutal French I had acquired in Paris.

There was no hiding the fact that my French should have been more fluent. I had lived in Paris for almost two years. I had attended lectures and participated in regular seminars. I had travelled extensively around France in my Peugeot. I should have been at least passably fluent in the language. But I had travelled with clergy from America or Australia, unfortunately never with native French speakers. I had lived in a hostel for priests, mainly among Americans and Canadians who had insisted on communicating in English and I had slipped lazily into the groove. While I came to understand what was being said in French, and while in time I managed to make myself understood to some extent, my stammering utterances, even at their best, were rough and brutal. I used only limited adjectives and adverbs, seldom subordinate clauses. There were no colours in my speech. I never succeeded in telling a French joke, or in using coarse, insulting language, or attending the theatre or, to my lasting regret, conversing with the pretty girls of Paris in their own tongue, complimenting them, teasing them. I had even muffed my simple lines of polite refusal one evening in *Pigalle*, when a woman of the night had made me an attractive offer to spend some quality time with her. Full of embarrassment and confusion, I had informed her that I did not want her services, that I was "an Australian". On reflection, it does not now appear to have been an adequate basis for refusal.

When it came to making contact with my table companion,

"Vous êtes français?"

was all that I could manage in the heat of the moment.

It was a question, not a statement. Just a simple question and spoken with a little stutter of hesitation. Not a smooth, James Bond approach, but I thought it would be a safe way to begin. We could move on, to my stay in Paris, perhaps her province of origin, to my country of birth, to the Goethe course and to an exchange of names. I was lost for something to talk about, though according to my friends I am a person who is seldom lost for a word or two. I did not realise that she was as fluent in English as I was – and superior in grammar and spelling. I had assumed that our only common language would be French, or some infantile form of German. I was going to have to muddle on in her language. In her soft, aloof voice, she replied, abruptly, casually,

"Non, ... française",

(leaning on the "e" at the end of the word, thereby correcting my gauche introductory gambit). I had asked her whether she was a French*man*. I had failed to use the feminine form of the critical word. How could I have made such a rudimentary, silly mistake? The full feminine form was in front of me, in all its beauty.

My table companion could have easily replied with a simple "yes", or maybe added –

"I'm French. You are obviously not French. May I ask where you come from?"

I was wounded. How insensitive! Who did she think she was? An innocent stranger had asked a simple, polite question which she could have answered graciously. Her reply seemed brutal and dismissive. She had replied with a conversation stopper – maybe not for others, but it stopped me. I was someone who was easily deflated. I could be toppled off my perch by the hint of an insult. My mother had been the same. My brother Sean and my sister Colleen were even more sensitive to any perceived criticism. An unhappy family trait.

My future wife was not naturally cruel. I was sure she meant no harm. When I got to know her well I would learn that she would never deliberately cause pain to anyone, though she could be disconcertingly direct. Furthermore, languages were her forte and accuracy her weakness. I was to discover these characteristics as we travelled together, but for the moment, I sat there, eating, seething. She sat, unaware of the circuit breaker she had activated.

"Well, bugger you", I thought. "That's the end of a promising relationship."

There was no further interchange. The conversation had been nipped in the bud before she had revealed her identity.

I took a few days to cool down. Maybe she had not meant to be so dismissive or perhaps I had been a little thin-skinned. (It was not the first time in my life, or the last, I had bridled when corrected. Anyway, it was true.) I had failed to sound the "e" on the end of the adjective. After almost two years in Paris, I should have acquired more facility with the language. It had been a small mistake and she should have been more gracious. But the French are like that and they have a reputation to uphold and cannot bear to hear their language mangled.

I was recovering – and she was attractive – a full, rounded figure; an aloof, untouchable aura. She had been blessed with beautiful, slender, delicate hands and she was French. I had fallen in love with the French and their culture. Maybe this was just her manner. Perhaps I could overlook our first encounter. So, after some reflection, I decided to give her a second chance.

One of her countrymen had wisely observed –

> "The day when a woman who passes in front of you gives off light as she walks, you are lost: you are in love. There is only one thing to do! Think of her so intently that she is forced to think of you."

Within a day or so we were reconciled. She enquired about my name, its Irish origin, my homeland and she informed me that she was called "Adela" – "Adela Rodriguez" – and she was from Toulouse. We were making headway.

The second chance had paid off and in the company of my new friend we drove through pine and oak forests, along narrow country roads, past well ordered lush fields, on mountain roads, to visit the gilded art-works in the gallery at Kassel – rich in Reubens, Rembrandts and Van Dycks.

As much as I had no idea as to who this young woman was, Adele was in the same boat – she had no notion of who I was. In Germany, just as in France, I dressed in mufti. I wore nothing to identify me as a priest – no little cross on the lapel; no Roman collar of course; no devout smile and no pious language. All she knew was that I was from Australia; that I was trying to learn some German; that I was a good ten or twelve years older than her; and that I spoke French badly. She had no idea that I was a Catholic priest until I disclosed my full identity, and then she took the additional information coolly in her stride. I was to learn that she takes all things coolly, in her stride.

During these summer months in Germany, the burghers of Paderborn were holding their annual carnival – crowds in the streets, flags, banners draped from windows, heavy German drums, base tubas, umpapa music, processions, powerful draught horses plodding out their rhythmic gait on cobblestones, local costumes in red and greens, flared skirts, old men ridiculous in skimpy lederhosen with lily legs and tiny hats, bratwurst stands, and flowing, frothing beer waved in time with the music and drained into happy throats. I wanted to be part of this festival.

When my beautiful French friend accepted my invitation to attend, I knew in my bones that I had to be super-cautious. I was swimming in uncharted waters, free of the usual, taut institutional lap-ropes, protected only by the fragile interior mechanisms that the system had tried to develop in me over a lifetime. My stay away from home was at an end and I was on my way back to the seminary. I had completed my task in Europe and was returning to the tribe, to the routine, to the world of my youth. While Paris had been spiritually and intellectually enriching, I had managed to maintain a firm self-imposed control. My stay had been enjoyable but I had had no real fun outside the ropes – no Follies, no ride on the Ferris Wheel, no marching in the streets, no masquerade balls. Brilon was a brief interlude and I was feeling a little "off the hook", far from home-base, with space to move, with limited time and no one to scandalise.

I knew in my heart that I had to be careful, but I did not want to be so clerically cautious that I smothered every natural, human, spontaneous instinct. She was surrounded with an aura of dignity, so I did not sense any immediate danger. I would be doing her no harm by showing a little interest. She was a stranger to my world and in this situation, off the beaten track, I was not obliged to girt my loins tightly and pretend I was a man without feelings. In the circumstances, my deportment may have been a little risqué, somewhat imprudent for someone in my position, but it did not offend the dictates of propriety, or compromise the virtue of my companion. Together we enjoyed the noise, the crowd, the procession and I rejoiced in her company.

One evening, late in my Brilon stay, I shared a meal alone with Adele in a quiet restaurant somewhere out in the German countryside. Apart from a milkshake I had shouted Anna Arnold in a milk bar in Sydney when I was fourteen, maybe fifteen, I had never been alone in the company of a pretty girl or a woman of my own age, in a private room, the corner of a restaurant, a theatre or on a beach. Up to that stage of my life, I had related to these mysterious and dangerous creatures as a son or a brother within the family, as a seminarian, and later as a priest to groups of nuns or to wives and mothers in the parish, to giddy, attractive teenage members of a youth club I had established at Avalon.

Until I held hands with Adele in the silence of the Brilon forest, no female had touched me since I had been a boy. Apart from that desperate seminarian, driven mad by devils, who had attacked me in the darkness of the winter toilets late at night when I was thirteen or fourteen, hugging, groping, pumping as I struggled to escape, I had had no intimate, physical contact since I had left home at the age of twelve to study for the priesthood. No soft hand had touched my body. I had received no pat of encouragement on the back, no kiss on the cheek, no hug apart from the ritual Kiss of Peace during High Mass in the chapel on Sundays. I had never walked arm-in-arm, hand-in-hand.

Late in my clerical life I discovered that not all my colleagues had survived the same way in the desert. As a priest, I remember how scandalised I was to find out that some of my confrères, even some of the older, more senior men, could not keep their extremities to themselves – employing their appendage to gratify their urges, laying impure hands on male or female, each according to his preference, or on more personal parts of their own bodies. One of my former students, after his ordination, penetrated a member of his parish and when she fell pregnant, he generously paid for the fragile life in her womb to be expunged.

One of my friends told me towards the end of his life, that as a student for the priesthood, even as he approached the time of his ordination, and later, after a year or so, as a young priest, he had continued to keep company, to proposition and to "fuck" at every opportunity – nurses, hostesses and secretaries, but seldom married women in case their husbands might complain to the Cathedral. Apparently, according to his own story, he was a man much sought after by eager women – a dream which many male members have shared. Why he entered the seminary in the first place, why he continued to present himself for priesthood with his unquenchable urges, why he remained in the celibate ministry for so long was a mystery to me and perhaps to him also. Clerical dalliances and affairs, house-keeping mistresses and male partners were not the rule, but nor were they apparently the exception. I had much to learn about the things they had neglected to tell me in the seminary.

During my few weeks in the little German town, the graceful girl from Toulouse had been much in demand among the international brigade of men at the Goethe – a band of Turkish men, a Quixotic Spaniard from Malaga and a lonely Danish sea captain who could not bear being separated from his wife and who needed to talk about her incessantly to Adele. Appreciative eyes followed her as she moved about. The male members, young and old, were fascinated.

One of the young officers in the local police force had driven Adele to her residential address when she had first arrived in town and had returned within the hour to press her for a date. The severe frau who was in charge of the house where Adele was staying and who answered the constable's knock on the door, had been far from impressed to have a man in uniform calling at her home so soon after her guest's arrival.

Towards the end of my time in Europe – for maybe a week, ten days perhaps, Adele seemed content to grace me with her company. Nothing complicated was going to happen in that time. For a few summer evenings, for too brief a time, we shared the simple pleasure of carefree walks in the forests and paddocks of the Sauerland. Shadows and unseen eyes haunted the forest on the border of the town at night. Stately trees, crowded in rows like cathedral columns, created long corridors which stretched far into the distance. The ground was soft under foot and in the evening as we walked together, as the sky glittered above us, there was not a stir of air among the trees. These were moments to cherish – a little space of happiness in the company of an angel.

In this nightly setting, distant stars shining in a foreign sky, with Adele strolling by my side, German cows were attracted by the murmur of our shadows and followed us in the darkness like dumb ghosts along the fence line. We paused to touch their moist muzzles. I lifted my head to draw deep into my body, the perfume of mown hay, of lush fields and cow dung. My body tingled with the simple pleasure of being there with this feminine presence by my side. I was far from home and surprised by joy.

We talked. I talked and Adele listened. I spoke of home. I told her about my mother and my father, about my life, my fears, my expectations. She walked near me, gently, without a word. I sang out into the still air, lifting my voice to the high and mighty trees, floating it out into the soft rural silence, to the tiny animals of the night hidden away under a blanket of darkness.

Before my departure, I purchased a gift for Adele. She was not at home when I called so I left the parcel with her forbidding landlady. On the back of a card I expressed the hope that the large, oven-glazed, earthen vase, would sometimes catch my friend unawares; that it would soften her heart, bring a smile to her pretty, peaceful face, tempting her to remember the darkness of German woods, the gentleness of silence, the vastness of the heavens, voices in the night, and two friends walking hand-in-hand. I presumed to invite her to write to me, in French – not in German! As she has often since remarked in passing, my German studies were not a great success because, unlike her, I left the Institute before sitting for the examinations. I had not made much progress.

With some difficulty, my French friend carried her heavy present on the train back to Toulouse and eventually to Sydney where it continues to contain large displays of flowers to brighten our home. When I recall that she also kept my note among her papers to remind her of our meeting and of our parting, my peacock feathers stiffen and spread.

Our encounter had been all too brief. I drove away in my Peugeot with tears streaming from the headlights, heavy air in the tyres, with a sad, sluggish engine, heading towards Cologne, to England, to visit relatives in Ireland, friends in Canada and the United States and eventually, to my home in Sydney. I assumed we would never meet again.

chapter fourteen

1974

BACK ON HOME TURF

I flew back into Sydney in late October 1974 and as I floated down over the harbour and the beaches, the excitement of arriving home began to tingle my body. The glimpses of my city underneath the wings were thrilling. One of the world's breathtaking sights was laid out beneath me. I was happy to be home. St Mary's Cathedral was visible from the air and as I flew over her, back to the Sydney Archdiocese, I knew I would have to keep my own counsel – knuckle under and remain alert.

The drive from the airport into the busy heart of the city brought me back to earth. While I had been flying high in the most elegant city in the world, I had forgotten the grey concrete buildings, the tangle of overhead wires, factories falling into disrepair, store-houses, frenetic traffic, trucks belching fumes, jockeying for positions in the narrow streets. As I travelled past the city scars of Sydney, counting her pimples and her wrinkles, passing the multi-storey growths standing like carbuncles on the hills and shores of a stunningly beautiful coastline, I was recalling the classical beauty of Paris. She had sparkled like a diamond with her broad boulevards, her tree-lined streets, her sculptured buildings, the footpaths cleaned and purified with cheap, black African brooms. She had her own ugly secrets, but they were hidden from sight. Beneath the bliss of my home-coming fluttered some doubts and regrets.

I had seen the world over the horizon. Some people on the other side were dreaming dreams; some asking real questions; many were not bothered by some of the beliefs and narrow opinions which had dominated my life before I had ventured out of the ecclesiastical kingdom in Australia. I had met men who felt free to explore ideas and state their opinions, without concern for what might be said at the Cathedral dinner table or on St Michael's golf course on Monday. I had discovered that the world was a big playground where many games could be played.

I had learnt to ask different questions, to seek answers in different places, to think thoughts, to follow leads. I was more independent, more confident, less committed to the tired party-line. Some of my childhood certainties had turned into suspicions and suspicions revamped as insights. The world over the horizon and new experiences on the other side, had cleared the cluttered decks of my theological mind and my spiritual life. I believed that I was in a much better position to determine to my own satisfaction, what was central to the system and what was the dry dust of centuries past. I had begun to scrape away the accretions which had accumulated like barnacles on the body politic of my Church.

And I had met a girl from Toulouse.

Within a few days of my return, after I had rested in the company of my family, after the family had recovered from the joy of my re-appearance among them, I made contact with the Cathedral. His Eminence Cardinal James Freeman, who had replaced Cardinal Gilroy in July 1971, invited me to attend on him in his inner-sanctum where I thought I should report on my Parisian studies. He seemed to show no interest in what I had been doing on the other side of the world. No questions. No comments. It was as if I had been grazing in the next paddock. I did not need to mention my casual encounter with a pretty French girl in Germany. It had been an innocent meeting at the end of my stay abroad and nothing terrible had happened. Maybe I had played ducks and drakes for a few days with his cardinal virtue of prudence. I had lowered my guard momentarily, but I was ready to crank up again, to take up where I had left off – studying and lecturing in theology – and to push forward.

Before I bowed low and withdrew from his Eminence's presence, Freeman issued an invitation to address his next clergy conference. It was an honour bestowed and it would complete his planned business agenda and fill in the time. It would establish me as a go-to expert in the minds of the clergy – or so I thought. I was ready to begin my work and anxious to share what I had experienced abroad.

On a hot, steamy, summer day in January 1975, the clergy from far and wide gathered in the crypt of the cathedral over the tombs of the Cardinal's predecessors. Some of the more canny clerics had stayed away. There was always a proportion of the brethren who could find an excuse to be out and about on urgent business. Those who turned up had to listen to tedious general business. They were impatient for the meeting to grind to an end so they could play golf, go to the beach, retire to a restaurant or a bar in the city, so they could spend time with their mates, or chew the fat and exchange the gossip. They weren't really interested in the proceedings. They were sweating inside their black suits, chocked tight by their white collars, ready to explode.

It was my turn. The Cardinal announced that Dr Geraghty had recently returned from Europe, that he had successfully completed a two-year course in liturgical studies and that he had invited him to address them on the latest, up-to-date trends in liturgical thought and practice in France. A gentle wave of murmurs and whispers filled the crypt. It wasn't easy to impress members of the clergy. Most of them had known me at Springwood in the early days, when I was a cocky boy of twelve or thirteen, in short pants.

The Second Vatican Council had concluded in Rome almost eight years before. The bishops of the world had excited great expectations which had reverberated round the world. Among many other reforms, they had foreshadowed and encouraged quite radical changes in the way Catholics prayed and worshipped. But the Sydney diocese (and Australia in general) was still moored, like a rotting hulk, up-stream, in oily, muddy back-waters. At the Council, our bishops (Gilroy himself, Muldoon, Thomas, Cahill, McCabe and many others) had batted on the side of the reactionaries. Many of the clergy had been reluctant to change, dragging their feet and resisting reform. Some were positively hostile and a few of the hardened Sydney clergy were itching for some target-practice, on the lookout for a fledgling about to leave the nest and take flight. I could not have been more exposed to a more unappreciative audience.

I told my colleagues something of what I had seen in Paris – the Sunday celebrations at the Jesuit church, *St Ignace* on the *Rue de Sèvres* where Father Gelineau had been the choir-master; the intimate and spontaneous Eucharists in the railway station at Montparnasse; the scholarly and pastoral work undertaken by the Liturgical Institute in Paris. The liturgical scholars and pastoral experts, in searching for ways to simplify our worship, had sought to return to the original spirit and the pristine forms of the early Christian communities. They were trying to devise ways to encourage everyone to participate in the theatre of worship, to modernise the rhythm and flow of the official prayer life of the Church.

Perhaps I was over-enthusiastic. I had learnt too much. I had experienced and taken to myself, a different style of liturgical prayer and practice. In the French Church, as far as I could see, there was nothing rough-edged, nothing sloppy and slovenly. After the disappearance of the Latin Mass, liturgy in Australia had become a bit hit-and-miss – a guitar, a few dreary hymns, a pick-up team of singers, muffled biblical readings, prayer formulas recited in a monotone. The Irish clergy had been energetic in building churches and schools, running housie-housie and banking money, but the study of theology or the meticulous and imaginative preparation of liturgical celebrations, had not been their long suit. Many Australians had come to expect a fast Mass on Sunday, preferably without a sermon. They would cross parish borders to avoid the tedium of a proper liturgical celebration.

In Paris, the French were celebrating with style – the preacher prepared his homily; gifted fashion designers produced an array of colourful vestments; the celebrants and their entourage processed with dignity and aplomb. The pace and rhythm varied throughout the celebration – reflective silences, powerful proclamations of the Word of God which everyone could hear and understand, prayerful responses, drums, flutes, bells, violins, cantors and soloists. Nothing was rushed. I had visited parishes and chapels in the cities and out in the villages, in cathedrals and oratories and as a general rule (though there were exceptions), both the people and the priest in France took their liturgy seriously. Whereas in Australia, quantity ruled – as many

Masses on Sunday as possible, for as many people as possible – in France the emphasis was on quality. Liturgy was religious theatre, a work of art, an act of personal and community faith. I had come back to the place of my origins full of ideas, throbbing with enthusiasm.

On that hot summer day in Sydney, the clergy were in no mood to listen and learn. They had nothing to learn, especially from the French, or from a jumped-up, over-educated junior. I could see as I was speaking that some were bored and others were hostile.

The Cardinal invited questions from the floor. This was the chance the larrikins sitting at the back of the crypt were waiting for to buy a few cheap laughs – all Monday golfers from St Michael's, all sitting together as they used to do in the seminary, ready to throw eggs and heckle. I do not remember at this distance who said what, but I do remember the feeling of being mocked and humiliated. As far as they were concerned, I was still that little boy in the seminary. I remember them from seminary days – they had been some years ahead of me and were larrikins then. They were not having anything of this liturgical bullshit. No frog was going to tell them how to suck eggs, how to improve on their priestly performance.

They knew what they were doing, what the people wanted and what was good for them. They had learnt all they needed to know years before, in the seminary. All this new talk about liturgy, about singing, active participation, symbolism, about style, proclamation – it was all nonsense. The people in the pews didn't need to be pushed and punched to accept change. They were content in their place. The Church in Australia was "relaxed and comfortable" well before John Howard made it compulsory for the nation. The larrikins up the back, the clerical bullies, nudging, winking, mocking, laughing, didn't need any hare-brained suggestions and were determined to keep the Fathers of the Second Vatican Council and a minor liturgist with new ideas in their places, as far as possible.

I was mortified. There was trouble ahead.

In the meantime, Adele and I continued to send and receive letters as I settled back into my clerical life. I worked briefly as the assistant priest in the parish of Malabar with Father Ford, before I took up a teaching appointment in the theological institute on the hill overlooking the village of Manly.

I stayed with John Ford for several months, laughing together, talking over personal things, sharing our philosophy of life, listening to music, enjoying his cooking and his conversation. They were days of summer joy and sunny re-adjustment.

I began to hear confessions again, to "say" Masses in a church, to preach the Gospel message and attend parish meetings. I continued to pray the daily Breviary, in French now instead of in Latin or English. John Ford had been sent to Malabar to replace the cranky parish priest, who had been run down by a local tram and killed. During his tenure there, the old fellow had done nothing to renew the parish life or to implement the liturgical changes coming out of the Second Vatican Council. John and I had remedial work to do.

We set about preparing the parish for Christmas. We established a parish choir for the Midnight Mass. We set up a little table in the centre of the church, covered it with a purple cloth for Advent and celebrated the Eucharist there, instead of on the heavy marble altar up the front of the church, away from the congregation. Together, we made some changes which failed to please everyone. There were some rumblings but they only lasted a few weeks. It was easy living and working with a good man who was ready to "give it a go". The recollection of those fun summer months on both sides of Christmas, ebbs and flows gently in my head and softens other darker memories.

For a number of years, John Ford had been a member of the staff at St Patrick's Manly where he had worked as a bursar, putting food in the mouths of hungry seminarians and replacing the slate tiles of the roof. His stay there had convinced him that the seminary was suffering from a terminal, institutional insanity and he blessed every day of his escape from the madhouse. While I was with him, he advised me almost daily not to go near the place.

> "Mate, you'd be crazy to go anywhere near that place. If they ask you to go back there to teach, take my advice and just say "no … NO". You'll go mad. It will destroy you. Stay away from there."

But I was keen to return to my books and to share what I had absorbed overseas.

As the summer months advanced, I was beginning to realise that this French girl had struck a powerful and unexpected blow in Brilon. I was struggling to regain my balance – I needed the space, the time to break from the clinch, stagger back to my corner, breathe deeply, to relax and clear my head.

While I was working in the parish at Malabar, I received the complicating news that the girl I had met in Germany was coming to Australia as an exchange French teacher. She was coming to Killara High School and intended to prepare a university memoir for her Master's degree on an Australian novelist, Kylie Tennant. By coincidence, she had been born in Manly and, like Adele, was a passionate advocate for voluntary euthanasia. Adele's university in Toulouse had offered a course in Australia and New Zealand literature which she had been following before we met. She was landing in my home town in May. It was going to be a rocky ride.

The news was unsettling. I had barely unpacked. I was settling back into a conservative, rigid, clerical world, re-establishing myself on familiar turf, knowing there would be some people watching my every move, knowing that I had left the scene two years previously with a feeling of profound alienation. I still wanted to give it my best shot and I knew Adele's presence in Sydney would be troubling, perhaps even a serious distraction. I knew I was sailing on turbulent waters, but I was confident I could weather the storm and navigate my way into calmer seas.

The moment I heard she was coming, I was both thrilled and struck with a sense of foreboding. One minute, I was accepting the inevitable – "that's it. I'm over the top. She's coming, and I'm going"; and the next minute I was gritting my teeth, preparing to dig deep, to welcome her as a friend, show her something of my country and wave her goodbye. She was soft and gentle. She was poised and elegant. But I had had a lifetime of formation in the seminary system to draw on. As it turned out, I was fooling myself.

I had already settled into the seminary at Manly and was lecturing in liturgical studies and the theology of sacraments to the senior students, when she arrived on my doorstep. She came with a gift – a copy of a map of *Le Vieux Paris* which I had requested. It was a splendid, sparkling autumn Sydney day in May 1975 with overarching blue skies and crisp salty air. I was waiting at the airport when Adele stepped off the plane, with electrified flutters in my heart and a bunch of roses in my hand. The endgame is history.

chapter fifteen

1975

A CRAZY STRANGER ON A TRAIN

L ate one night (before Adele had made her appearance in Australia
but after I had unpacked my clothes and books and spread myself
out in the magnificent Gothic building on the hill overlooking the
village of Manly) I was travelling through the darkness on a rattling,
suburban train, returning home from the western suburbs of Sydney
and hoping to catch the late ferry to Manly. I was alone.

An elderly woman moved from her seat on the other side of the
corridor and sat down next to me. A stale, cream overcoat edged with
acrylic fur, enveloped her weathered body and she was hiding her dry
face behind an enlarged pair of glasses and a thick layer of powder. A
collection of rings decorated the fingers of both hands. A blue rinse had
stained her crinkly straw hair, but it was gradually beginning to fade.

I was tired and cranky, but the old "boiler" refused to be ignored. Her
eighty-one year old husband was sitting in front, chatting-up a younger
woman. He had had an argument with his wrinkled woman, so they
were not talking to one another.

From Strathfield to the Quay my companion narrated the story of her
life – where she had been born; the places she had lived and with
whom; how long she had lived with each partner. "I am British, you
know". She had fought in the war and had been wounded twice.

While she was talking to me, ignoring her man, the old lady was
scrutinizing me, but she couldn't make me out. She asked me whether
I was married.

"You should be, at least you should have a lover. I've been married five times – and there were many others beside. I'm married to that old bugger in front of you and, because of him, I've had five dollars deducted from my pension. He wouldn't know now where to find it and even if he could, he wouldn't know where to put it."

At that stage, I had some idea what she was referring to. She didn't know it, but she was injecting a little sanity into my turbulent life.

I was happy teaching at Manly. I had a group of six or seven enthusiastic Jesuit students who travelled from Pymble twice each week to my lectures. Years later, Hugo Dillon joined me on the Bench as a judicial officer. Father Frank Brennan SJ went on to fame without fortune in Australia and Father Ronald Anderson SJ (now deceased) became a gifted theologian and physicist at Boston College. The whole student body seemed very interested in what I had to tell them. In those days, liturgy was a new field of study which had emerged in France and Germany at the beginning of the twentieth century and which had flourished since the Second Vatican Council in the mid 60's. Those young, Jesuit novices were my best students. I imagined they were coming down from their novitiate house to soak up this new learning, but one of them told me years later that they were escaping from the monastery to spend a few hours sun-baking and surfing at Manly.

In addition to my liturgy lectures, I was conducting an advanced seminar on the ordination of women. This was before the topic had hit the Vatican wall, before Catholics were forbidden to mention the subject even among themselves and before its rejection by the Pope had been classified "infallible". My seminar was creating some interest and attracting some female participants from outside the college. I was receiving encouragement inside the seminary, but outside the scene was bleak.

However, though I was reasonably content in my closed world at St Patrick's, the student numbers had seriously declined. We were talking to an ever-decreasing cohort. I could see the writing on the wall and I had that gut-churning feeling that I was wasting my life, that my narrow education and stiff lifestyle had removed me and my institution from the world of ordinary street people. Reluctantly I had come to accept that the bishops and senior parish clergy, were determined to maintain the status quo; sinning against the light; clinging onto power and ignoring *The Signs of the Times*.

I was nearly forty. Though I had made a permanent commitment in the blindness of youth, I was wrestling with the existential problem as to how, given that I was to persevere to the end, I would spend the remainder of my days. Most of the old ones seemed to fade away in dark, cold, inhospitable presbyteries, often respected but loved by no one in particular. It was a daunting prospect.

As I sat on the suburban train that night, I knew that I did not want to travel alone on trains and aeroplanes, to walk alone through streets, to be a solitary figure at parish parties, to hurry through museums with no one to turn to, no one with whom to share a smile. I could feel that my life was empty of joy and laughter. From being an intense, virtuous little boy, I had become a serious, controlled, lonely member of a cast. I was longing to burst out of my world and discover a joyful, carefree, dancing, private existence. Was that too much to ask?

The old siren got off at Central. With her boyfriend she disappeared into the night, to give him another opportunity "to find it", or maybe to find another, more expert partner. I caught the last ferry from the Quay to Manly.

chapter sixteen

1975

DOING SOMEONE'S DIRTY WORK

Seven or eight months after my return home, I was chuffed when someone invited me to give a talk on the Sacrament of Penance to a group of lay-people in the Eastwood parish. For some weeks the priest in charge, had advertised the event in his bulletin and from his pulpit. I was to make my appearance on a Monday evening sometime in late 1975.

The Eastwood parish was well known to me. A classmate, Peter Ryan, had been a curate there and, much to Monsignor Veech's chagrin, I used to spend time in the presbytery with some of my shady colleagues before Peter died in 1969. Tormented by the nightmares of the Second Vatican Council, Tommy Veech suspected that we were plotting sedition. We should have been, but we weren't.

Some days before my talk, I telephoned the parish priest (whom his clergy mates knew as "Abo" because of his year-round golden suntan). Father Jack Haseler loved the sand and the surf of the northern beaches and proudly exhibited a special brand of bachelor bravado.

I rang to let him know I had not forgotten about the talk and to apologise that I would not be able to share his evening meal as he had planned – or so I thought. Without warning and entirely unprovoked, Jack let off a firecracker over the telephone. He had been waiting to hear from me. I should have contacted him earlier. He seemed angry and ready for "a punch-up".

Abo Haseler began by informing me of the time-honoured rule which governed his turf.

"I have to warn you, mate, that no one ever preaches bad
news on my patch."

In his domain, there would be no carping criticism, no unpleasant, negative comments and no new, destablising ideas.

"I don't want anyone coming into my parish, ruining the
sheep in half-an-hour and leaving a mess of shit for me to
clean up."

"But why are you saying this, Jack? What brought this on?
Who have you been talking to?"

It was an obvious question but it put the fighting Abo on his back foot.

Lamely, in search of some plausible reason, any reason, he said that he had been listening to one of my ten-minute published tapes on the Sacrament of Penance and that he disagreed with what I had to say. But I wasn't fooled. I knew Jack Hasler was not the type to be listening to anything mildly theological or spiritual. He was a muscular Christian. Anything intellectual was off-limits.

The theology and the historical development of the Sacrament of Penance, was one of my specialties and destined to be the cause of further unpleasantness down the track. It was true I had recorded a tape on the subject, but I hadn't made any startling comment to which he could possibly object. Abo was stalling.

I was somewhat stunned. His unfriendly outburst upset me and he was denying, rather too vehemently, that he had made his silly rule just for me. He started to argue that private, individual confessions, as practised in Australian parishes, had served the people's pastoral needs well. Saturday afternoon confessions and the school children's monthly twenty-second's penitential cleansing, before First Fridays had proved a beneficial, pastoral practice. I had good grounds not to agree, but in the interests of peace, and forever conscious of my status in the hierarchy of the clergy, I replied that the practice may have been good for some, but that it had damaged many.

As usual, I fell straight into my junior, compromising position. I was anxious to keep the peace and be part of the team, though for some reason I could never pull it off. The system had not trained me to deal with conflict and besides, I did not want to alienate a popular senior member of the clerical mafia.

In truth, I believed the practice of private confession, as it had been practised for generations in the Sydney parishes and throughout Australia, had trivialised a sacred sacrament which should have played an important part in the life of any struggling Christian. Confessions on Saturday afternoons or evenings in parishes like St Joseph's Neutral Bay where I had grown up, or on Thursdays before First Fridays in the schools, had been like dipping thousands of sheep, indiscriminately, one behind the other. The process had been as crass as drive-ins at McDonald's or as vulgar as "up the Windsor Road" car sales. It had functioned as a blunt mechanism to control the rank and file.

Haseler began to rubbish the Manly seminary and the young men who were turned out from there after seven years of routine training – fledgling priests inflicted onto unsuspecting parishioners and parish priests. He thought they needed to be "bum-hardened" in the seminary, so they could endure the inevitable kick in the guts afterwards. The young clergy were too negative, too critical and too intellectual. They had no devotion to the Rosary and they were not interested in parish novenas or working to continue the regular housie nights. They were useless – some of them dangerous.

Abo was a bully and, like most bullies, he prided himself on his ignorance. But his clergy mates admired his macho style. He used to race fast cars, played cards into the early hours of the morning and drank his whiskey straight. He rode a surfboard with the best and water-skied like a champion. He was welcome at any party in town – plenty of laughs around him. A physically attractive man with a loud personality and celibate. The women loved him. Since the beginning of Genesis, it seems that some members of the female team have been attracted to forbidden fruit – or so I've been told.

But Jack was also a man's man. What endeared him to many of his colleagues was that he was anti-intellectual and aggressively reactionary. It was a popular stand among some of the clergy, especially the more senior ranks. Jack was a fully paid-up member of the old brigade, whose world was founded on blind loyalty, military obedience, on acceptance of simple dogmas and on an unquestioning faith in the Vatican, but not in the Second Vatican Council. There was no denying that in his own presbytery he was an affable and hospitable host.

As we settled into our telephone conversation, Jack mounted his hobby horse and rode her with energy. He joined in the old clergy attack against "book-learning" and indulged in the senior parish priest's defence, based on experience in the field. I sat with the blower to my ear, thinking my own thoughts, amazed by the vehemence of Abo's outburst, wondering what on earth had set him off.

They were all the same, clerical versions of Bruce Ruxton – the Tosi brothers, Lou and Frank, the Paine boys, Frank Mecham, Les Baggott, Bishops Bull Muldoon, JimmyCarroll, Algie Thomas and Bishop Bill Murray – Abo Haseler and his push. They all presumed they had been blessed with the common touch and that they had their fingers on the pulse. They had the answers (all supplied years before in the seminary). But only a handful of their parishioners were asking the dusty questions for which they had the formula. Their clerical life had isolated them. The sweet, fawning talk of a coterie of their special parishioners had spoilt them. Ordinary people communicated with them in ritualistic jargon. The collar, the cassock and the pedestal, had removed these black-coated men from the grubby, complicated realities of life. There was no table at which they sat, where people could look them in the face and tell them "the God's honest truth". They saved up their personal lives for Monday's at St Michael's Golf Course, or the local squash court, or Lewisham tennis courts where Abo and his episcopal mate, Bill Murray, and others played together. For the remainder of the week they were clerics on duty, stiff agents of the Roman Catholic Church which was centred in the Eternal City and which was, in turn, the spokesman for God himself.

I remained silent while Abo Haseler was lecturing me. He was spilling his ecclesiastical spleen while I kept my stupid, rebellious ideas to myself. It was the only way I knew how to survive in that world. While I was confident that I did not have all the answers (or even all the questions), I was certain that Jack and his ilk did not have the mindset to identify the real questions troubling the Church and society, and that he was not "within a bull's roar" of discovering the answers. His theological mind had been travelling in neutral, perhaps all his life.

Finally I forced myself back into this terrible conversation. My paranoid traits began to surface. I was under attack and I felt compelled to defend myself – my faith, my loyalty and my love of our Catholic traditions. When I had been under attack before, I had found it demeaning and unfair. There was nothing to be gained by remaining silent – I had tried that. Bullies never let their victims join the team and they had me marked out.

I told Jack that what I loved about my Church was that we had always been, even from the beginning, a group of sinners. The people in my Church had always done wrong and had made countless, serious mistakes over the centuries. But of course, my remarks were falling on deaf ears. I could imagine the puzzled looks, the vacant eyes on the other end of the telephone. What was Geraghty on about? Haseler's Church was triumphant and infallible. She was the pure and wrinkle-less bride of Christ. We were living in different worlds and I was in hostile territory.

Abo Haseler changed direction. He upbraided me for not contacting him earlier, so he could have cancelled my engagement. In allowing entry to his fiefdom he was doing me a favour and he would not tolerate any undermining of his authority, or any "funny business" in his parish.

What did he mean? He had known where to contact me. Rumours had obviously been circulating. In a smart, off-handed way, I replied that I could solve his dilemma and save him any embarrassment. I would simply cancel my engagement.

He was not pleased. He had advertised my talk two Sundays in a row and he insisted I honour my undertaking. Furthermore, I had to assure him I would push the party-line – and I knew which party he was talking about – but that was a bridge too far.

I ended our conversation adding, cheekily, that I anticipated we would meet up at the talk. It was a Monday – the clergy day-off. He was certainly not going to be there to listen to anything I had to say. It had been a long time since he had had to sit and listen to someone talk theology. He had his usual plans to play tennis with his mates at Lewisham by day and to exchange gossip over cards at night.

When I was in Wollongong the following Easter, the bishop casually enquired as to how I had fared with the parish priest of Eastwood. The knowing whisper behind the episcopal inquiry registered, but I chose to play dumb. I told the story of my telephone conversation with Abo as though the bishop and Father Haseler were total strangers. When I had concluded, I looked into Bishop Bill Murray's dark eyes set in his grey face and enquired –

"But how did you know I had been at Eastwood?"

Of course, I knew the answer. Splutter, splutter. He was a member of the Monday clergy tennis club. He had obviously peddled gossip to his mates about an earlier appearance in Wollongong during the winter season.

I had accepted to present the keynote address at a weekend convention of lay-people and the whole of Wollongong seemed to be in attendance. I saw a number of my close friends in the audience – Bryce and Kathleen Fraser, the Wands, the Driscolls, the Diamonds, the Morrisseys and Father Clem Hill. They were a small group of Catholics who, unlike many of those who had deserted the pews, still cherished some hope in the future of the Church. But it was a hope spiced with a level of well-grounded cynicism about the clergy.

I was staying in the bishop's house with my classmate Michael Bach. It was Sunday morning and the clergy had gathered for breakfast, dressed to their necks in long black cassocks, paying court to their bishop, as we were being served by a small team of Maltese nuns and eating our eggs off Royal Doulton with heavy silver forks.

Over breakfast, Bishop Bill apologised for not being able to attend the convention. He was particularly sorry he was going to miss the keynote address. He had tried to rearrange his program, but unfortunately, being a busy bishop, his presence was required elsewhere.

When breakfast was over, when Bill had pushed himself away from the table, changed from his red-piped cassock into simple clerical black, displaying just a hint of red beneath his Roman collar to mark his elevated status, he drove away to Sydney.

It was the football season and the Balmain Tigers were playing at their home ground that Sunday. Bill was a fervent supporter and religiously committed to attend as often as he could. The committee had reserved a permanent parking place at the home ground for their episcopal patron.

Now, with tongue in cheek, with little of the anger of former years, I can say that I am no longer as critical of Bishop Bill for his decision to watch his team play rather than put in an appearance at his diocesan convention. Even bishops have to relax occasionally. I am older, perhaps wise, and I expect less from people now than I once did – I am not as priggish as I used to be. At least, I think that's the case. What seemed so important back in 1975 has gradually changed its colour. Whatever his priorities for that day, the bishop's urge to prevaricate reflected badly on him and on the culture of the firm he was part of.

In 1975 however, I was still a super-serious cleric. I considered the lay convention was an important event in the religious life of the diocese, an event which the bishop of Wollongong, save perhaps for a death in his family, should have attended. He also had much to learn.

That mid-year meeting of the laity in Wollongong proved stormy but not because of my talk. A few days before several girls had been expelled from the local parish school for misbehaving during a weekend retreat, and at the same time the bishop had made some controversial, insensitive statement on East Timor which had hit the press – he had supported our Federal Government which had abandoned the local Timorese people to persecution by the Indonesian Government. (Those with an acute social conscience were livid). The parents of the girls were up in arms. Wollongong was in turmoil and the bishop was looking for someone to blame.

Bishop Murray needed someone other than himself to take the flak. (For the record, I had left the meeting when some angry lay-people began discussing local issues – social justice, the autocratic governance of their diocese and the absence of their bishop.) His failure to attend the conference had not gone down well. Harsh remarks aroused some mirth. Out of some false sense of loyalty to the hierarchy and as a member of the fraternity, I had restrained myself from revealing that their bishop was busy barracking for the Balmain Tigers in Sydney. But even in those days, there is only so much one can do to protect those at the helm.

In brief, putting the pieces together, I concluded that the episcopal tennis player had told his mate Father Haseler, his version of what he imagined had occurred at the seminar in Wollongong – Geraghty was a trouble-maker. Bishop Bill had not said a word to me but Haseler had assumed his mate's burden.

"Just leave it to me, Bill. I'll sort Geraghty out for you."

And he did. He did not confront me with the facts. He came at me with clouded half-truths covered in smoke. He was fighting his mate's battle and putting in the episcopal boot.

Now Bishop Bill, a school-boy pugilist himself, was anxious to know how I had fared in the ring against his side-kick and I was determined to give him an ear-full of material to entertain his mates in between sets on the following Monday.

I was making my Easter appearance in Wollongong, in April the following year. As Dean of the Cathedral, Michael Bach used to invite me to preach each year at his Easter ceremonies. I did this for a few years, without incident. I would preach the Easter message on Holy Thursday, Good Friday, Easter Sunday – nothing controversial, nothing heretical. Then in 1976, without a word passing between us, Bishop Bill simply froze me out. I turned up as usual in answer to Michael's invitation, slept and ate in the bishop's house, attended the ceremonies, but Bishop Bill himself took over the microphone and the preaching duties. It was his right – he was the bishop.

Bill Murray repeated his smutty jokes for the benefit of his clerical colleagues in the common room, watched the sport on television, drank his whiskey, but never acknowledged the elephant in the room. One of his monsignors was not so shy.

After the Holy Thursday ceremonies, including the washing of the feet, decked out in his canary suit, red robes, frills and laces in abundance, Monsignor Herb O'Reilly turned to me and, in his soft Irish brogue, as nice as you like, informed me that I was not welcome in his diocese. He said that I was a "fecking troublemaker" and that I should go back to Sydney and never return. By September of the same year he had gone to God and I was about to go into exile.

As you might imagine, I was somewhat taken off guard. Monsignor O'Reilly had made his assault on the visitor in the presence of the assembled clergy, immediately after the Mass of the Last Supper, during which we had pledged our brotherly love for one another. No one uttered a word. There was a long pause. What was going to happen? Would we all pretend that we had not heard? Would Geraghty attack the throat of the Monsignor? Were feathers about to fly? But one of the senior priests broke the ice. Full of clerical outrage and angry conservatism, he made his contribution.

"Yes Geraghty. You heard what Herb said. Fuck off. You're not welcome here. Just piss off."

And eventually I gathered myself up and did just as Father Peter Moore advised.

chapter seventeen

1975
A NEAR-MISS

Not long after Adele had made her appearance in my home paddock, I was faced with a near-death experience which proved much more edgy than the wobbles I had felt as a puppy priest at Cronulla.

After I had introduced my French visitor to an old friend, Carmen, and her husband in their home on Sydney's north shore, Carmen unexpectedly came out of the cupboard in an attempt to further disrupt my life. She may have meant well, I'm not sure. Seeing sparks arcing between myself and Adele, she must have guessed that I was struggling to maintain my balance on the high-wire. I had revealed to her and her husband before I had left for overseas that I was feeling uncomfortable in the service. They knew I had been having trouble with the college monsignor and the system and now Carmen was determined to rescue me. Perhaps she thought that I was on the verge of destroying all I had worked for and she wanted to prevent that catastrophe if she could.

Maybe as a true friend, Carmen saw herself as my saviour. She may have thought that from my youth I had been starved of intimacy; that I needed someone understanding to satisfy my cramping hunger and that once I had tasted of the forbidden fruit she could provide, I might rest easy. My cravings might be assuaged and I could return to my life's work.

My friend did not explain what she saw as her mission, but what she was doing became apparent once the fog had cleared. She was offering herself to me. She was taking advantage of my alienation, clutching at the opportunity she had been waiting for, or alternatively, in all generosity, sacrificing herself for my redemption. She was an experienced woman who could treat me to the delights of a close encounter, without any fatal repercussions.

Carmen was the mother of several teenage children. Extravagant, expensive, chunky rings and bangles glittered on the extremities of her fleshy body and pearls glowed in the cleavage of her full breasts. She used to smoke dope before it became compulsory, and fill her scatty, tangled head and her ultra-modern living space with rock-and-roll music turned up to deafening decibels. She was a wild cougar.

For most of the time Carmen had been kept within some acceptable limits by her gentle partner, though, if what she said was true, she would break out now and then – to sleep with some well-endowed hombre just for the thrill or to engage in some other outrageous misbehaviour. My sister Maureen had introduced me to Andrew and his wife and some years later they had honoured me with their presence at my ordination. I had visited them from time to time and enjoyed their hospitality. During the lonely years when I was labouring over my doctorate thesis, when I was stressed and struggling to cope, I used to visit their home and sit at their table. They had both supported me in a hard period.

When what was happening in my life dawned on Carmen, she was onto me – on the telephone to me at Manly every other day, talking at length. She understood the pressures I was under. I was often in her thoughts. Could she help me in any way? We should see one another more often. She was keen to know me better, to be closer to me. She insisted that I chill out at her place whenever I needed to.

When Carmen invited me to come to dinner on Saturday evening, I had no reason to be suspicious. I had often eaten at their table, alone with her and her husband, sometimes with their other guests. I thought of myself as part of their family. It was an era when priests were treated as special creatures, when good Catholic folk considered themselves privileged to entertain the clergy, when members of the celibate club found some consolation from their solitary existence in the warm home of a Catholic family. I naturally assumed that Andrew would be at home with his wife when I came to dine.

But I was wrong. Carmen was home alone in the house. Loud music filling every crack and cranny, upstairs and down. She was dressed in flaming red with her ample bosom on display. An invisible mist of French perfume floated in the air. I presumed that Andrew was working out the back in his study and that he would appear in due course. Eventually, after a drink and a little chit-chat, I enquired about him. At the last minute, he had to attend a meeting in the city. Unfortunately, we were alone for the evening.

I was uneasy. I had never been alone with Carmen before or with any other fully developed woman who was presenting her qualifications for my private viewing. Adele was my only close female friend and she had always dressed with elegant discretion. What would we talk about? Why hadn't she rung to cancel the occasion when she had found out that Andrew would be otherwise engaged?

We began by discussing my current situation – the bishops, some unpleasant fellow priests. Adele was not mentioned. There was something upstairs she wanted to show me. I forget how this arose and what she said, but it was something more subtle than the etchings on the ceiling in her bedroom. At the top of the stairs the conversation became more personal. She had always admired me. She was sorry I was so unhappy. Perhaps she could be of some comfort. After all these years we should be closer.

I was beginning to freeze. At last I could sense real danger. She was standing too close to me, invading my personal space. I hated that. She was beginning to touch me. Since my first years in the seminary, I had bristled when someone tried to touch me or trespass on my territory. How was I going to escape? How could an awkward thirty-seven-year-old, celibate bachelor, remove himself from this situation without offending a giddy friend and her husband?

She took hold of me and began to cover my face with kisses. She planted her painted lips on my dry mouth. She poked her tongue right in, past my teeth. I was shocked. I tried to keep talking and to move away. I was turning my head from side to side, but she kept coming. When she began to grope about in my private parts, I stepped back, broke away and hurried downstairs in a state of confusion.

It was nice of her to offer and she was at least partially right. It was true that I was longing for intimacy. I needed a partner – someone more than a friend. I was lonely and vulnerable and Carmen had picked up the vibrations. But it was impossible for me to cooperate in her plan. I could not relax and bury myself in her mature body. She was not the person of my dreams. She was a friend – I was a friend to her husband. I had played a priestly role in their lives. The person they had welcomed into their family had been Father Chris, the priest. In those circumstances, I could not relax and let the current take me downstream. I told her I felt a sense of loyalty to her husband Andrew; that if I were to cooperate with her, his friend, the priest, would be cheating on him and he had been good to me. We had shared so much over the years, but I was not about to share his wife with him. I thought this was the best line of attack;

> "No. No. No, Carmen. I'm out of here. We'll pretend this never happened. Thanks for thinking of me, but this would only complicate my life and yours."

And I fled.

Some might think that a little sex would have been harmless and that an occasional sexual encounter can be fun. I was not brought up to think so. In later life I have come to understand that the sexual act itself is not nearly as serious or earth-shattering as the high priests of morality have made it out to be, in their dreams, in their doctrine. Without the least experience, or else based on illicit and guilt-laden encounters, the clergy speak of the act of intimacy in hushed tones; as though each encounter is the mighty act of creation; as though it carries the most overwhelming implications; as though they knew what they were talking about. The truth is that after the thrill of first love, the activity itself is sometimes rather mundane, if not a little risible. It can be amusing, empowering, relaxing, exhilarating, embarrassing, disappointing. In the modern world, given all the precautions, it is generally not all that serious. The sexual interaction with a wife or partner, however, at least to my mind, was special. The intimate relationship between two lovers should be precious. From my point of view, it involved a deep and personal trust, and a spiritual duty of faithfulness. A loving sexual encounter involved an opening out towards the other, an exposure, a spontaneous giving of her most valuable possession – herself. It was a glorious way for any human being to communicate with another. Tampering with this intimate, exclusive relationship could be dangerous and was often destructive. People did often tangle and mangle the relationship, compromising their intimate communion, but in doing so, they caused pain to others and often suffered heartache themselves.

Anyway, I fled. I was conscious of the fact that I had sailed close to the rocks in a violent storm and was lucky to be alive. Carmen had been about to devour me. Of course, I did not entertain the idea of discussing our little Saturday night encounter with her husband. Nothing much had happened, so I thought it was best to forget his wife's moment of madness. Though on reflection, I could see that a good deal of planning had been invested in the evening.

Some days later I received a telephone call from Andrew.

> "I hope you had a good evening with Carmen last Saturday, Chris. I'm sorry I had to attend a meeting in the city. It was unavoidable. I just want you to know, Chris, that whatever happens between you and Carmen is OK with me. I hope you understand."

I did understand alright, at least as far as the essentials were concerned. I never found out whether they had agreed to assist a desperado whom they loved, or whether I had been chosen as a temporary distraction, a substitute, an amusement for someone who was insatiable and whom Andrew no longer sought to satisfy. I assured Andrew that I understood and hung up.

That was the end of our friendship.

chapter eighteen

END OF '75 – BEGINNING OF '76
JEUNES FILLES EN FLEUR

As the year advanced and as 1975 turned to Autumn and Winter, I was spending more time in Adele's company. I was showing her around my territory – the Botanical Gardens, Bondi Beach, the northern beaches and the spectacular headlands. We travelled to Katoomba in my old Peugeot and walked in the shade of the Jamison Valley. We visited the national park to the south of Sydney, rowed a heavy boat on the river, strolled the paths near the edge of the ocean and sometimes visited the theatre together.

These outings and my visits to her flat were thin slivers of time stolen from a busy schedule at Manly. I was conscious of the tensions which had so easily become rooted in my soul. I was anxious that no one should see me out in public with a pretty girl on my arm. What other couples were doing openly, without complication, was forbidden to me. I used to look furtively over my shoulder, or search the faces in a theatre, walking down city streets, in the hope that I would not meet an old parishioner or someone I had taught. It was silly. Sydney was a small town and I was reasonably well known, at least in some paddocks. For a time, my heart was filled with anxiety – a life in turmoil.

In January 1976, I delivered the keynote paper at a theological seminar for students and spent several days at St Leo's University College in Brisbane, where the students were relishing the opportunity to do some "clergy bashing". By this stage our Church leaders were bleeding from multiple self-inflicted wounds. They had shot themselves in both feet and sustained serious brain injury. The students had lots to say and I provided an outsider's attentive ear, to a litany of complaints about a team of old men living in an ecclesiastical Disneyland.

My sister Colleen had arranged to spend a fortnight with a few of her girlfriends on the Gold Coast, south of Brisbane. She had recovered, somewhat, after being abandoned by her second-grade husband and left without resources to care for their two little boys. The tears had ceased; the anger had subsided and she was getting on with her life. My parents had offered to look after the boys while Colleen had a few days with Jan, Jannie and Susie. They had supported my sister, like women tend to do, through the hard times, and they pressed me to join them down the coast.

From Brisbane, I travelled by bus to Surfers Paradise with my budgie smugglers and sun-cream, to meet up with Colleen and her gang. I bunked in with them in a flat overlooking the beach and shared a bathroom with four spunky females in their late twenties. I am a little embarrassed to admit that at the age of thirty-seven, this was a whole new experience. Apart from a few days in Paris consoling her after the agony of rejection, I had never spent any holiday-time with my young sister. Nor had I had the pleasure of eating and drinking, sitting around watching television in swimming gear, shopping, looking in windows and just talking with a clutch of pretty, feathery hens. They were fun women and those were fun days.

The girls were not treating me as a piece of forbidden fruit. I was the brother of one of their mob. They were not distant towards me, or careful of what they felt able to say. Nor were they flirty, or seeking to shock. They were relaxed and natural together, laughing, chatting and enjoying themselves. It was exciting to waste a few summer days with Colleen and her young, attractive, carefree friends in bikinis. We laughed and talked, we walked the streets together arm-in-arm, looking in shop windows, we prepared food and shared glasses of port late into the night.

This was not a near-death experience, but it made me stop and reassess where I had come from and where I thought I was going. I began to realize how monotone my life had been, and how different from other people's lives. I began to appreciate how much I enjoyed female company. I could feel a fatal attraction deep in my body. I became aware of the price I had to pay for the choice I had made in my youth and I began to question whether I could live the life of a celibate priest, even if I wanted to.

chapter nineteen

1976

A LETTER FROM HOME

In July 1976, while I was still teaching the students at Manly, lecturing in Liturgy and running an heretical seminar on the ordination of women, I received a letter from my mother.

This was not one of those periods (like my two years in France, or the many years I had spent as a student in the seminary), during which Mum used to write a page or two to me in the neat, rounded running-writing she had learnt in a Queensland country school. She always used to begin her letter "My dear Chris" and she never told of any turmoil or dramas within the family (though I later came to learn that in my absence, on occasions, sparks used to fly in the family home in Florence Street). No. She wrote during a period when we would speak on the phone from the south coast at Manyana several times each week, but this message was too important for a telephone-call.

Her letter arrived unexpectedly.

"My dear Chris,
Just a few lines to let you know I am thinking of you and to tell you I love you very much, and that your happiness means everything to me and I know your father's sentiments are the same.
You have been struggling against great odds this past couple of years and I know any decision you make won't be made without a lot of thought and prayer.
Even if you decide to leave the priesthood, your fourteen

years has been well spent and I am sure you will never be forgotten for your unselfish efforts during that time.

You are welcome here as soon and as long as you want to come. Try not to worry too much. It will all work out in the end.

I'm not much good at these kinds of letters, Chris. Guess I need practice.

We are all both well and contented.

Love,

Mum".

This was one of my mother's letters which I kept. Even now, after all these years, tears cloud my eyes as I read her generous words.

Top Left: Brother and Sister (Colleen) – circa 1968. Top Right: Reverend Dr Christopher Geraghty, D.D.
Below: Father Hughie Boland of Avalon and his curate.

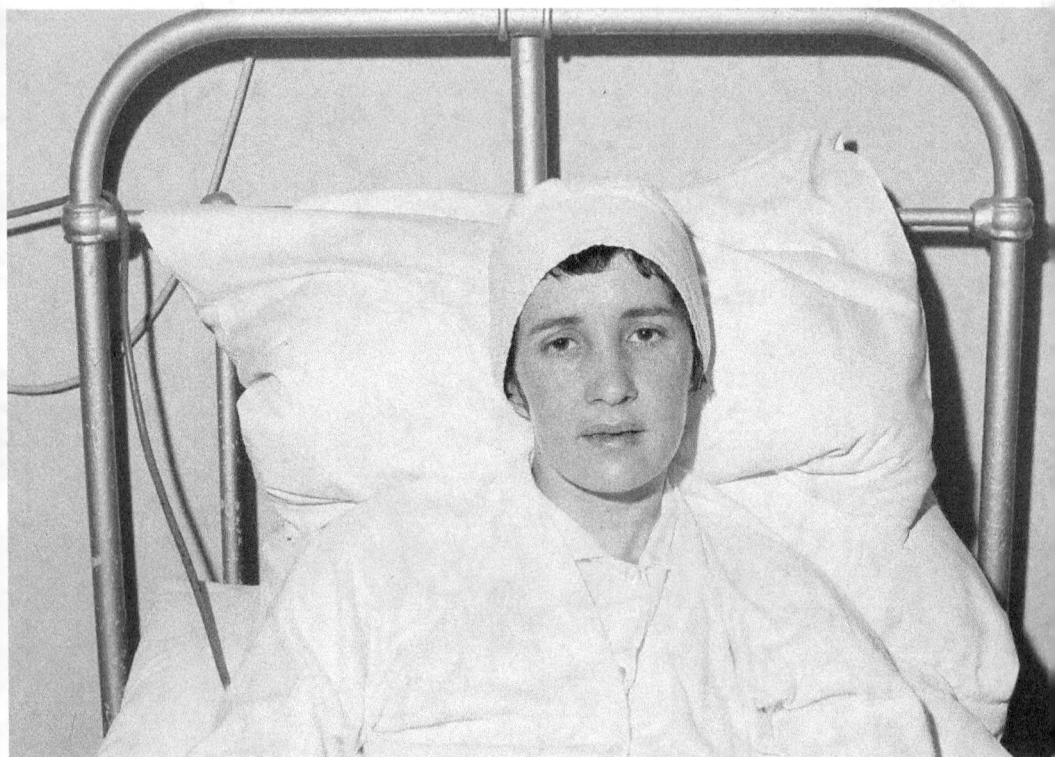

Above: Sister Christine Mary nee Maureen Yvonne Geraghty.
Bottom Left: A French girl and a Sydney priest in Brilon. Bottom Right: Adela Rosa Rodriguez.

Above: The Fraternité in Paris, in winter.
Below: Bride and Groom in Toulouse, October 1977.

Right: Judge Geraghty.

Below: On holidays in Provence.

chapter twenty

1976
A CRITICAL DECISION

While she was in Australia, Adele travelled through the red centre, camping under the Southern Cross, sharing her sausages with manic bush-flies and breathing in the dust of the outback through the bus window. She went as far as Perth and the quokka colony on Rottnest Island.

She had toured the Barrier Reef. She had joined a bus party of campers in New Zealand, wading through rivers and climbing snow-covered mountains. She had been entertained by warriors performing the terrifying haka. She had flown to Fiji with a group of teachers, slept in thatched villages, watched sure-footed, grinning natives dancing on hot coals, forded rivers and gambled with her life as a passenger in a rented vehicle on narrow, ochre-coloured roads, landing in remote communities, where village royalty had received her as a foreign queen.

My French companion had been busy down-under, travelling happily without her Australian patron. I would receive an occasional card from the back-of-beyond, which recorded a typically neat summary of events. Later I watched the slides and listened to the commentary she had composed in preparation for sending a tape-recording of her Australian adventures to her family in Toulouse.

I missed her when she was on tour, but I accepted that these trips were part of her Australian adventure and I was committed to a timetable of lectures at Manly. My increasingly precious quality-time in her company was limited to day trips out of Sydney and to visiting her compact Seidler flat on McMahon's Point. My total commitment to the education of seminarians and to my way of life, was cooling. I was beginning to find my way towards the escape hatch.

Adele had floated a vague desire to tour the Apple Isle, hinting that I might like to go with her, and I was seriously tempted to accept her offer.

But even during those months, I was not stupid. I realised that a decision to seize the day would be at odds with my chosen way of life. I had never done anything like that before, but I did not want such an opportunity to slip away. It was a lovely offer and I knew what it meant. I did not know what the future might hold and the chance might never reappear.

So I acted impulsively, in the full knowledge that too much reflection might end in a fatal refusal. I was in no mind-frame to take a dispassionate, considered decision. I was surrounded by trouble; angry and depressed; infatuated and in love.

For some months in 1976, more months than I care to remember, I was living a double life. Parallel to my public life on the staff of the seminary, I had a secret life – at least in so far as a priest's life in Sydney could be secret. I suspected that clergy rumours were spreading energetically. I was teaching theology, fighting with a number of bishops and senior clergy, and at the same time keeping informal company with a young woman. I was aware that my life had become a bit of a shambles but I needed space to breathe. After such a long time chained to the institution, I needed time to think, time to decide, space to feel, to grow in confidence, time to experiment and experience a different life. I was treading a path other men had negotiated in their youth.

According to the narrow Church world in which I had lived my life, I found myself engaged in a relationship which was considered improper. Hundreds of millions, billions of men and women over the centuries and on every continent had fallen under the spell of someone special, spending weekends arm-in-arm, holidaying together and making love under trees and under bedcovers. Not the slightest complication soiled the hearts of these people. They had not been tormented by any crisis of conscience. They could dance, laugh and make love without a care in the world. Being together physically was a neutral, pleasurable experience. What made the communion good or bad was the participants' status in society, their state of mind and the circumstances in which someone would, or might, be hurt by such an intimate relationship.

In the heat of the moment, I agreed to team up with Adele on a ten-day trip to Van Diemen's Land.

As we hurtled down the highway in a rush to catch *The Empress of Australia* across the Tasman, I was feeling like a man on the run. The further I travelled from my home base, the safer I felt. Another part of me, however, was ever alert that someone would confront us and demand an explanation. I had spent my whole life answerable to others and it was difficult to escape.

At Devonport, we drove out of the hold of the ship, down over the ramp, onto land and away. Tasmania looked like a land of plenty – green and oozy lush, with pockets of contented sheep, mountains in the distance blanketed in snow. We were together in a distant space in paradise and I was beginning to feel a little like a normal invisible person.

Tasmania was a quaint island on the edge of Western civilization – a gentle, slow, tranquil land. Grey stone bridges over glistening streams which were carpeted with shiny, smooth stones. Old homes, busy kitchens with large, open hearths, long, wooden tables, butter churners, meat safes, candle makers, old tools, fat luxuriant gardens, soft grass for picnics, stables, elegant carriages, working drays, blacksmith's hammers and anvils, old cupboards and dressers, four-poster wooden beds covered in lace, Devonshire teas with cream and apple jelly jam – Tasmania had preserved the relics of its colonial past. Its history had been reconstructed as a fairytale, made up of happy memories and tokens of a simple life. No haunting relics of conflict, of murderous, bludgeoning acts of violence, torment and blood spilt, of human flesh eaten, of vicious genocide.

We moved happily, from youth hostels to caravan parks where we would hire a tiny self-contained unit for the night. We camped in the open under the clear sky – a diminutive couple observed from distant stars. We cooked on my primus stove, boiled the billy and slept snug in a warm, downy sleeping bag, inside the red igloo tent I had inherited from my ugly ex-brother in law. Timid animals – possums, field mice, a curious wild cat – visited our freezing campsite during the night to scavenge for left-overs.

Fishing boats laden with prawns; fresh fish cooked on sparklingly clean public barbecues in the park; a rainy, wintery night in a neat caravan park unit, with facilities to cook, to wash hair, to shower and relax in front of the television – my life was different, if only for a brief interlude.

The youth hostel at Burnie, where Adele and I renewed our friendship with a Canadian wanderer whom we had met earlier in a log shelter near Lake St Clair, was crowded with weary road warriors. A tube of smoke drifted up the old stone chimney and out into a crisp heaven. The warden in charge, John, wandered in around 6 o'clock, a little drunk after the local football match and a few drinks with his mates in the pub. The grubby back-packers had already draped themselves casually over chairs or stretched out on the floor to watch a television program and discuss plans for the next day.

By the following evening the crowd of itinerant visitors had departed. Adele and I were the only guests and Warder John was relaxed and flying high – talking freely, laughing and telling stories. He brought out a flagon of fortified wine and, in breach of the house rules, invited us to partake. Adele politely refused but I felt obliged to partake. I had drunk a few tumblers of his poison when suddenly my companion decided to take himself off to bed. But before leaving me he looked across the communal table, straight into my face, and said –

"Take my advice. Hang on to that one, mate. She's a beauty. Don't let her go. You should take extra-special care of her or someone else will nab her."

I agreed and it proved good advice.

chapter twenty one

1976

THE CATHOLIC WEEKLY

A t this end of my life most of the details hardly matter. It was so long ago and so much has happened in the world and in my life. Few people still living will remember even a skeleton version of the facts. Maybe a few, when pressed, could dredge up some frayed memories of the incident, but the details are mostly lost in the frail cobwebs of the past.

But I remember – I remember well. The facts and the personalities surrounding those events of 1976 are etched into my memory like rivulets of bile. What occurred here in my hometown, over a period of six or eight months, was to determine, at least in part, the remainder of my days.

If *The Catholic Weekly* incident had never happened, if Frank Mecham had not taken up his censorious red crayon, if Paddy Murphy had never become involved and made his flattering assessment of my loyalty to the system, I might not have gathered the courage to leave the nest in which I had grown to manhood. I may never have spread my wings and floated free on the wind.

At one stage, long ago, and for more years than I care to admit, the events of '76 dominated the screen on which my life was projected. This distressing experience used to act like a hot curry, which would pervade every corner of my mind and flavour my religious thoughts.

But the passing of time and the blossoming of a new life, the love of family and friends have gradually eased the sting in the curry. Age and a broad experience of the world outside the narrow confines of the institutional Church, produced a whole new context in which to remember and weigh the actions and the motives of the players. The events which proved overwhelming at the time, eventually faded back into the gentle ebb and flow of my existence.

As I now recall, flickering shapes appear out of the shadows – Darby Mecham with his corrugated iron grin and Toto Murphy, who was once a clerical policeman, walking his beat in the corridors of the seminary, imposing discipline and order on the scrubby students. Both were Manly men and are now dead. My friends have warned me that I must not speak too harshly of them now they are gone, that I must try and see through compassionate eyes the peculiar, mythical world in which they lived. I do, however, have some facts to recite for the record and some observations, which may not please those of their lost world and who might still hold them in high esteem.

Out of the mists, appear the ghost of David Coffey, President of the Faculty; Bob Stapleton, the editor of *The Weekly*, who was made to walk both sides of the barbed-wire fence until he was totally knackered; Eddy Campion, who emerged from this minor theatrical performance as a hero of the piece; Michael Mahony who, as a young priest, was sent into battle by faceless elders to fight a cause, and on a side, which he himself must have found distasteful; and further back, in the distance, covered in fog, other figures – Jimmy Freeman, Jimmy Carroll, Bull Muldoon; the wily Gerry Gleeson; John Marsden of Campbelltown; Ian Allan, secretary of *The Weekly* board; and many citizens, clergy and nobodies who wrote to me, or to *The Weekly*, to the Cardinal, to the Sydney Morning Herald, expressing their thoughts and unleashing their fury.

In November 1975, Bob Stapleton telephoned the seminary at Manly, looking for me. Since his return from his studies in Rome, he had risen through the ranks to become the editor of *The Catholic Weekly* and he wanted to invite me to write a series of articles on the Sacrament of Penance for his paper.

The Church throughout Australia (and in the diocese of Sydney) was in the difficult and slow process of reluctantly reforming its penitential rituals and other areas of its liturgical worship. The Vatican had revamped its ceremonies and rituals, and consequential edicts had emerged from the centre of power. In place of the rather dull routine of monthly or weekly private confession in which we had all been schooled as children, Rome had devised three different forms of the sacrament, thereby assuring some flexibility in the pastoral experience of seeking forgiveness of our sins. *The Weekly* was looking for a series of authoritative articles to inform its readers of the changes and the purpose behind them.

At the time, I happened to be the emerging expert in Australia in liturgical studies. I had recently returned from Paris where I had made a special study of the history and pastoral practice of Penance in the Roman Catholic Church. I had worked with the principal author of the three new penitential rites – Father Pierre Jounel – and I assume that the editor had thought I was in a privileged position to present a series of articles for the readers of his *Weekly*. I agreed with him.

The Weekly made a mistake. As it turned out, I was not the appropriate person to deliver what they wanted. I was a lecturer in the senior seminary for budding clerics in Sydney. In Paris, I had come into contact with thinkers, scholars, with ideas, influences and with unknown forces. By contrast, *The Weekly* was a flabby, devotional purveyor of pious good news to the regimented masses on the underside of the world. It reported first communions, Papal appearances, miracles, blessings of schools and churches and confirmations performed on a multitude of children, by photogenic local bishops in their party hats. It acted as the agent of the hierarchy in their attempts to reassure an ageing and unquestioning laity, that all was well. Nothing hard-edged and nothing difficult to swallow. Colourful cup-cakes and bread-and-butter custard. No controversy. Roses from heaven. Comfort food and soft drinks.

But, flattered by his offer, I accepted without much reflection. It was a mistake. I should have known that while the world had been changing radically, my Sydney Church had stubbornly turned its back on change, smiled knowingly, patronisingly, at new ideas, ignored the aspirations of its lay members and remained blissfully unaware of their needs. Ecclesiastical leaders, bishops and monsignors wanted to hold onto the decaying thought-patterns and practices of the 40's and 50's, which were (like themselves) relics of the nineteenth century. They had not embraced the vision of Good Pope John. They were suspicious of "the world", frightened of change, anxious to preserve their sacred past in frozen form and unwilling to trust the Spirit to lead them out of the desert into the future.

Because of my jaundiced opinion of *The Weekly* I accepted their invitation, subject to one condition. Without hesitation, the editor agreed that no changes would be made to my text without first consulting me. There would be no difficulty. I would be consulted on how my articles might be edited for publication, I would maintain full control over my material and if there was any disagreement which could not be resolved, I would have the last say. I had his word on it and he was an honourable man, but, like me, without the worldly wisdom of the viper.

In response to Bob's invitation, and in my tiny running writing, I wrote four lengthy articles over the summer holidays. I was aware that some of the faithful pew-polishers in Sydney might be startled by my material. For those who simply presumed that what they did in church had always been done and what they believed had always been believed in all parts of the known world and in every century back to Peter and the Apostles, the bare facts of the historical development of the Sacrament of Penance would have proved confronting. For pious Catholics who had learnt from fossilised parish priests and religious teachers that monthly confession was almost obligatory; for clergy trained to believe that weekly confession was highly recommended; for pious folk who had heard that those saintly figures closest to God used to confess as often as twice, three times a day – for these believers, it might have proved disturbing to discover, for example, that many Christians had lived in a world in which the Sacrament of Penance could only be offered to a sinner once in his lifetime. The practice of private confession had been unknown for many centuries. Over the years, Christian communities had developed a number of different forms of forgiveness. For some centuries, sinful Christians had sought forgiveness and reconciliation through a long process of public penance which had been linked to the seasons of Lent and Easter. It might have been unsettling to find one of their local clergy asserting, in their pious *Weekly,* that in his opinion the form, frequency and circumstances in which the Sacrament of Penance was offered in local parishes, had tended to trivialise an important sacrament. It had created many pastoral problems as well as providing a fertile field for the blossoming of serious psychological disorders (such as debilitating obsessions and compulsions, as well as various forms of anxiety disorders and depressive states).

About the middle of March, I delivered my four articles by hand to Stapleton and, with his assurance in mind, promptly turned my attention to other things. Sometime later, I happened to see a recent copy of *The Weekly* at the back of some country church and I turned the pages to glance over my fourth article. The by-line read –

"Rev. Christopher Geraghty DD, M.Th (Paris), lecturer in Liturgical Studies and Theology of Sacraments at the Catholic Theological Faculty of Sydney, in the fourth and last in a series of articles, explains the background of the new form to be used in the Sacrament of Penance."

In the light of the undertaking given by the editor, I began by casually scanning the text. I read through the columns and I read them again. Something was wrong. This was not my work. My words had been edited and changed. No one from *The Weekly* had rung me. There had been no consultation as promised.

I lost no time in telephoning Stapleton. I began by telling him that I had just read what purported to be my fourth article when he interrupted me. Father Frank Mecham had offered to take the articles home to his presbytery and to "look at them". My article had been slashed, not by the editor but by the chairman of the board.

I was furious and Stapleton knew it. I was outraged that *The Weekly* had felt at liberty to publish, under my name, an article which had not come from me – a fury further fuelled by the fact that the editor had not kept his promise.

Father Mecham was well-known to me from my seminary days. As a student, I had been exposed every day for a year to his pseudo-scholastic mumbo-jumbo (though his long, unexplained absences from the college had provided some temporary respite) and from where I sat in the pecking order, he was a harsh, robotic, steely man. I acknowledge that others whom I respect speak well of him as a teacher of classical and *koine* Greek, but their opinion is not generally shared.

The fact that later, for some years, Frank Mecham became the official spiritual director of seminarians, was unfortunate for all concerned. He seemed incapable of exhibiting feelings of compassion, gentleness and humanity. He was tough and unyielding on us and on himself. It had been of some amusement amongst us that Frank had advised those among us who were dull or desperate enough to seek his guidance, that it could be a mortal sin to break the rules of the college. Even though mortal sins were exceedingly common, his advice was patent nonsense. In those days, it was easy to become an enemy of God. One could do it almost by accident. All of a sudden an otherwise good person could be damned for eternity to the fires of hell, to live in the bottomless pit, separated forever from divine light and happiness – eating meat on any Friday throughout the year; missing Mass on Sunday without some reasonable excuse; entertaining salacious, sexual thoughts – any number of omissions could do the trick, but breaking a seminary rule achieved an even higher plane of absurdity. This was the man who had volunteered to "correct" my articles.

Frank was a safe member of the club. He would not hesitate to use the red pen in what he considered to be the higher interests of the organisation. He was a paid-up member of the ecclesiastical thought-police and proud to make his contribution. Scandal was to be avoided at all cost, and his attitude was typical of the clergy of his generation. The parish priest of Kensington, for example, Father Lou Tosi, is said to have once proudly boasted to a group of fellow priests –

"I'd be happy to commit perjury in the interests of the Church."

On hearing his boast, one of the team was heard to mutter under his breath –

"The Church might be better served if he were to commit adultery."

At my request Stapleton returned my original handwritten articles and as I turned the pages, the extent of Frank's handy-work became obvious – additional paragraphs in red; words, tenses, meanings changed; paragraph after paragraph, sometimes pages, scored through, in red ink. The evidence was startling – my writing in black ink, his in red. Darby Mecham had spread himself all over the original pages, distorting the story of the development of this sacrament and imposing his own reactionary views.

A Faculty colleague at Manly, Eddy Campion, was keen to examine the black and red redacted text and, after a close inspection, he put together a four-page, roneoed critique of Frank's hatchet job. *"Doctoring the Facts : A Case Study in Partisan Censorship"* circulated among some clergy and journalists in Sydney and even penetrated *The Weekly Catholic* compound.

Campion circulated his essay in Sydney on April Fools' Day 1976, and within a few days it had travelled along the clerical high wires. Stapleton rang me to complain. Campion had concluded in his critique that a faceless censor had doctored my work; that the sub-editing process had revealed a strongly partisan, conservative, theological prejudice. Most of my more incisive reflections had suffered under the power of the red pen. What was left was second rate and, in some instances, quite banal. At one point, Eddy wrote –

> "In a fine piece of historico-theological writing, Geraghty
> reflects on the tensions that could be caused by this change.
> These reflections go deeper than any other part of the article.
> None of this appears in *The Catholic Weekly.*"

In hindsight, a telephone call, perhaps a personal, unannounced visit to my study at Manly might have been more healing than Frank's one-page, non-committal note which was written in an attempt to place his problem on hold. He should have known that Geraghty was a "squib"; that he would go to water if he had been approached in a proper manner. But there was no personal contact, no conversation.

On the 2nd April Campion forwarded a letter to the president of the Catholic Theological Faculty, of which he was himself a member. He was following up his *"Doctoring the Facts"* paper with some initiatives the Faculty might consider. He gave President Coffey four suggestions (undoubtedly made with his soft Irish tongue in his ruddy cheek). To appreciate the comedy of Eddy Campion's suggestions, you would have to visualise the male and clerical make-up of the Faculty, the Monty Pythonesque seriousness of its members and the cold, formal relationship between the "professors" and the students.

Eddy thought that the President might feel "impelled" to call an urgent meeting of the Faculty personnel to discuss the situation; that the united Faculty might feel moved to condemn the unwarranted attack on a member's professional reputation and find a way "to right the wrong". He also thought that they should call another extraordinary meeting of the Faculty theologians, to show solidarity and support for one of its members. These meetings never took place.

Campion suggested that the President might convene a public meeting in the city, to protest against the activities of *The Weekly's* censor. He thought such a meeting would appeal to public opinion within and outside the Church and would highlight the hidden vice of partisan censorship. This suggestion was also ignored.

Finally, he informed President Coffey that *The Catholic Weekly* board would be meeting on Friday 9th April. He invited him to cancel lectures for that day and organise a peaceful demonstration of staff, graduates and students outside *The Weekly's* office.

"Campbell Street (on the edge of the city) lends itself readily
to such a peaceful demonstration."

Campion thought that the students and staff of other theological colleges in Sydney might be willing to show solidarity. Leaflets for distribution to bystanders and passers-by could be prepared and a loud hailer for a speech by Coffey himself could be borrowed. Campion was an old Peace campaigner from the Vietnam War days in Sydney and he thrived on protest marches and demonstrations. He was having such fun.

The fact that Eddy's letter was addressed to David Coffey made his suggestions all the more ridiculous. President Coffey was a gifted theologian and a cultured man, but he was not a man of humour or passion. He was aloof and grey, stiffly formal, rather cerebral. The image of him shouting in public over a loud hailer, stirring the masses, causing trouble in the streets – had a touch of the absurd.

An undignified battle had broken out. Letters went back and forth between me and *The Weekly*, the skirmish was receiving coverage on the commercial television stations, letters to the editor were appearing in the daily press and I was receiving copies of letters of outrage addressed to Cardinal Freeman or to *The Weekly,* from members of the clergy, and ordinary laypeople and academics.

I had stirred a hornet's nest and while *The Weekly* was ducking for cover, Father Mecham did not appear to understand what the fuss was about. He had simply done what any clerical editor would have done with the material presented by a member of the clergy – changed it, modified it to assuage the delicate faith of the little people, to avoid scandalizing the ignorant.

Like many of the clergy of his generation (and some of my own generation), Frank had the happy belief that what he had learnt as a child, out of the penny catechism and his own personal practices and devotions, had been in some way instituted by Jesus himself in his lifetime and had remained substantially unchanged down through the centuries. His theology was almost totally ahistorical. It was not based on scholarly research but depended on Roman authority, on the Pope and on his personal gift of infallibility. This form of Roman theology had been standardised and canonised sometime between the 1850s and the 1950s. The techniques of historical research which European scholars had finely tuned towards the end of the nineteenth century, had been arrogantly condemned by the Vatican and her censors and resisted well into the late twentieth century.

Until my troubles with *The Weekly* I had never set foot in a solicitor's office. But I was friendly with a solicitor and a junior barrister, so I sought advice from both of them – the standard free advice for clergy.

I regret that, covered in indignation, I turned to the law for some resolution to this problem. In this, as in most other situations, in family disputes, in criminal trials, often in commercial disagreements, the law is powerless to provide a satisfactory answer. My problem was beyond the rule of law. It had no power to remove the hurt. The law could not raise its healing hand to touch my anger or my disillusionment. She is a blunt tool. She can sometimes provide a degree of superficial certainty for the sake of the smooth function of society, but she is incapable of solving problems and doing justice in complex human situations. Those who entrust their lives to the rule of law are condemned to disappointment. Perhaps my barrister friend knew that but I doubt it – like me, he was young.

I visited John Marsden in his offices at Campbelltown. He had once been an angelic priest-apprentice at Springwood. He read the papers and advised me to insist that *The Weekly* present a full apology, in a prominent place on page-one, and publish my articles unaltered – perhaps in a booklet format. In addition, he thought, I should claim some compensation and mentioned ten thousand dollars. Apart from the suggestion of an apology, his advice was unhelpful but as a novice in a war-zone, I was in no position to judge. Seeking to stress the gravity of what they had done, I communicated Marsden's legal advice to *The Weekly*. That was another mistake. *The Weekly* informed the clergy and the clergy responded with outrage.

Later in April 1976, I received a disgraceful letter from the secretary of the Catholic Press who mangled the facts and distorted the truth. It was obvious I could not trust the people I was dealing with. I could see them backing and filling, the spinning wheel turning, weaving their message. The board was in a bind. One of its members had breached the code of ethics which the Australian Religious Press Association had adopted. They were reluctant to admit guilt and like John Howard, to perform the simple penance of an apology. They adopted the usual strategy of bankrupt politicians and high clerics – pull down the shutters; raise the drawbridge; pretend you are innocent; deny everything. (The cause of "truth and justice" would eventually prevail because teacup storms eventually lose impetus and the mighty Roman Church can outlast the fleeting lives of protesters.)

Ian Allan asserted that the directors believed the problem was largely due to "a misunderstanding of the brief" that I had received. Like Mecham, he was rewriting history – busy constructing a convenient but false explanation after the event. Stapleton and I alone knew what my brief had been.

Geraghty was being spoken of everywhere – in the priest senate in Sydney; in the meetings of the Theology Faculty when I was not present; on television; in the newspapers, even in Melbourne. Suddenly I was a public rebel. For Catholic-haters, for Church critics and the indifferent, I was providing proof that my Church bore the mark of an institution which relied on spin and propaganda, which demanded blind obedience, which needed to sanitise the events of history and which was indifferent to due process. They were having a field day. On the large screen, the events themselves were so tiny they were almost invisible but they provided a window for outsiders to peer in on the life of the Church in Sydney.

Once again, like my Springwood days, I was playing on the boundary, in the long paspalum grass, among the bush flies. I had always been on the outer but until that moment, I had refused to accept this was my natural position – that this was where I was destined to play. I did not enjoy the feeling of being different, but I had to accept that I could not belong – I would never belong. I was a stranger among my own brothers and a threat to the Church in Sydney.

Someone from *The Weekly* had also informed *The National Times* that their failure to consult me about changes to my material, had been "due to an oversight". But there had of course been no oversight – that was nonsense. Their clerical censor with the prophylactic pen had simply assumed that he could do whatever he wished with the material in front of him, that the author was subject in all things even to minor authority and that Frank's iron-fist was free and unfettered.

For some months, Archbishop James Carroll had been tapping out some Morse code messages for me. He and some other bishops were concerned about my informal, non-clerical dress in the corridors of the seminary. I was not walking about naked – I was wearing a skivvy and corduroys. The authorities must have been confident that the rumour-mill would reach me, and it did.

In his presbytery at Woollahra, Archbishop James Carroll was a man of influence. The clerical ghosts who walked the corridors upstairs, were silent witnesses to the coming and goings of the highly placed Labor-Party, right-wing, machine-men who used to visit the grey eminence under the cover of darkness. Political plots were hatched at Woollahra – deals were done, shadowy figures arriving late at night, unobserved by their political opponents.

The Archbishop was a canny fox. He used to lift his nose in the breeze to detect any rumours, gossip, innuendoes or any information which might prove politically useful. A mutual friend reported that the Archbishop thought Geraghty had become a "prima donna" in the diocese. He might have been right, though it was not an image I had of myself. I had found a flutter of freedom while I had been away in Paris, but as far as I was concerned I had not given him or his diocese any real trouble – no fraud or drunkenness, no public scandal. I was not picking up desperate gays in public toilets and I was not living in concubinage or knocking off the housie takings.

Being in charge of education in the diocese, the Archbishop was a member of the executive committee of the Theological Faculty at Manly and one of his duties was to attend Faculty meetings. Each time he was circularised about a meeting, he would agree to attend but, true to form, come the day he would fail to appear. Perhaps his migraine held him back, maybe he had more important, secret matters to attend to or perhaps he thought the Faculty was a lost cause. Bishops did not have to explain.

Although he seldom attended meetings, Jimmy did not relinquish his power. By ruling through the telephone, he was not forced to be part of any open discussion. He did not have to expose his thoughts in the public arena, his ideas and prejudices were not the subject of any refining discussion and he could ring whomsoever he liked, plot secretly over the telephone and let his wishes be known without scrutiny. No minutes to file in the archives.

Though I had received a permanent appointment as a member of staff, Archbishop Carroll secretly, by telephone, began to advance the issue of my retrenchment. No-one confronted me with his plan. I found out about this move some years later, when a friend let slip that at a special interim meeting of the Faculty at which the Archbishop had made a special appearance, John Walsh, David Coffey and Bishop Pat Murphy had spoken up on my behalf. When Carroll had announced that he was under pressure to "do something about Geraghty", the meeting had advised him not to move against me, at least in his capacity as a member of the council. The Faculty invited the clerical mafia to bear in mind that Geraghty was the one who had been wronged by *The Weekly*.

I was surprised to learn there had been at least some muted support from my confrères. None of them, except Pat Murphy, ever spoke with me. I was hurt when I learnt, much later, of the secret move against me. In my innocence, I would have expected to have been consulted and confronted before being forced to drink the poisoned chalice. I had been part of their system for all of twenty-four years and they still presumed they could decide my future and discuss my life, (like they had when I was a student) without consulting me, as though I was just a number.

chapter twenty two

1976

VISITING THE BEAST IN HIS CAVE

I should have been annoyed with the Geraghty women for inserting themselves into my professional life. I might have been cranky if I had known at the time, that my mother had plotted with my sister to confront my Archbishop, in his den. I would have been embarrassed to discover they were outraged enough, to do what I had to do for myself. But when I later heard of their assault on the Cathedral bunker, I could only laugh and sympathise with their feeling of helplessness in the presence of my pain. I understood their anger at seeing their son, their brother, wrestling with an ecclesiastical blob. My sister Colleen later, laughingly, described the one-act piece as it had unfolded.

My mother was not as meek or as reticent as she used to imagine. She could interrogate with rough questions that penetrated to the heart of an issue, without first dancing round to soften the ground. In the family and among her friends, she was renowned for her letters of complaint to government agencies and large corporations, and for the results she could achieve; apologies, free biscuits, theatre tickets – anything to appease and placate an unhappy consumer. Colleen was also not known to take backward steps in a crisis. I suppose you could say that this was a Geraghty trait. She could be ferocious in argument, vicious in the heat of battle, unreasonable and mad with self-righteous anger – parading like a frill-necked lizard. Like her mother, she was protective of the members of her family, especially her three boys. I am pleased to record that in my fight she was on her brother's side.

Out of the blue, a strong, female tag team had made an appointment with His Eminence to meet him at the Cathedral, at the seat of his power. My mother and sister had hatched a plot to stalk him, to strike him in the eye and leave him in no doubt about their concern for their boy (even if no one else "could give a rat's arse" about how the petty battles he was waging on multiple fronts were bringing him down). They were determined to make their stand as members of the Geraghty clan. They had discussed the situation in the kitchen at home in Florence Street and they had decided to take the initiative and to goad the dragon in his pit.

The operation was covert and its chilling details remained secret. Occasionally, in later years, Colleen would let drop some delicious morsel – flash-backs often accompanied by giggling laughter. My mother was less forthcoming. Only once did she make some passing reference to her visit to the Cathedral. Piece by piece, knowing the protagonists, I will now attempt a reconstruction of the encounter.

On the appointed day in mid 1976, in preparation for the appointed time, the two Geraghty women took out of their wardrobes dresses that would hide their cleavage, pulled on their panty hose, painted their faces and made their way up the oak-carved stairwell to the red, carpeted first floor of the cathedral presbytery. The general clerical staff who ministered daily to all and sundry around the Cathedral, to drunks, druggies, prostitutes, visitors from interstate and overseas, all worked on the ground floor of the sandstone building where the clergy also used to eat three times each day, in seniority.

The important activities of the Archdiocese took place higher up, on the first floor, where members of the special branch had their offices. Cardinal Gilroy used to interview the rich and famous, members of the clergy and visiting bishops, in an office where he was surrounded by the many trinkets and baubles he had accumulated over the years, gifts from different countries and from various dignitaries. His interviews used to last exactly fifteen minutes, four an hour, as regular as clockwork throughout the morning. Cardinal Freeman, as his successor, had inherited the same strict timetable. He had simply taken over the routine practices left vacant when Norman Gilroy had disappeared to the clergy retirement village at Randwick.

The Cardinal's private secretary also had his cramped office on this first floor. A cabal of secret, powerful, elderly clerical advisers, people like Monsignors Wallace of Darlinghurst, Clarke of Earlwood, Keller of Caringbah and McCosker of Ryde, all met in the inner-sanctum to whisper to the boss the advice they thought he wanted to hear. The ecclesiastical stock exchange, the corridors of infallible power, the religious wheeling and dealings for Sydney, Australia and the world, were all secreted on the first floor, in an area heavy in wood-paneling, haunted by celibate ghosts, shaded in suffused, tinted light which filtered through stained-glass windows featuring religious scenes and saintly giants of the past. It was a rarity to hear the twitter of female voices disturbing the solemnity which pervaded the Archbishop's elevated world.

The two women were respectful and suitably hushed as they made their way up the carpeted staircase to the first floor. A little overawed, they waited their turn in silence. At the appointed hour, the humble secretary ushered them into the majestic presence of his Eminence. He was robed in a long cassock with red piping and bright red buttons. A flaming sash which was wrapped round his ample waist draped itself down his right leg almost to his buckled shoes. Jimmy rose from his plush chair to meet the little women. Like most elderly clerics, he had learnt to be wary of women, but nonetheless, he was always the gentleman. He was warm in manner and manly. As a fledging priest, he had studied Dale Carnegie's *How to Win Friends and Influence People* and had learnt how to put others at their ease. He had a common, popular touch – not stiff, icy or princely like his predecessor.

The Cardinal extended his right hand, inviting his visitors to display their respect and deference. My mother and sister did not hesitate. They were not anarchists. They were reverent and obedient, but within limits. Jimmy was doing something Jesus would never have thought of – a gesture foreign to the Christian ethos, an act which some might consider scandalous, and knowing the man, it was a gesture which would have made Jimmy feel uncomfortable. But after all, he had accepted to be a prelate of the Roman Church, though her imperial and byzantine traditions made some awkward demands on him. My mother and sister went down on their right knee in the presence of his

Eminence, clasped his soft hand gently and moistened his episcopal ring with their painted lips.

The introductory play-acting was complete. The holy women of Neutral Bay sat self-consciously and, with their knees held tightly together and their handbags on their laps, began to explain the purpose of their visit. They were worried. They had noticed a change in my demeanour. They saw how isolated I had become in the diocese, how anxious and withdrawn, how depressed. The energy and enthusiasm of the man they knew had disappeared. At least by inference, they were inviting the Cardinal to lighten their burden, seeking some assurance that all would be well. They wanted to know that the man-in-charge was aware of my plight; that he was in there fighting by my side; that he would work towards some remedy; that he would intervene and show some pastoral concern.

While they were explaining the purpose of their visit, the Eminence remained seated in silence, listening. Then to their amazement, as though in some kind of answer to their plea, my mother and sister sat listening to the Great One recount the many problems he had to face, day after day. His was a terrible tale. Every fifteen minutes, four times an hour, with no warning or respite, he was confronted with a different problem – often serious, mostly insoluble. Politicians, bishops, nuns and brothers, lay-people complaining, one after another, in procession, visited him in his prison-parlour on the first floor. What could he do? How could they imagine he had the answers? He felt powerless and exhausted.

A little stunned, they listened for as long as politeness demanded and then my mother interrupted to inform his Eminence that she had not come on this special mission across the harbour to listen to his problems. If he wished to discuss them he could arrange a separate interview. None of his concerns were on her mind at that moment but she was prepared to discuss them at a later date, on another occasion. She had come to discuss her son's predicament with her Archbishop and pastor. Jimmy's male ruse was not working. But he had no answers. When the fifteen minutes had ticked over, he pushed himself away from his desk, extended his jewelled hand again for the ritual obeisance, and smiling kindly said to these two cranky women –

"Settle down, girls. Don't upset yourselves. Don't get your knickers in a knot. It'll all work out somehow."

The Cardinal was a man who liked to have the last say – something cute, something smart. But his two visitors hated being patronised.

They were, both of them, irate. They had arrived angry and upset. They were more annoyed by the realisation that the little Stanmore-parish-priest-come-Archbishop-of-Sydney, was not up to the task. They had tried, but it was obvious to them that there was no hope of help among the upper echelons of the hierarchy. Freeman was a good man in an impossible job. His exalted position loaded demands on a little man which he could not carry.

1976

USING THE WHOLE RING

Sometime after my mother and sister had visited him in the middle of 1976, and without knowledge of their meddling, I too arranged a private meeting with the same Eminence. I didn't want to, but I knew I had to speak with him. I removed the jeans and the rolled-neck skivvy I used to wear in the corridors of the seminary and which had so enraged the senior clergy of Sydney and bishops beyond, and, for a change, dressed up in my best clerical suit and shiny Roman collar. I parked my Peugeot under the shade of the Cathedral and ascended the same polished stairway to the engine-room of the Archdiocese. I was early for my appointment. I had been trained to military precision at Springwood and Manly, to be in my seat in the chapel, at my desk in the classroom, before the final bell had rung. I had been drilled to be on time.

As usual, the Cardinal's secretary was busy at his clerk's desk. It was hard to imagine how he filled in his day, though I have come to realise that a large part of the bureaucratic art is learning how to look occupied – how to stretch the available work to fill the daily time-sheet. He was not as attractive as many secretaries, or as well-trained. He was not wearing high heels to show off his shapely shaven legs and to please the boss. He was one of the few secretaries in the city, perhaps the only one, who dressed in a neck-to-ankle cassock. He performed most of the mundane tasks of any personal assistant – typing letters, answering the telephone, making appointments, keeping the diary, running messages, covering for the boss. This priest was exercising the mysterious calling he had received from on high, as someone between a batman, a chauffeur, a butler and a secretary.

Father O'Sullivan greeted me on my final visit to my lord. I sat nervously on a Queen Ann style chair, watching the secretary fuss around – doing a little one-finger typing, answering the telephone, making a record in his boss's appointment book.

As the polished brass handle on the heavy door of the inner-sanctum sounded a faint click, my nerves froze. Father O'Sullivan rose immediately, but without haste, glided to the door and ushered his superior's earlier visitor out as far as the top of the staircase. He returned to announce my attendance on the Archbishop. The clock was running and my allotted fifteen minutes had started.

As I made my gesture of humble reverence to his Eminence, he extended his wrinkled hand adorned with the episcopal ring. Freeman made this gesture with a rather more casual air than his predecessor, as if, like any fair-dinkum digger, he was reluctant to invite such a gesture of subservience. I took hold of the limp hand of authority, bent my knee as was the custom in the Middle Ages in the presence of kings and emperors and, with my dry lips, kissed his golden ring. It was over in a flash and I began to tell my lord and liege, my Archbishop, his Eminence the Cardinal, Sir James Freeman, who, in some strange way, had always been able to maintain the image of the little battler from Stanmore, that I was in trouble. There was no mention of my mother and sister. I provided him with an outline sketch of the fronts on which I was fighting – as if he didn't already know. I told him of my attempt to confront the secrecy and cowardice of Bishop Thomas of Bathurst, who had banned me from his domain without notifying me; the Vatican pettiness of Archbishop Cahill of Canberra and Goulburn (but that's another story); and the tribal bullying of Bishop Bill Murray and his tennis mates. He would have heard already the details from a number of sources at episcopal conferences and clerical meetings. The scandal vine which entangled the clergy was strong and vigorous. My fight with *The Catholic Weekly* and Father Darby Mecham as chairman of the Board was public knowledge. The details had been presented on every television set in Sydney. There had been letters and articles in the daily newspapers in Sydney and Melbourne. It had been the topic of special business at the Archdiocesan synod of priests. Geraghty's punch-up with the establishment had been a *cause célèbre* for a few months and was not yet at an end. There were some heavy rounds yet to fight.

I informed Cardinal Freeman that I suspected his auxiliary bishop, Archbishop James Carroll, was manoeuvring in the darkness to have me removed from my teaching post at Manly. Carroll was a schemer, a back-room, secretive operator whom the poet James McAuley, years before, had captured in a verse of his epic poem *Captain Quiros* –

"His (Cardinal Gilroy's) close adviser was a canonist,
Well practised in dissembling double thought
In double speech; skilful to wind and twist
All meanings till they cancelled in pure naught.
Holy detraction was his special flair,
And the light verbal web flung in the air
Entangling others for the ends he sought."

Archbishop Carroll was applying his special skills to my case.

Jimmy Freeman listened. He did not seem surprised. Nor was he angry, or argumentative, or anxious to offer advice. I told him I had lost my way; that I was seriously depressed and angry; and that I had been wounded by the way my religious superiors and brothers had felt free to deal with me. I reminded my shepherd in the Lord, that all my life I had been a loyal member of the institution, a seminarian from the age of twelve and, though still very junior, I had been a member of the establishment, as seminarian or priest, for twenty-five years. I was a member of the brotherhood. No Anglican, or Protestant, or Jew, no heretic, no traitor. I was not the enemy. (But even then I was conscious that when a member of the tribe has to plead his own cause to the chief, the die had already been cast and the end was nigh.)

Cardinal Freeman asked no questions. He was not concerned to cross-examine me to identify any additional, perhaps more personal, reason for my deep disaffection. We did not speak of Adele, of how I felt towards her, about our outings, my visits to her flat, her recent presence in my life. We only had fifteen minutes and it was almost exhausted.

The Cardinal appeared weary. Perhaps he was finding it difficult to bear the burden of office. He was a simple battler who had accepted the lonely job of commander-in-chief. After he had listened in silence to my story, Freeman began to speak. He too had problems. I was to listen to the same spiel which I later found out he had tried on my mother and sister. He was condemned to sit as a prisoner in his Cathedral office, receiving a different visitor each fifteen minutes, attending all day to a litany of complaints, disasters, failures and expressions of frustration or anger. He heard reports of what priests had said from the pulpit, about priests who were rude, or alcoholic, or grasping for money, lazy, too old, too cranky, too narrow, coupling with married women or interfering with little boys. The stream of complaints was endless. One after another his visitors arrived, to up-end another load of decaying bones in his study and then leave.

The Cardinal seemed sad and isolated. His life appeared unnatural and the pure message had somehow become obscured. The institution had taken over and imprisoned all of us, and he was caught tight in a trap of expectations, bureaucratic functions, institutional values, decisions he should never have been required to make and penalties the Gospel would never wish to impose. He worked long boring hours each day, in a room which was a cross between an office, a clerical den and a museum. His work-space was over-furnished, frigid and antiquated. The customary portrait of the reigning Roman Pontiff hung in a position of prominence. Paul VI looked tormented with scruples and somehow aware that he was in a place which would have seemed comical to Jesus.

Like his predecessor, Jimmy was surrounded by knick-knacks and bric-a-brac, gathered as gifts from all corners of the known world. Not one item in the room, including the Archbishop himself, resonated with the tone, the character of the Gospel message as preached in the early Church. The gold cross and chain which hung around his neck, the episcopal ring, his red piped cassock, the formal portrait of the Pope, the shining, sanded floor, the Persian rug, the antique desk – all seemed to mock the simple message of the poor, itinerant preacher. While I was teetering on the edge of flight, the Cardinal was condemned to serve out his sentence of life imprisonment. He rose from his chair to indicate the conclusion of my quarter hour. The chimes had sounded.

> "Well, Chris, that's your fifteen minutes. You can leave, but I have to stay to attend to someone else. I have to listen to problems every morning, one after the other".

I was embarrassed. I did not know what to say to comfort his Eminence. I took his soft hand, genuflected, and paid my last respects. Then, just for a moment, Jimmy Freeman hesitated. He shook my hand, looked me straight in the eye and said in his characteristic, manly drawl –

"Let me give you just one word of advice, Chris, before you go. Keep you left hand up as your guard and use the whole ring."

Those were my Archbishop's last words to me. He had always had a fascination with the noble art of boxing. There was still some fighting to do. We were never to meet again.

1976
BISHOP PATRICK LEO MURPHY

In about October, as President of the Faculty, Bishop Murphy came visiting at Manly – a meeting which proved to be a mixture of gentle confrontation and civilized conversation.

We settled down in the very room he had occupied when he had been teaching in the seminary (the den I had visited on occasions when he had been the professor of dogmatic theology and dean of strict discipline in the late 50's and early 60's, when I was trying to be an obedient student at St Patrick's) and we discussed *The Weekly* fiasco.

As a student at Manly, I had had daily contact with Pat Murphy. He had conducted a compulsory class, five days a week, in Dogmatic Theology. Three times a day he walked among us to the top table in the refectory for his meals. When we needed correction and discipline, it was he who used to deliver the lash with a heavy hand. In all those years, his eyes had never sparkled; his belly never shuddered in fits of laughter. I had never seen him smile. There was no music swirling in his head, no spring in his step, no joy bubbling in his heart, no dancing on his face. He had been a living, breathing, moving embodiment of all things serious and drab. From time to time, as infrequently as possible, I had visited him in his dark, book-laden office on the first floor, to receive correction for a minor breach of discipline or perhaps some punishment. The clerical way of life was so harsh, the presbyteries so lonely and the senior men so humourless that perhaps the training program, which old men had devised in the seventeenth century, at the time of the Council of Trent, and which Paddy was policing, had been the best way to prepare a young man for the priesthood in Australia. But I didn't believe it then and I don't believe it now.

In late January 1974, in the middle of winter, while I had been studying in Paris, Pat Murphy had arrived and booked into the *Fraternité* where I was living. He was on a cheap trip, engaged to act as a chaplain on a migrant boat back to Sydney. In addition, he was on a mission from the Archdiocesan headquarters to seek advice from the experts in Paris, as to how to divide the manpower and spoils of a vast diocese like Sydney into three smaller domains – Parramatta, Broken Bay and a much reduced Sydney. He had asked me to accompany him to *Notre Dame* Cathedral to act as his interpreter.

I remember well, walking the streets of Paris, striding alongside my former Dean of Heavenly Discipline. Heads turned as people of all ages and genders, from various parts of the world, paused in amazement, transfixed at the sight of my companion. Dressed in their colourful caftans and high fashions, the Parisians had seen almost everything. Nothing could surprise them – until Doctor Murphy passed them by. His wardrobe and accoutrements proved an international knock-out on the Paris catwalks of style and fashion. He wore black, polished policeman's shoes with rounded toes, a black suit with his pants cut to accommodate two people, a Roman collar, a black '40s hat with broad brim, a black Humphrey Bogart gabardine overcoat tied tightly around the waist, and black gloves against the cold. The dean of years past marched down *Boulevard St Germain* with me by his side in the maroon polo-neck jumper that Carol Ryan of Avalon had knitted for me, on past *Metro Mabillon* and onto *Boulevard St Michel*. The streets were crowded with students and hippies, some in the most outlandish gear. Paddy trudged on, totally oblivious to the entertainment he had brought to the city of chic. My friend was indeed, both inside and out, a man from another planet. Suddenly, out of left-field, an irreverent larrikin had appeared, doffed his musketeer hat, bowed low in a mock gesture while Pat thundered on.

Later, when Toto Murphy (which was Dr Patrick Murphy's nickname in the seminary) was visiting me at Manly, we had a full and frank discussion. His position was simple. He wanted the embarrassing *Weekly* matter resolved with the least fuss and as soon as possible. The solution was in my hands. I told him I was angry and that I was not about to back away. The tide had turned and for a change, I was in control. I had been wronged and everyone knew it. It was a weird feeling confronting a senior cleric, my old dean of discipline, the president of the Theological Faculty of Manly. He argued that what I was doing would damage the reputation of the Faculty – that elite team of scholars which had been slaving away for almost twenty years, under the controlling hands of Madden, Veech, Muldoon, Tierney and himself. As far as I could see, their achievements were miniscule. At least this minor skirmish would bring them some notoriety.

We talked on, heading for an impasse and when I offered to resign, Paddy panicked. He seemed to realise suddenly that I was serious. Some compromise could surely be reached. In the end he asked if I would be prepared to consult with the politically astute Gerry Gleeson of the Premier's Office, who had offered to broker a compromise with *The Weekly*. I agreed. Reports dribbled back afterwards, suggesting that Murphy had formed a favorable impression of our meeting and some days later, I was dining with Mr Gleeson at his home in Strathfield.

Gleeson's summary and interpretation of what had occurred at our private meeting, later came back to me when my friends, John and Barbara Coburn, recounted what he had told them as they were standing together on a smorgasbord queue one evening at the New South Wales Art Gallery. According to them, Mr Gleeson had told them that their friend Geraghty was in deep trouble. I was, for a fleeting moment, the talk of the town. I suppose Gerry Gleeson's version was a reasonably accurate summary of the situation.

My priestly life was sinking deeper into crisis. I was fighting on too many fronts. By July or August 1976, apart from Eddy Campion who had stuck his neck on the line, I had lost confidence in the members of the Theological Faculty. In my censorship dispute with *The Weekly* and with Archbishop Carroll trying secretively to remove me from my teaching post, I felt that my confrères at Manly had proved themselves cowardly. I did not know at that stage that several had spoken up *in camera*. The members of the senate of priests in Sydney were hiding. Archbishop Freeman had been unwilling to interest himself in the difficulties I was facing, though I was still a member of his diocesan team and he had been urged by several people to intervene. My mother and sister had concluded that he was reluctant to pull on the gloves and enter the ring – useless in a fight.

I was suffering from irritating skin rashes and fits of anxiety were causing shudders in my soul. There was not much fun in me – no laughter, no dancing. My mind had filled up with mud. I felt paralysed – unable to decide whether to change my life, or to climb back into the nest; to give myself to someone, or dedicate myself to a cause; to turn back, or go forward into unknown territory.

I had not imagined myself as a disturber of ecclesial harmony. From an early age I had cooperated without question, institutionalised myself; I had studied and prayed hard for years. Now I felt ostracised and on the verge of failure. I felt at that time that the religious leaders that I had paid so much notice to, were the whitened sepulchres of the new covenant, like the breed of vipers of messianic times. However, over time my assessment of them has softened a little. I see them now as old frogs thrashing about in an evaporating pool, full of wind, croaking out the same old message in the night – obedience, submission and conformity in all things.

chapter twenty four

1976

PUT ON THE SPOT

"What power and clarity lies in the word!
In the unfettered, carefree word!
The word that is still spoken in spite of all one's fears."
    Life and Fate by Vasily Grossman.

After more than thirty years, the Five-Ways Hotel remains a throbbing watering-hole for Sydney-siders from the eastern suburbs.

Sometime in about September 1976, Adele and I were faceless in the swirl of the crowd eating and drinking, laughing and talking on the balcony under a blue sky. She was far from her home on the *rue des Prêtres*, off *the Place des Carmes* in Toulouse, and I was well away from my home paddock on the other side of the harbour. We were no-bodies there in Paddington and I was feeling quite safe.

As we sat in the sun looking at each other, touching across the table and talking, I found myself searching, hesitantly, to put flesh on feelings I had until that time only half identified in the turbulent shadows of dreams in the night. Blurred phantoms were hovering over me and I was in unmapped territory. I had some important things to say, but I had to watch my step and tread carefully. Once I had found the words and put some flesh on my fuzzy feelings, those hidden feelings would be out there, in the open, exposed for others to see. They had been thoughts – my thoughts, secret thoughts. But when spoken out loud to another person, they would be out of my control. They could wander about on the earth like banshees, taking on all kinds of shapes.

I had invited Adele to lunch with me in Paddington. I needed to discuss the possibility of a future together, though even at that critical stage I was tempted to continue just as we had been. I hesitated before stepping out into the currents which could sweep me up and drown me. It was a hot, sweaty, lazy afternoon in Sydney and the summer blow-flies were out and about. I was aware that what I had half-planned could be a gamble which could easily end in disaster and that even at this late stage, I could pull out without a word.

Deep breaths, sweaty palms, heart pumping as though a heavy, thunderous wave was banking up out the back, breaking, rumbling in and creating panic down deep. Thoughts germinating into words began to take root and constrict the muscles in my throat. After all those years of training, was this what I really wanted? What might be her reaction? What might be the unforeseen consequences of what I was about to say? This afternoon encounter could prove disastrous. But I felt that I had already journeyed too far and there was no turning back. So, I blurted out my feelings to my companion as we sat at table on the balcony.

I was in love with her. I wanted to spend the rest of my life in her company. There, I had said it. Despite the high walls which had kept me safe, years of seclusion in the bush, years of isolation on the headland on the hill – I had fallen off the battlement and was sliding over the precipice. As my stomach was tumbling in a whirlpool of emotions, it was strange to hear myself giving voice to my feelings.

Adele must have known long before that I was madly in love. Throughout my life, since I had been a little boy, even when I had held back, when I had consciously controlled my tongue, despite my efforts to hide and prevaricate, people had known what I had been thinking and feeling. It was beyond me to play poker like Paul Newman in *The Sting*. In spite of my best endeavours to appear compliant, or respectful, or submissive, my world had been a book open for others to read and now, despite my vows and my way of life, my beautiful companion could peer straight into my soul.

Adele must have known, if only unconsciously, that once she had made her appearance in Australia, my private and clerical lives would become messy. I had felt for a long time, before I had left for overseas, that it was not going to be possible to live the lonely life I had chosen in my youth. But while the Roman collar had been choking me, until more recently I had been unable to plan a route of escape. Now, just possibly, there was a path to be found out of the labyrinth.

I revealed to my luncheon partner that I was giddy with a desperate longing to be part of her life. While I had become hopelessly preoccupied, she had given no hint, at least in word, as to what she really thought or felt. Did she think that she and I might have a future together? Did she imagine that she might one day be my wife? Was there someone else in her life? I didn't know – she hadn't said. But we had been spending time in each other's company, humming the same song. We had been walking hand-in-hand – we were on touching terms.

Hesitantly, I waded out deeper into the conversation. There were sensitive areas I needed to explore. We did not share a common faith, or a common culture. She was a *pagan* – or perhaps I should simply say a non-believer – and since my childhood I had followed the Christian way. I would not, I could not, surrender my faith in the God of all Christians as revealed in the Gospels, in his son Jesus and in his Holy Spirit. My life had been geared to a Christ-like code of behaviour. I felt that even if I was alienated from the ugly institutional Church system in Sydney, I wanted to cling steadfastly to my life of faith and to our Christian traditions. I knew that I was, deep down, a religious person.

From my adolescence, I had been buttoned-down and aloof. My life had been lived out on stage, in school or clerical uniforms, in the sacred vestments of an angelic altarboy, a pious seminarian and a consecrated priest. I had answered to the expectations of others. I had thought their thoughts, and in lieu of a healthy emotional life, I had developed a steely armoury of spirituality. Now for the first time, my life was spinning out of control. There in the glare of the summer sun in Paddington, I felt happier than I had been in recent years. But I also feared that I was about to be sucked up into the eye of a violent storm. With my head spinning and my heart singing, I knew I was on the threshold of a chaotic and dislocating period of my life.

It is strange and confusing to recall the details of that luncheon. Before I had come to the point, I remember telling the woman who would soon be my wife, about the problems I was facing with bishops and *The Catholic Weekly*. I heard myself telling her that I was anxious to regain some control of my life, to become more committed to teaching on the theology team at Manly. I knew I could not return to the cloudy old days, but I wanted to reclaim some balance in my life, without forfeiting the new ground I had claimed. I do not know what I was thinking or what I was meaning to say. I was talking to myself, talking nonsense. I was fooling myself.

Adele has always been incisive – some might say blunt. Though over the years she has gradually become more talkative, at that early stage of our relationship she was a woman of few words – placid, at peace in her gentle world. She was more inclined to listen, to wait and observe.

"Chris, are you truly happy in what you've chosen to do with your life?"

She had put pressure right on the wound and her question immediately unsettled me. I knew I was not happy. I hadn't been happy for such a long time. But I had not admitted my aching discontent even to my parents, or to my brother, my sister, or my friends. I had hardly admitted it to myself. I had hidden my dissatisfaction under waves of activity. Perhaps Monsignor Veech had seen that discontent when I had been part of his teaching team at Springwood. There was no need to confirm Adele's suspicion. She knew the truth.

But Adele pursued me down a narrow gulley, into my soul.

"How long have you been unhappy?"

It had been a long time – yes, years. I had been unhappy teaching in the seminary at Springwood, before leaving to study overseas. An alien in the ranks of the clergy; attacked by silly, pompous bishops; trapped and broken in a top-heavy, sluggish institution. The old brigade was clinging onto their power and privileges like falling angels grabbing onto thin clouds as they tumbled into oblivion.

Gently, Adele sought to understand why I had been unhappy. I spoke to her of the soulless institution, its secrecy, its mistrust of me and others, of its tendency to trivialise sacred things, of its unreasonable demand for total subservience and of its drive to inflate its dogmatic currency. I had found myself part of an institution which had too many dogmas, too much money, too much property, too many regulations, too much power, and which was dominated by too many old men. It was hard to imagine a wandering preacher in Palestine, with a few mates and no home, planning to establish an international enterprise with offices in every town and city in the known and the unknown world, and with its head-quarters in Rome.

I tried to explain to an unbeliever my complicated, personal faith life, but she did not understand the ins and outs, the twists and knots of my ecclesiastical world. She was puzzled. From her point of view the solution was simple – if I was unhappy and the situation was that horrible, give it all away and move on. She listened for a short time and then delivered her knock-out blow. Quietly, gently, she probed under my guard:

"Has anyone, over the years, shown you any affection? Do you feel you've had enough love in your life?"

For a moment I heard again the rattling sound of a train underneath me, as it sped through the darkness. I saw again, the elderly woman in her moulting fur coat, decorated with cheap jewelry, smiling at me.

I did not reply. I had no answer. Love and affection had been sucked out of my life in the seminary. The dean of trivial discipline at St Patrick's, had informed me that he had been watching me closely and he thought that I was far too close to my family. If I wanted to be a good, holy priest, if I wanted to model myself on John Vianney, the patron saint of parish priests, I had to turn my back on my siblings and my parents, surrender my life to God and, while living in the world, remain a stranger to it. I had not known at that stage how crazy St John Vianney, the Curé of Ars, had been.

Love and affection were dangerous forces. Young priests and old were expected to survive without them. None of us could hope to be successful as agents of the divine – representatives of Christ, celebrants of the Mysteries, as commissioned officers of the Church – if we were looking for love and affection and if we longed for warmth and intimacy from a woman – or from a man. We were dedicated to resist the forces of nature.

Had I found enough love and affection in my life? Does anyone ever find enough love? Who can claim that he has received enough affection in his life? My emotional life lay before me. Adele had penetrated my protective shell. Her simple questioning had disarmed me and I felt that the emptiness in my heart had been exposed to the summer glare.

chapter twenty five

OCTOBER 1976
TETHERED BY THE SHORT AND CURLIES

Negotiations with *The Weekly* continued. My solicitor friend told me that Bishop Murphy had let it be known that the members of the board would not budge; that they knew I was not a troublemaker at heart and that I could be trusted to do the right thing. The bishop thought the problem would go away. He thought that I had always been loyal to the institution and that in the end, I was one of them and would see "reason".

My solicitor's report came as a cruel blow. "They" had concluded that they had me (literally and figuratively) "by the short and curlies". The reaction was all the more painful because it was essentially true. After bouts of depression and sleepless nights, I had determined to put the incident behind me and to move on. I had in fact reached the end of my rope. The stress had been too much to bear. I had decided to instruct my lawyer to run up the white flag. They had read the tea-leaves correctly. I was a product of the system. My superiors felt they could hit me and I would lie down. There was no need to worry about right or wrong; about ethical imperatives; no need to restore the balance; or reach out to a wounded brother in the Lord.

While the wounds are now healed, at that stage I was deeply affected by the treatment I had received from *The Weekly* and its board. Darby Mecham and his posse had treated me unjustly and then decided they did not need to admit their fault. They had played the game like true right-wing politicians. He and his team, Bishop Murphy and the others, presumed to take advantage of my "good will" – or in another world, to exploit my weakness. They were not interested in issues of right and wrong – only in politics and preserving a public image of always being right. How the world has changed!

As soon as I had had time to reflect on the message my solicitor, John Marsden, had delivered, I began to relax a little. The stress began to seep out of my facial muscles. This was the end of my clerical journey. It was as though the sinful cynicism of the bishop and the board had given me permission to let go. They were liberating me. I had a flight to catch and a life to live, and they could "go to buggery".

I had not learnt at that stage of my life the important lesson that every member of the human race must learn to live in conflict. I had not yet discovered that life was a struggle; that some people and most institutions could be dishonest; that all of us have to fight for survival. Pushing, shoving, manoeuvring for advantage, challenging, flexing muscles, confronting and threatening, were essential features of our human condition. I had been protected in my family and in the seminary from dealing with this aspect of the human condition and now, I had to learn survival skills as quickly as possible. I had much to learn about the world, about my Church and about myself. I had invested too much of myself in an institution which, in ways I couldn't have seen, in ways I had refused to accept, was twisted and stained. One could not give one's self to a bureaucracy without being gobbled down, digested and eventually expelled.

The human beast needs at least the occasional moments of fun. We need to feel the breeze on our face and enjoy the freedom, the opportunities to laugh, to mock, to ridicule. I had been a priest from head to toe, twenty-four hours a day, twelve months of the year – loyal in the face of stupidity; a standard-bearer for a movement of ideas and ideals in which I believed – and at the same time, for official teachings which I regarded with suspicion and some with disdain. I had been bullied by bishops and told that I had to endure it all for the sake of the Gospel. I had arrived at the cross-roads and was faced finally with a real decision.

Time would prove that Frank Mecham and Toto Murphy would be a blessing in my life – a blessing for which I continue to thank them and the Lord. Soon after I had heard Murphy's assessment of me and of his confident assertion that nothing needed to be done, I was on my way – out of there and onto the highway.

To this day I do not know whether my solicitor had been telling me the truth. I did not, myself, hear Paddy Murphy say that *The Weekly* affair would eventually lose its steam because Geraghty was a loyal, obedient member of the Church. Maybe he did say it and maybe he didn't. It does have the ring of truth. In those days the elders of the Church did truly believe they held the levers to control lives. It was something that Bishop Murphy could have said, but I will never know. Marsden is dead, and so too is Murphy.

John Marsden had a colourful reputation. I came to know him better when I was working as a barrister and receiving the occasional brief from him. He did not always speak the truth. As a solicitor, he was inclined to write his own script. From personal experience I knew that he could massage the facts and varnish his instructions. Maybe he imagined that Bishop Murphy had told him I was a push-over and that in the end when "piss came to shrug", I would not cause trouble. Perhaps my solicitor had had no meeting with the bishop. It was not beyond him to have made the whole incident up. Maybe he wanted to close the file, especially since he was acting *pro bono* for a friend.

In one sense, it does not matter now. I believed him at the time and it was almost true. If Bishop Murphy had truly expressed those sentiments, he had almost been right. When Marsden spoke to me, suddenly I realised what I had become – a patsy for the institution, a number in the system, a part of the machine which they could grind down and discard as they saw fit. They were almost right, but they had stepped over the mark and advanced just too far.

It took some years for me to look at *The Weekly* events dispassionately, from a distance. Now I can see clearly and accept that that stage of my life was a story of betrayal and bastardry.

chapter twenty six

1976
FLYING THE COOP

M y world had imploded since returning from overseas and rather
than letting go and strolling confidently into the future, hand-in-
hand with Adele, I was struck down with a profound sense of failure.

I constantly obsessed in my turbulent mind, about how men of the
institution had treated me. I was smarting from the years I had spent at
Springwood, trying, without success, to dance to Monsignor Veech's
sepulchral music. I recalled how summarily Algie Thomas had dealt
with me – listening to rumours at the episcopal conference and issuing
secret decrees in his diocese forbidding "his" nuns from having any
contact with me, then telling me lies; how Jimmy Carroll had been
secretly trying to remove me from my teaching post; how *The Weekly*
and Toto Murphy had presumed that I would lie down like a beaten
bitch; how members of the clergy team had marginalised me. I
understand that each of the players in my little drama, had they been
asked, would have had his own story to tell. But back in those dark
days, I was not painting on a large canvas or in some other cleric's
colours.

I had woken every morning for too long, with a sticky glug of
sadness in my throat. I knew that as long as I knuckled down and did
not seek to explore other paths while I drove sedately along the Pope's
highway – turning up for lectures, mouthing their weary orthodoxies –
I could journey smoothly in the rut. The hit-men of the system had
beaten me. I could not stay.

I had finally worked out how the firm functioned. My Church was like the Commonwealth Bank, like BHP or the Murdoch press. There was one boss, a cohort of sycophantic middle managers and a tribe of little Indians. Like the other institutions, my system cynically mixed fact and fiction together, until it was unable to separate truth from horse-dung. The CEO in the Vatican governed the international organization by threats and secrecy. The Jesus message was lost in a theological drain, in interminable reports and internal memos. Like the modern Liberal Party, the State Labor Party in Sussex Street, the company employed right-wing, reactionary spin doctors and advertising gurus to relate to the masses and waste their money. All shadow and little substance, all show and no guts, wasting time with endless pomp and ceremony, with internal disputes, legal processes, enforcing minute law and rigid order. No humble search for truth at the top, no genuine reverence for lowly office workers, no respect for their shareholders, no social conscience, no genuine desire to serve, to come alive, to grow or to include the unwashed masses. You might conclude that I was pretty alienated. If so, I think you'd be right.

Towards the end of 1976, without a word to my bishop or my colleagues, I pulled down the books I had accumulated lovingly over years. Books which had decorated my study and nourished my mind, volumes I had collected from the bookshops of Europe – I withdrew these books from the light and confined them to the darkness. In the corner of my empty study at Manly I stacked thirty-odd brown boxes filled with my precious library. Until I had space for them again in my life, they would stay buried alive in the seminary, inert and without sparkle. I packed my few belongings, my underpants and shaving gear, my Bible and Breviary. I left my black cassock hanging in the cupboard. I looked around my spacious study with its million dollar view of the northern coastline as far as Palm Beach and without a further backwards glance into the dark corners of my spiritual cave, I drove through the solid sandstone gates of St Patrick's, down the hill and out into the unknown.

Knowing what I knew about the clerical rumour mill and sacerdotal thirst for gossip (in this regard priests were at least on a par with journalists and prostitutes, with barristers and judges), I had been reluctant to disclose to anyone the details of my personal life. As I look back, I can see that I was suffering what was known as "a nervous breakdown". I was seriously depressed to the point of constant weeping and remain surprised, and somewhat amused, that no one of my colleagues seemed to make an attempt to contact me to see how I was travelling, or to perhaps help me.

To this day, for more than thirty years, I have had no official contact with the institution. I presume I have been removed from the clerical rolls, but I do not know. My priestly faculties – to preach, to hear confessions – were conferred by Cardinal Gilroy *"usque revocetur"* – that is, until revoked – and I have received no notice that I was ever officially divested of these powers. I still have the document in my filing cabinet, ticking away.

The silence was puzzling. I did not know whether my superiors were relieved that I had finally thrown in the towel and left the ring, or whether they were so embarrassed by the way they had treated me, that they could not bring themselves to face me and to make overtures to seek an amnesty. On reflection, and knowing what they used to be like, I suspect those self-righteous prelates and senior priests breathed a communal sigh of relief and simply moved on.

I had played a part in the Sydney Archdiocese media campaign, preached in almost every parish church of the diocese, lectured religious women throughout the state, given retreats, written articles, lectured and advised students for the priesthood – and my sudden departure was greeted with silence. I had passed twelve years as a student in the seminary before my ordination, laboured for a doctorate in theology, lectured in both minor and major seminaries and in the end, when all my chips were spent and I was looking bankruptcy in the face, there was no offer of a little bank-roll to get me on my way – no advice, no whisper of interest. Instead, I heard the roar of silence. In those days (times are different now), the clergy tended to treat deserting colleagues like rats abandoning a happy vessel.

Years later, my friend Peter Marr enquired as to whether any member of the clergy had officially made contact with me after I had gone AWOL. He was surprised to learn I had departed at night in total silence. He said he had always thought of me as someone more influential, better placed than he had been in the Archdiocese, more senior, more established, with a higher profile and yet, even he had been contacted after his departure. In fact he had found it difficult to have his name removed from the list of clergy in the diocese almanac. For years after he left, even when he was married with a family, he had still been officially listed as "on leave".

Peter had been sitting at home among the mess in his flat in Fairlight, looking over tiled roofs towards St Patrick's College on the hill, when the telephone had rung late one night. He had already consumed several cans of beer. He had finished his daily toil of cleaning toilets and public bars in hotels throughout Sydney. (He was managing a little cleaning business while at the same time struggling, like me, through the Barristers' and Solicitors' Admission Board law course.) He was tired, relaxing in an alcoholic haze, thinking of turning off the television for the night, when the telephone had rung.

The call had sounded three years after he had abandoned his duties in the parish of North Leichhardt.

"Is that you, Father Marr?"

Peter was puzzled. Hardly anyone was ringing these days and it had been some years since he had been addressed by his paternal title – a blast from the past. Hesitantly he admitted the caller was indeed talking to "Father Marr".

"This is Father Roche."

"Oh, yeeees ..."

There was a pause. Who was he again? Who was to speak next?

"I've just been going through the records and found that you haven't paid your contribution to the diocesan Sick Priests' Fund for the past three years."

"Oh, haven't I? That must be right."

Pause –

"The years have passed so quickly. What have I got to do? How much do I owe?"

Of course he had not made his regular payment to the Sick Priests' Fund. He had been out on his own, cleaning toilets, removing vomit, studying, driving his little van round the city, drinking, struggling to survive, forgetting about the fund and everything associated with it.

"You owe three years' contribution and, with your seniority, that would amount to fifty-seven dollars and fifty cents."

"Thank you, Father, for contacting me. I'll send you a cheque in the mail."

Peter put the receiver down, scratched his head, opened another can and burst into laughter. This was the only official contact any member of the Archdiocese had made with him since he had left – the sole expression of interest. (Peter had fathered two daughters before he succeeded in having his name removed from the list of clergy.)

After twenty-five years of service I might have expected at least a certificate of merit to hang in the trophy room, or a friendly handshake, a slap on the back and good luck wishes or perhaps a gold watch. Maybe a telephone call or a letter from the Cathedral. Or perhaps a discrete visit from a clerical emissary to enquire of my health, my intentions, my state of mind, an expression of concern or a referral to a counsellor.

For many months I was reluctant to return to the long corridors of the seminary to recover my books. Then one night, under cover of darkness, I crept back into the building through the back-door to rescue my muzzled library. As I was tiptoeing along the timbered, upstairs corridor, one of my former teachers, and later a colleague, Clem Tierney, made one of his rare appearances outside his room, on his way to the communal bathroom. Even in the austere life of a city hermit, nature still made her demands. Like a timid animal, all aquiver, he was startled by my figure in the darkness, muttered a greeting, made a few polite inquiries and scurried away. It was like old times. We were strangers passing in the shadows of the seminary, just as we had lived when we were neighbours in the corridor.

At one stage while I was teaching at Manly, Clem had taken some six-month's long-service leave and disappeared. After two or three months it transpired that he had not in fact left the building. He was spending his leave in his room, feeding himself and avoiding us. Even when he had been on duty, Clem had avoided staff meals or our community gatherings. He used to stay in his room, surviving, as the gossip had it, on Arrowroot biscuits, emerging only to deliver his regular lectures on Sacramental Theology and then slinking back to his study. I had been sharing my life with a highly-strung hermit, with a shy nocturnal creature – brothers in the priesthood, colleagues in the seminary but strangers in the world. Eventually, under the glazed eyes of his fellow lecturers, Clem suffered a complete breakdown and was taken screeching from the building by his brother Eris.

Anyway, on this last occasion, I loaded the boxes full of powerful knowledge into my rusting Peugeot and drove away, down the hill to The Corso, across the Spit Bridge to North Sydney where Adele and I had purchased a terrace house. I laboured up and down the staircase of our home (a renovator's dream – screaming for painting), up a rickety step-ladder I had borrowed from Max and Linda Jones who lived round the corner, and loaded each box through a manhole, into the ceiling. I stacked the boxes one on top of another on a make-shift wooden platform laid across the old roof-beams and hoped the weight would not collapse through the cracked ceiling. My library went to sleep there above our matrimonial bed for a number of years, gathering dust, growing old and out-dated, ignored by me as I went about the reconstruction of my life. I had a lot of baggage to throw overboard – or, to be more accurate, I had jumped ship, leaving most of my heavy baggage behind.

In retrospect, with a modicum of experience of the ways of the world, it is breathtaking to think that the authorities would have let me drift away, without any attempt to recover me. No international company in the real world, could afford to have let my defection pass without some review and report. Perhaps middle management should have shown some interest in exploring the reasons for my unscheduled departure. I suspect they already knew the reasons, but could not face the truth. At the very least, the institution had invested some of its substantial assets in my formation – and would later complain of its wasted expenditure.

So, in October 1976, leaving Manly with tears in my eyes, I drove alone to a friend's holiday home near the beach at Avalon, to a house overlooking the fairways and sandpits of the local golf-course. The rooms were cluttered with an overload of Queen Ann beds, dressing tables, chairs, dressers and family photographs of yesteryear in heavy silver frames. There was a large portrait of the master of the house above the bricked fireplace, looking stern with his compact moustache, side-by-side with a portrait of the lady of the manor, wearing Edna

Everidge styled white-framed glasses. A pungent odour of must filled the house, heavy layers of dust covered the furnishings and handfuls of naphthalene had been sprinkled like confetti on piles of folded blankets.

I stayed in Avalon, on my own, for a few weeks. Baking in the summer sun, crying, feeling extremely sorry for myself, looking with half-interest in the daily newspaper to see what type of jobs were available, bursting into tears and wondering what the future held – a nervous breakdown was in full bloom.

My bills were no longer being paid and there was no one now to prepare my three meals each day or to pour the tea from silver services each morning and afternoon. I was alone sitting at the meal-table in the kitchen. My student audience had disappeared and the servant nuns were gone. There would be no free medical and hospital treatment, no ten percent clergy discount, no cheap holidays and no free meals at restaurants. My days, day after day, were no longer packaged neatly into that majestic, Gothic building at Manly where I had eaten, studied, lectured, prayed, slept and socialised. If I was lucky, I would eventually have to make my way through the impatient city traffic to an office, appear in collar and tie at my desk close to 9am, fill in forms, make reports, look forward to the regular Thursday salary envelope, weekends and annual holidays, pay taxes and rent, gas and electricity bills.

It was a strange feeling at the age of almost forty to be forced to learn the ways of the world. I was going to be answerable to others in ways I had never been. Yet no-one would be telling me what I had to believe, what to think, how to behave in my free-time or what to wear in the privacy of my own room in my home. In my new life, if I wanted, I could be outrageous, drunken, debauched, critical, mocking, truthful, direct and no one should be scandalised or offended. I could be myself – my best self, or my worst. I would no longer be representing anyone, any ideology or institution. I could enjoy a private life. My friends, if it pleased me, could be independent of my work colleagues. My working day would be limited to eight hours and the rest of the day, and all the night would be my own. Almost nothing I would be doing was going to emit supernatural, eternal wavelengths. I would not be dealing with issues of salvation, with death and mortal sin, or with moral imperatives – only with temporary, transitory issues; health, exercises, banks, amusement and relaxation.

For some time my contact with reality was somewhat warped by my anger and depression. I shunned contact with my confrères and I was furious with the mechanical men of the institution who had claimed so much power over me. I couldn't read, or listen to the radio, or submit myself to the sludge of daytime television. I couldn't think or pray. A paralysing laziness took possession of my mind by day and came with me to bed at night. Simple tasks, buying bread or a few eggs, were postponed until tomorrow. Washing, shaving, eating – the ordinary mundane functions – demanded more energy, more motivation than I could muster. I lay on the balcony in the summer sun and suffered – waves of loneliness, tears of self-pity, a sense of irretrievable loss, a longing for death to take me away.

As far as my clerical brothers were concerned, I had contracted some form of spiritual leprosy. Rumours were swirling around and beginning to take flight. I was concerned that my parents would be saddened when they heard what was being reported. Among their friends, and in the parish, they had enjoyed the comfort and the status of a priest in the family. Everyone had told them that their Christopher displayed the marks of leadership. People had been saying that one day he would be a bishop, perhaps even a member of the College of Cardinals. Who knows? Men with far less talent had succeeded and nothing more illustrious could have been imagined. But I could not turn back. My parents would have to weather the storm and deal with the opprobrium as best they could. They too, had a reality to face.

While the trembling moment of my departure would be the beginning of a new life (challenges, children, a warm home, an exciting profession, a loving partner), the future had not yet moved into my frame of vision. I could not have seen the journey I was about to undertake – the conflicts, the successes, the joys. I was locked in a lonely world, not looking to the future, but desperate to escape the mess my life had become.

Unlike today, in those early days it was distressing to look back over my shoulder to examine the path I had trodden. The narrative of my life had congealed inside a fragile human being who was camping in a friend's holiday house or later, alone in a one-bedroom bachelor flat in Epping. I was riddled with doubt and bitter with memories.

But I had to think about myself and my own sanity. Though I knew others would be upset and scandalised, I had to turn away from them. Some young religious sisters, some seminarians had come to draw strength from people like me. They saw us as the hope for the future of their Church and we were becoming increasingly rare in the business. Many had left the service, but some of us had held on. Though I felt guilty that my abandonment would generate distress and further confusion, for the moment I could not be concerned about others. I had to consider myself, my own survival, my mental health, the future of my little life.

Adele was in Sydney, still occupying her apartment in Blues Point Tower and still looking from her sitting-room window across Balls Head, down the Parramatta River. After I had recovered my composure and was feeling better, I used to visit her. As I was beginning to find my way on shaky legs, she made me feel that I did have a value. I was happy in her company. I knew that I had to find a job, earn a living and fend for myself. I had to pretend, at least for awhile, that I was coping. She must have been wondering what was happening under the waves to this man, whether he would ever find his way out of the heavy clerical surf and whether he could offer her anything.

We would go to the theatre, catch a film, visit the zoo, travel to Echo Point at Katoomba, or stroll hand-in-hand in the sun along one of the northern beaches. From time to time, she would visit my little flat to check that everything was proper, that there was food in the cupboard, clean sheets on the bed and no dishes in the sink.

As far as I can remember, it was in the first few months of 1977, after our lunch at the Five-Ways, that I began pestering Adele for an answer to my attractive offer, first made in the pub, to join forces with me in marriage. At the time I was jobless, my personal life was a mess and I could claim no translatable qualifications – but I persisted. I had leapt from the nest high up on the cliff and, after some hesitation, after a few tentative flaps, I was flying. I was off the ground, spinning, giddy, away and on my own.

Adele did not reply, for or against, to my proposal. There was no hurry, she said, and I could understand why she was hesitant. Who could blame her? I had no reason to expect a positive reply. Even so, I had decided that even if she were to refuse my generous invitation, I would not be dragging myself back into that narrow space and returning to Manly – too many things had happened.

My French visitor left from Mascot on Friday 1st July 1977. She had been two years in Australia and she was going home to Toulouse, to her family, to consider my insistent proposal, to reflect on her future. She left me in a state of terrible uncertainty. She was going for who knew how long – perhaps forever. What hope could I cling to that she would return, that she would decide to leave her family and her country and accept my offer to fuse our empty bank accounts? Sydney would be empty without her.

chapter twenty seven

1976-1977
PENNILESS

My life had been simple and unsophisticated: food, drink, a few clerical companions and somewhere to study and sleep. In the 60's, a clergyman owned a black suit, two or three Roman collars, a pair of swimming togs, a few T-shirts and a pair of football shorts. In the 70's, I had also acquired a pair of corduroys and a polo-neck jumper which were causing trouble in the ranks. As a priest, it had not entered my head to waste money on a pair of brown shoes, a tweed jacket or a cravat. All food tasted the same as it had in the seminary – sausages and gravy, rump steak and potatoes, lamb and soggy vegetables with no dressing, spices or condiments and a cold beer (Tooheys or Resches) and red or white wine – which I had not begun to drink until I was almost thirty. I was frugal by nature, and by training, and someone had always been there to provide for my basic needs.

But life had changed. Now I was penniless in the world. My meals were not on the table waiting for me. I had to shop in supermarkets and pay the lady at the check-out. Yesterday, the daily newspapers had appeared miraculously each morning in the common room. Now I had to pay for a copy of the Sydney Morning Herald, in order to see what jobs were on offer and whether someone might find me useful and want to give me a chance. What does an unemployed theology professor, at the age of thirty eight, do? Where does he begin looking for a job?

I searched the *Positions Vacant* section in the newspaper. With dull eyes and a brick in my chest, I scanned through the employment notices each morning. Being the end of the year, there were vacancies for teachers of English or mathematics, for modern languages, but most of the notices were for positions in Catholic schools and I had to accept that any application would inevitably meet with rejection. The official institution knew how to exclude. Since the 70's, times have changed.

There were also vacant positions in schools for teachers of physics, chemistry, geography, and others in the public service, and jobs for salesmen, accountants, solicitors, mechanics and tradesmen, but I was qualified for nothing. The only personal reference I had, the one which would accompany my every application, came from Father Michael Bach, who happened to have become the parish priest of Bulli before he too decided to desert the ship. In a few short paragraphs, Michael recommended his old mate for his integrity and his general academic attainments. What more could he say?

In desperation, I submitted myself to a series of questionnaires and interviews at a placement agency in Martin Place. Polished desks, glass panels, pretty secretaries with gleaming teeth and shapely legs on high heels. The office radiated a glow of success, but the smartly tailored young executive who interviewed me, was not confident he could place me with anyone in his stable of companies. He invited me to leave my details and he would contact me. But I was too much trouble. I was wasting his time. I did not fit the mould – too old, too inexperienced, and over-qualified in an unmarketable field. A square peg when all the holes were neatly rounded and smooth.

His Honour Mr Justice Bill Perrignon, a portly acquaintance of my friend Sausage Hogan, agreed to give me the benefit of his worldly advice. I met this dour, judicial officer in his mouldy chamber. Bill was known to his friends as "The Giant Panda" and like a panda, he listened in some abstracted manner for as long as he needed to and then delivered a short judgement. He was a practical man – he had to be. He had eleven little mouths to feed before he and his wife could sit down at table. Anyway, he told me that I was starting very late and that I should not set my sights too high and that I had little to recommend me. A job in the State public service was my best option – perhaps my only one. I would have to begin at the bottom, but by sixty-five I should have a modest pension to support me in retirement. He was not optimistic but to be fair, my prospects were bleak.

While I was camped at Avalon, I answered an advertisement for a factory worker with Tubemakers at St Leonards. Unlike my other applications, I was granted an interview with one of the company managers but jobs were not easy to come by. Rampant unemployment was on the rise in Sydney in the late 70's. I was starting out at a difficult time. I did not have the appropriate training or experience. The interviewer thought that I might soon grow bored. It had been a long-shot anyway.

I had to find a real job – something I could do. I made contact with a middle-eastern gentleman who was running a taxi- drivers' course out of a scungy backroom, on the first floor of a shop-front building in Oxford Street. At the time my head was full of porridge. I thought that maybe taxi-driving would let me hold a wobbly line for a few months, giving me space to settle and decide where I was going. I paid the scruffy one-man-band one hundred of my precious dollars and booked in.

For some weeks I attended endless sessions of map reading. I had to learn the principal streets in the city and suburbs, where to find main railway stations, theatres, sports ovals and hotels. I attended these weary lectures with other desperate aspirants, some speaking broken English at best and others no English whatsoever. We were Vietnamese, Chinese, Turks, Lebanese, Chilians and one Australian of Celtic origin (myself) – a mixed bag struggling for survival. I was accustomed to attending lectures, taking notes and absorbing information. The group at the institute in Paris where I had studied, had also gathered from all parts of the world. But my taxi-group was not as prestigious and the quality of the lectures left much to be desired. It was not easy for our untrained, overweight, Turkish teacher to communicate to a multicultural gathering, the knowledge necessary to satisfy the licensing authority, but he was running a business, so he collected the money and presented a series of heavily accented monologues. His students were in and out without ceremony and if they failed the Road Traffic Authority test at the end, they paid more money and went round again. The owner didn't seem to care.

When I had completed the course and memorised some of the principal pages of the Sydney street directory, I sat for the Authority's test and as usual, passed. But this time, it was without distinction – *no magna cum laude* or *très bien* – only *assez bien*, or *not so bad*. I received a plastic card with my mug photograph in the corner and my licence number. Suddenly I was a self-employed businessman.

Armed with my new licence, I made my way from Avalon to the ABC taxi centre at the Shell garage in Artarmon where the manager took a few moments to explain the system. I would pay the faceless owner of the vehicles for the hire of one of his cabs and any money I could collect in addition to the hire charges and my daily petrol expenses, would be mine. I could begin the next day. The day-shift started at five-thirty in the morning and concluded around three in the afternoon.

I didn't want to waste any of the rental time, so I presented myself at the depot the following morning before the sun had made an appearance and when the streets were empty. The cabs were waiting in lines, looking tired and hung-over. The manager pointed me in the direction of one of his older jalopies. The tyres were bald; a shudder in the steering column; the brakes were soft; the springs in the driver's seat collapsed into a hole and the upholstery was of dirty, brown vinyl, tattered and torn. Inserting the key and turning over the exhausted engine, I began my taxi-driving career just as the horizon was ablaze with fiery reds and edges of soft pinks. Mine was destined to be a short and extinguished career.

Though my taxi felt wobbly and dangerous out on the open road, I drove furiously for my first day. Despite the training at the taxi school, I could not seem to manage the two-way radio, so I was reduced to picking up the odd passenger who hailed me from the curbside. The teacher had not told me that I should focus my effort on the more lucrative areas of Sydney. I did not know that I should have been hovering in the eastern suburbs or loitering on the lower North Shore. I went wherever my passenger took me, as far as the outer Western suburbs, then turning around, made my way back, fare-less, into the city, to begin again.

Those summer days were hot and sticky. Some of my passengers were cranky, or hassled by whingeing children. My elderly passengers were surprised when I offered to help them with their parcels and groceries up the steps and in through their front door. Mine was a service which taxi drivers normally did not provide. I didn't know.

Strange as it may seem, I had never ridden in a taxi before – and this was only my first day.

About midday my cab collapsed into a heap of junk. It just stopped and I was off the road, idle and without a fare, losing revenue, for some hours. When I rang the manager at the ABC centre, he did not seem surprised or concerned. He told me to keep the cab for a further shift – no extra charge. I returned to home-base at Artarmon at about nine o'clock that night, exhausted. I had been on the road for fifteen hours, without a *smoko* or a meal, battling traffic, scouting for work. Lecturing at Manly had been a breeze in comparison. I counted my takings for the day, paid my lawful debts and pocketed ten dollars. Taxi-driving was not going to make me rich any time soon.

I wondered how the other drivers were making a living and feeding a family. I thought there must be some knack, some inside information which I needed to learn before hitting the big time. If everyone was to function at my standard, there would be no taxi-drivers in Sydney. I presumed some of the drivers were making a living. They must have been able to hunt and gather for their families. There had to be something else to this business, some key to success and I hoped I could pick it up quickly.

The next day I turned up, bleary eyed, again just before sunrise. I took delivery of a different, sloppy machine. As the sun rose in the sky, so did the Sydney temperature. My cab was not air-conditioned, so the century temperature and unpleasant hot wind made driving intolerable. I kept hearing the machine-gun announcements on the two-way radio going off like fire-crackers, but I was too slow to beat the other drivers to the button. I kept searching for clients off the street and felt that I was probably in the wrong business.

Driving in the city was torture. In the heat of the early afternoon I picked up a young mother and her daughter and as I drove through the haze and the heavy traffic, the little girl in the back complained she was feeling sick. The baking temperature was beginning to trouble her. A sudden burst of recycled ice-cream and lolly water gushed from her innocent mouth, spraying the back seat and the floor of my cab. The harassed mother apologised, paid the fare and hurried away. Holding my breath and with windows down, I drove to the nearest garage where I cleaned the back section as well as I could. It was not enough. The interior continued to glow with the smell of summer vomit. Passengers complained and even I, the driver, couldn't bear it. The heat, the traffic, the smell, the competition, the financial rewards – this was not for me. Without further reflection, I made a sudden career decision. Two days were enough and I would have to find something else to do.

I drove the clapped-out, putrid ABC vehicle back to base, settled up with the manager and closed the trapdoor on another stage of my life. This time I didn't have to delay fifteen years before deciding I was in the wrong line of work. My licence had a little less than a year to run, but I would never need it again. The outlay of one hundred dollars for the course and the cost of the license would be a neat deduction on my eventual taxable income.

My sister Colleen was worried about me and anxious to support me during those dark days. Her new husband, John Byrne, was managing an export meat business in an ugly area close to the railway yards near Rozelle. So my first real job came by the grace and favour of my brother-in-law. He did not require any formal application or need to read my only reference or sight my CV. He knew I needed to fill in my days and have some money in my pocket at the end of the week, so he offered me a job – a menial, servile job, but a job.

The work was repetitive and exhausting. My priestly training had not prepared me for heavy, constant, repetitive bending and lifting – repetitive bending, yes, but heavy lifting, no. I was spending hours on the road, driving a grubby, clapped out Holden utility with *Harris Meats* painted on the side, carting boxes of meat to different locations throughout the city, parking in back lanes and struggling in and out of freezers.

The work was ideal. It required no intellectual input. These were simple, labouring duties; my days were occupied; my energy was expended; I had money in my pocket; I could buy groceries; and I was not lying around morosely, wiping tears from my eyes, sighing like a teenager on drugs, like a broken down half-man.

Harris Meats was a temporary job until after Christmas. In order to restore some semblance of sanity, I moved out of my isolation at Avalon and parked myself for a few weeks with my mate, Father John Ford. In the meantime, he had moved from the parish at Malabar to the little inter-city, harbour-side parish of St Bede's in Pyrmont and he was a perfect companion in my frail condition. He was always in a good mood, he asked no questions, he applied no pressure and there was no unspoken criticism or clerical expectations. He cooked dishes that the Italian house-keeper at Malabar had taught him to prepare and shared his simple life with me in my distress. Together with others who know him, I've canonised the man while he still lives among us.

Then in about April, and with the assistance of the society of St Vincent de Paul and my sister Colleen, I moved into rented premises in Epping and began answering a few advertisements in the hope of finding permanent work. Late at night, after delivering meat, I wrote out applications – for the position of lecturer in liturgical studies at the Catholic Teachers College, Castle Hill; for the chief executive officer of the Workers' Education Association in Wollongong; and for the position of public relations officer at the Hornsby District Hospital. With a spark of hope but little confidence, I sent my letters off with a copy of my one character reference and waited. The bureaucrats and clerks seemed to process my applications with an agonising delay.

In January, I attended the baptismal party of Pat Martin's second daughter. Pat and I had been together at Springwood and Manly. He had worked for the bank before he had heard the call and was therefore, technically, a "late vocation". We had been ordained to the priesthood in the same class of '62, but it had been five or six years since I had seen him and in the meantime he had surrendered his faculties and left the service. At the time, I was still unemployed. The taxi business had been a flop, *Harris Meats* had put me off and the gathering was amused to hear me recounting my exploits – all that is, except Pat's brother, Jack. He was an old Newcastle boy who had served in the Second World War and who had survived on his wits, with little formal education. He was in charge of a freight business and had men employed on fork-lifts and front-end loaders, moving cargo and containers around wharves and sheds. Jack listened attentively to my story – a priest, a doctor of theology, a healthy body of almost forty, who was seriously unemployed. He was feeling sorry for me and offered to find me a job. I would have to sit for another examination – for my fork-lift driver's ticket – but that wouldn't prove a problem. The telephone remained silent and nothing came of his offer.

chapter twenty eight

1970'S
TO DIG, I WAS NOT ABLE

L ike many retired priests, I was finding it difficult to land a job which would pay the rent and support a family. From a high position in a parish or a school, suddenly we were on the lowest level of society – untrained and out of work. We were all starting behind scratch, way behind. Like me, some drove trucks or taxis. Many worked as officers in the Department of Probation and Parole where Father Roger Pryke had landed a responsible position and, being a failed priest himself, he could provide an inside running for other clerical desperados.

Some of us, frightened to branch out too far, sought comfort in what they knew. They began teaching, or tried their hand as civil celebrants, officiating at funerals, marrying believers and unbelievers, divorcees and atheists, sometimes blessing the union of gay men and women and burying whoever came along, in some cases even household pets. It was a job, even if the pay was modest. My mind was always turning over for new job opportunities and business ventures. What were we as ex-priests, suited for? How could we use our expertise? I had a few ideas.

In more recent years, fuddy-duddies in the Vatican have become anxious that there is a dramatic shortage of exorcists practising their arcane trade (though there are still some exorcists hard at work in parts of Africa and South America). Dom Gabriele Amorth, the Vatican's chief exorcist and the honorary president of the International

Association of Exorcists, claimed to have performed 70,000 exorcisms. Father Gregory Jordan SJ, a Jesuit well-known for his work at St Aloysius College in Sydney in the 70's, was a member of the association and the official exorcist for the Brisbane Archdiocese. Those in the Vatican who were in charge of providing these essential services were keen to commission an expert *Exorcist Maximus*, who would reside in the Holy City and would be in charge of making sure that every diocese on the globe enjoyed the services of a trained and ordained exorcist. Even for a modest fee, I was thinking there was considerable money to be made for an enterprising businessman. I confess that when I was searching for a job, I had not realised that there might have been a business opportunity for an active exorcist in the Sydney area. It makes sense. The devil and his little ugly helpers were everywhere.They had taken up residence in the brains and the bowels of many Sydney-siders – armed robbers, drunken louts on Saturday nights, wife beaters, financial advisers, drive-by shooters, climate deniers, CEOs of public companies, bankers, spin-doctors, corrupt land developers, scientologists and Opus Deists. They had even taken up possession in the sensitive loins of some members of the clergy.

> "As I have not ceased to warn you, the evil comes from within (the Church) and from very high up. There is an authentic rottenness, and at times it seems as if the Mystical Body of Christ were a corpse in decomposition, that it stinks…"
> St José María Escrivá de Balaguer, founder of *Opus Dei*.

Though those on the inside have always known it, the little people and the outsiders are now aware that the devil and his many minions have been active among the executive members of the institution. The sexual drive and the terrible need in an authoritarian system for secrecy have been exploited by the devil. But they had not been the only port of entry for him to take possession of the superior ranks of holy mother Church. The power structures, the unquenchable thirst for control, the tightly closed categories of orthodoxy, the paranoid concentration on the minutiae of the law, the widespread acceptance of superstitious and idolatrous practices as well as the evil spirits of ambition, ignorance and arrogance, deceit and stupidity have provided fertile soil for the devil to play havoc.

When the devil saw that God had sent his son to earth as a travelling, homeless, dusty preacher and that this divinely touched man was defying the religious establishment, exposing its stupidities and emptiness, Satan knew instinctively he was facing a challenge to his influence and that he had to devise a strategy to combat the forces of good. He had to inspire Jesus's followers to build big churches, collect baubles, dress up in extravagant gear, talk a strange language, complicate a simple message in heavy formulae, multiply regulations, exclude the little people, the twisted, the ugly, the stranger, the homosexual, the black and the female, invest in real estate and establish an international firm with a branch office and personnel in every large city and colonial outpost throughout the world. He watched on as God's special messenger invited his friends to remember him in the context of a simple family meal, breaking and sharing bread, passing around a cup of blessed wine. He knew what to do. Create an entanglement of theological interpretations and overlay the memorial communion with an evanescence of byzantine ritual and high-camp ceremonies, tie the simple event to a priestly caste of men, to a hierarchy of ranks which would inevitably distract and pervert the message.

There was much work to be done, many devils to be dealt with and money to be made.

A whole new field of employment had been waiting to be tapped by the local labour exchange. Priests and ex-priests, like me, would have had no need to attend training courses to obtain the necessary practising certification. Before my ordination to the priesthood and as a necessary prerequisite, the bishop had inducted me into a series of minor orders including the order of exorcist. By profession, like every other priest, in the seminary I had been ordained as an exorcist. I had been given the incredible power of driving devils out of those who were possessed, away from rivers and trees, from dogs and swine.

Before launching myself and taking up this new opportunity offered by the Vatican – before advertising my special services, being a raw or rusty practitioner, instead of the taxi-driving course – maybe I should have thought of undertaking a few hours of in-service lectures, of accessing the new material on some of the available websites and answering a bank of multiple-choice questions to up-date my skills. The trade of exorcism had probably changed a little in more recent times – new devils and evil spirits to learn about; more powerful ritual formulas; more potent holy water and spells; a range of overpowering incenses; different threats and chants; more colourful vestments. There was always something new to learn. The next step in the process would have been to make an application for a special federal government grant, for someone launching a new, boutique business. Finally, before erecting the sign over the door, there was the important question of a suitable fee for service. Professional fees would vary according to the extent of the possession and the number and power of the devils in residence, the difficulty in removing them from their dwelling and the exorcist's experience as a professional as well as his prior success rate. Two-storey houses would be more expensive than a single-storey home and multi-storey buildings and factories, more costly again. Like weddings and funerals, driving devils out of a high-profile celebrity, a film star or a cardinal could attract a handsome fee. The Vatican was opening a niche market which could have easily been exploited by an enterprising ex-priest on the make. Exorcism was certainly worth considering. It would simply have meant exercising a power which had already been conferred and which had lain dormant for years.

But I must confess that the possibilities offered by my enrolment in the order of exorcists, never entered my muddled head. Anyway, I was no entrepreneur and I was not inclined to go back into the business of religion. Marriages, funerals and exorcisms were no longer my scene. I had to look elsewhere.

chapter twenty nine

1977
TO TEACH THEOLOGY AGAIN?

The postman delivered an invitation to attend an interview for a position at Castle Hill. The Catholic Teachers' College had advertised for a senior lecturer in sacramental theology and liturgical studies and in a moment of desperation, I had applied. Providence was looking after me. Because of my overseas qualifications and my teaching experience, I was confident that I would stand out, head and shoulders, over any other applicant. All things being equal, the job was mine if I should want it.

I was a little hesitant. In my clearer moments, I could not bring myself to believe that the organisation I knew and the Mullahs in charge would roll over and make room for me. They were not inclusive men and they were a long way from being aware of the role they had played in my life. I was naïve enough to think that since the college was a tertiary institution and government funded, that the faceless clerics might be slow to apply the veto and that this might be my chance to pick myself up and get started.

Come the day, I put on my black suit (the only business clothes I possessed), selected a non-descript tie from my range of two and drove to the old De La Salle college on the outskirts of the city. The principal of the Teachers' College, a Marist Brother, greeted me at the door and ushered me into the reception parlour. Inside, I found President David Coffey D.D. sitting in the corner, dressed in clerical grey and wearing his shiny Roman collar. He did not stir himself, but nodded in my direction as though he barely knew me. He looked embarrassed. I was embarrassed – and surprised. He had been a senior seminarian at Springwood and Manly when I was enrolled in the lower ranks and we had worked together at the same establishment for some years, but we were never close.

The Marist Brother introduced me to the other gentleman. Mr John McCarthy was unknown to me. He was a big man, physically impressive, friendly and urbane. We shook hands. He turned out to be the John McCarthy, now a Queen's Counsel of the Sydney Bar, a lifelong comrade of Premier Bob Carr and the Labor Party, a confidante of Cardinal George Pell and now the Australian ambassador to the Holy See, but in 1976, he was just a humble barrister.

I sat on one side of a mahogany table, McCarthy on the other. Coffey remained seated in the corner with his gaze fixed on the floor, as if the die had already been cast and the meeting was just a formality – a waste of time and demeaning to all involved. The brother, dressed in his religious habit, a rope around his waist, a crucifix hanging from a string around his neck, took his position on the side, out of the firing line. The principal inquisitor opened the bowling with the new ball and continued to unleash his body-liners until stumps were drawn. There was only one area of the wicket on which McCarthy trained his missiles. The cross-examination of his victim had been carefully crafted. He probed; he pushed; he persisted; and I realised almost immediately, that there were no runs to be scored and that I needed to be cautious. He had found his length early and I had difficulty reading the wicket and getting my eye in. Perhaps I should have come with my solicitor to advise and protect me. McCarthy was working to entice me into a web of damaging admissions. He had been trained to sculpt his questions, to build momentum, to lead his innocent prey into cul-de-sacs and dead-ends. I had to play this game carefully to avoid the pitfalls and circumvent the traps.

The inquisitor's line of attack was to bowl hard and fast at my off-stump, attacking my approach to the ill-fated encyclical of Pope Paul VI, which had dealt aggressively with artificial birth control. He was not interested in my qualifications, my publications, my teaching experience, or in any plans I might have for teaching courses in liturgy and sacramental theology to the students of the College. Our interchange focused entirely on the encyclical *Humanae Vitae,* on papal authority and the control of women's reproductive organs. Whatever swallowing a tiny pill and controlling a woman's ovulation cycles had to do with celebrating the mystery of God among us, completely escaped me. But given the political and practical wiliness of McCarthy's principal, Archbishop Carroll, I would be amazed if the inquisitor was straying outside his bowling instructions. The invisible captain's orders would have been simple and succinct –

"Get him out of there, John. Bowl hard and fast. Aim at his head. Just get rid of him once and for all."

Where had this budding Torquemada sprung from? I understood why Dr Coffey was in the field, at long-on. He was the President of the Theological Faculty in Sydney. And I understood why he was saying nothing – I had left his team in embarrassing circumstances. I could see why the Marist Brother as principal of the College should also be playing in the team – the successful candidate would be a member of his staff. But who was this McCarthy? Within the diocese, there were wheels within wheels of which I had no knowledge. The organization was crossed and criss-crossed with corridors and dark passages of power. Unbeknown to me, we had been surrounded by spivs and spies who had infiltrated the system. Pious knights who had sworn an oath of secrecy were scrutinising and reporting on the members of the minor clergy. These people would later become known as *The Temple Police.*

McCarthy of the Bar was a rising star in the right-wing of the Labor Party and an obedient follower of Rome, so on and on he went with his interrogation. Thoughtfully, he constructed the questions and carefully, I provided the answers. I knew that my responses were unsatisfactory. One answer only generated another probe into the heart of my orthodoxy. I was like a rabbit caught in the diocesan searchlights, looking for a burrow to crawl down.

There was nothing about sacraments, nothing about liturgy, or about the mystery of the Church, or about the social and political dimensions of worship, or the structure of the Roman Catholic Church, or the Second Vatican Council, or about the bishop of Rome, or the position of the Pope within the hierarchical structure of the Church – only the notorious Pope's letter, French letters and the pill. The inquisitor was determined to extract what the successful candidate proposed to teach students of liturgy and sacramental theology about sinful means of controlling pregnancies.

Back in the 60's and early to mid 70's, as a junior priest I had narrowly avoided the Pope's harsh and unwelcomed letter to his people. In 1968, when the students were rebelling on the streets of Paris and Lionel Rose was becoming a world champion, I was lucky to be back in the seminary rather than sitting on hot Saturday afternoons in the confessional, fielding curly questions of conscience from irate sinners and exhausted mothers. In the outside world the indecisive bishop of Rome had exploded a suicide bomb among his clergy and loyal Catholics. He had incited a crisis of conscience among those who were remaining faithful to the Roman version of the Christian tradition, while the rest of the world greeted his message with yawns of indifference or ridicule. Pope Hamlet had emerged from the Vatican shadows to freeze orthodoxy, create divisions and generate erosions within his Church and inside the ranks of his clergy.

But I had been living far away, on top of a mountain, and outside the danger-zone when the earthquake struck. So much had passed over me in the 60's – the Vietnam war, the anti-apartheid rallies, the tragedy of Biafra, the world's first heart transplant, assassinations, the bus ride to Moree and even the Beatles. I had somehow also avoided the tremors caused by *Humanae Vitae.* The students for the priesthood were all males and birth control was not on their minds. They were not sexually active – or so I thought. Let me rephrase that. They were not *supposed* to be sexually active. I had a lot to learn about life and the world, about the Church and its officers and about students for the priesthood. When I later told my wife about a young priest who had hanged himself after he had found out his girl-friend was expecting a baby, Adele's response put me a little off-balance. According to her, we should have told the seminarians during their training that if they were to engage in sexual intercourse with a person of the opposite sex, they should wear a fresh French letter. In fact, she thought the authorities should have given a packet of condoms to the newly ordained as they left the seminary and made them routinely available to members of the clergy – she had practical solutions to any problem.

Although the storm created by the Vatican prohibition almost passed over me without my getting wet, I had had my own ideas. Happily, I could keep them to myself – at least until McCarthy had me pinned on his rack. I thought the Church had shown far too much interest, for too long, in seed spilling and in the pleasurable exchange of human juices. The officials had become obsessed with sex, especially the sexual behaviour of people other than the clergy. There were more important human activities to concentrate on – other critical issues about which the Church had, by and large, either sent out muted messages or remained silent on – global poverty; the distribution of wealth (including Vatican wealth); over-population of the world; war; the sale of weapons of destruction to mad dictators; and the treatment of the mentally ill. Do I need to go on? On the question of sex, those who were saying the most knew the least. In addition, it was to become clear that they had serious problems to address in their own backyard. Now, not only was the little pill under challenge, but so were the questions of papal authority and the credibility of the institution. The Mullahs had gone too far and the clerical power base was coming under attack. The bishops were busy inserting their ringed fingers in the dyke up to their armpit, but gushers of rebellion were breaking out all over the place. In my humble opinion, the encyclical letter had been an act of pure folly which was destined to change the ecclesiastical landscape forever. Pills, diaphragms, French letters, rings, abstinence – who cared? What had Jesus said about any of these matters? The people in the pews were voting with their feet and bums.

Fortunately, in 1968 I was safely in hiding among men who were in training to keep their private parts to themselves. I was not regularly put on the rack like my clerical mates, by troubled mothers with their heavy burden of children, finances, mortgages and a husband who expected a little affection. I was relatively free of trouble, until McCarthy came poking around, checking up, getting rid of me. Remembering Cardinal Freeman's advice, I danced and stepped around the ring but at the end there was no doubt who the victor was and who the victim. The interview at Castle Hill was small beer for McCarthy, but it was a job which had to be done properly. He had been briefed to expose my under-belly. He had to show I was not to be trusted, that I would be a danger to the Church and hostile to the angels if I were given the position. The bout had been fixed. I was judged "not suitable" for the position which they had advertised. But they had to continue the pretence.

Some weeks later, after an appropriate delay, the principal of the college regretted to inform me I had not been successful. There was the usual spin to soften the harsh message of failure – so many applicants; a number with very high qualifications; difficult to make decisions and so forth.

I knew it was not true. There was no one in Australia at that time more qualified or experienced than I was in such a specialised field. The decision had not been difficult to make. It had been made from the beginning. They had made a fool of me and I had made myself look silly. Though I felt humiliated by the game of charades involving President Coffey and John McCarthy, though the position might have been a convenient place to start a new career, I look back and bless the captain and his fast bowler. Success in my semi-clerical application might have proved the kiss of death. I might have been locked into a second-rate teaching career with no path of advancement, going over familiar ground, dancing around inconvenient truths, suffering institutional burn-out and the enmity of petty men, without the challenge to strike out for freedom. My guardian angel had been looking after me.

1977
CHIROPODY

I was still sitting on the jetty, holding a thin line in my hand and waiting for a nibble. I had not received any reply from the Hornsby Hospital. Of course my application to work as the public relations officer for the northern region of the Health Commission, had been a gamble with long odds. Perhaps the position had been filled. Maybe I should reel in and cast somewhere else, but I wanted to check whether I still had bait on the line. When I telephoned the hospital, the receptionist put me straight through to the chief executive officer. But mine was not a call Stan Williams, the big boss, would normally have taken, so his secretary referred me on to someone in middle management. After a brief, pleasant, conversation with a faceless bureaucrat, I hung up. The position had not been filled. There was still hope.

The background to what happened next within the hospital in Hornsby came to light years later. I had spoken to Art Sidaris, a handsome young man who was one of twenty or so mature-aged students who had joined Stan William's special course in hospital administration. Mr Williams had passed on to Art the ninety-odd applications he had received for the position, with instructions to select the ten best applicants for interview. On the day I had telephoned, Art had just finished working through the pile of applications and had finalised his list. I was not on it.

Art later told me that he had been impressed by my interest in chasing up my application as no one else had bothered. The truth was that, being unemployed, I had nothing better to do. Anyway, Art Sidaris had formed a good impression from our brief conversation. When he went back over to have another look at my *curriculum vitae* and my character reference from the parish priest of Bulli, he had concluded that I deserved a chance. So he included me on a revised list of eleven candidates.

Mr Williams and Dr Jim Lawson interviewed the chosen few. I had had no experience or training in public relations. There were formal courses at various technical colleges throughout Sydney, but I had not attended any of them. I had come with little to recommend me, but the other applicants must have been horrible. It was miraculous when I was declared the winner of the competition and offered the prized position. At last a real job, with a desk, an office, a salary package each week and tax deductions. I was part of the real world and on my way.

Late in March 1977, early on a Monday morning, I presented myself in Stan William's office at Hornsby Hospital to commence my new career in public relations. It was like my first day at school with newly sharpened pencils and a clean slate; like my arrival in the darkness at Springwood in 1951 as a fledgling seminarian; like presenting myself as a novice teacher at Springwood. I was trying to fly without falling on my face, flapping furiously to stay in the air.

The public service gazette had advertised a position vacant for a chiropodist to work in the northern metropolitan region. Being a kind of maverick administrator, a creative bureaucrat, Dr Lawson did not think the organization needed a chiropodist – or if it did, he chose to forego that service. People's toenails would just have to fend for themselves. He needed a public relations worker to raise his profile in the health world; to establish programs to educate health workers and the public; to create a niche for health news and education on Sydney television; to produce video tapes for schools and generally liaise with the gurus of the mass media. So he employed someone who knew nothing about feet, or about public relations, to further his goals. I was employed as a chiropodist; paid as a chiropodist; classified as a chiropodist, but engaged to exercise my initiative, in whatever way I chose, to expand Jim Lawson's vision of preventative medicine and to set him on the road to glory.

Years later, during my swearing-in ceremony as a judge of the Compensation Court, my past came back to haunt me. The chairman of the court, His Honour Judge Frank McGrath, in his welcome speech, recited a few salient facts of my past and referred to me as the "reverend toe-cutter" come to judge the workers of New South Wales.

When I received the nod to join his team, Jim Lawson was on the move. His letter offered me the exalted position of *Regional Public Information Officer* (officially to be known as *a Chiropodist*), with a salary of $11,747. This glorious figure would rise to $12,041 after one year of "satisfactory service". I accepted the position for six months on a "trial basis". I was desperate. Despite my inexperience, I accepted the position without the least hesitation. I launched myself on a happy journey of three years with Jim Lawson and his team of health workers, staying in service with them until January 1980.

Fortunately I was the first public relations officer for the region, so no one had set the standard or established the rules. I had an "open slather". I had not realised that bureaucracies, by their nature, tend to expand and grow. I started like a wasp, as a lone insect in the corner of a large office area. Within a few months I had found a nook for myself, built a nest and within the year, I was caring for three other hatchlings – Tony, the camera operator; Jason, the sound recorder; and Tom, the Health Commission's face on television. I was supposed to be in charge.

I felt awkward in the Commission office at Chatswood. My fellow workers knew of my previous life and naturally assumed that they had a clear idea of my values, my beliefs and what had happened to make me change my direction. I felt exposed and they seemed wary. While they knew about me, I knew little about them and had had no life experience dealing with others in a secular setting. I didn't know which of them were Catholics and who were heretic or heathen.

It had been comfortable living with others in a world where one shared beliefs, a lifestyle and a basic philosophy, where nothing was seriously challenged and where the limits were clearly drawn. I had experienced troubling tensions and wounding conflicts, but deep beneath the surface there had been a rich seam of realities which, on one level, I could share and celebrate with my brothers. We had been energised from the same source, shared the same creed and gallery of heroes, numbered in the same institution. That's where I'd been all my life – home, school, seminary and diocese.

After a lifetime, I had cut myself adrift from this safe mooring and was now sailing in unchartered waters. I knew practically nothing of the world of those whom I was interacting with on a daily basis. It was a surprise to find that very few whom I was in contact with were interested in religion, even less in ecclesiastical affairs. Almost no one gave "a tinker's curse" about what the Pope or the local bishop had to say and yet, these matters had been centre-stage since my childhood. Those who might have entertained a vague interest in such matters, used to deal with me in a completely different way than they would have done a year or so before. I had lost my place in the sun.

When I started in my new job at the Commission, I was wearing the same baggy, black suit with the charcoal grey strip (the crutch was almost between my knees before it became the fashion). It was the same suit I had worn for some years at Manly. I had had no money to go looking for another. I also had two or three shirts with collars (only white ones) and two ties, until I was able to purchase a few extras from St Vincent de Paul for weekly rotation. I must have looked stand-out drab in the office at Chatwood, but I was too conscious of the other things happening in my life to be concerned about my dress sense. My external presentation was the least of my worries. I was anxious about how I was fitting in and how my fellow workers were dealing with a self-conscious ex-priest. What did they think of me? Was I doing the job, or failing miserably? What were the stereotypes, the prejudices my fellow workers had of a spoiled priest?

I was like a new-born foal struggling to its feet, trying to stand still and look normal. I was determined to survive and, at least to some limited extent, I had the ability of hiding any feelings of inadequacy and masking my discomfort under the cover of a smile. I could make-believe that I had not heard the sharp remark, that I had not understood the snide comment or the inoffensive throw-away line which I took to heart. In the seminary, I had learnt survival strategies which now proved useful.

A dizzy Pommie red-head named Rita used to mother the new arrival from her switchboard, giggling in her outrageous, provocative manner. She was great fun and we seemed to hit it off. She liked me and the big boss treated me with respect and welcomed me as a member of his crack team. I look back with affection and gratitude to the friends I made at the Commission – the researchers, the nurses, doctors, dentists, inspectors and secretaries. Unknowingly, they assisted me on my excruciating transition from the Roman collar and black suit, to colourful bow-ties and cuff-links.

Naturally, although I had heard nothing on the subject from Adele, I had vague plans to marry and start a family, perhaps purchase a home and run a car. On the edge of forty, I was in a hurry. I had to re-fashion myself. I was no longer an altar-boy at Neutral Bay, a page-boy in Eucharistic processions, a seminarian, a young priest, an energetic preacher, a flamboyant celebrant or a professor of theology. The world I had constructed had disappeared into the mud and I was now a faceless figure lost in the crowd. After moving upwards, throw-over-throw, climbing ladders, reaching goals – with one throw of the dice I had to return to the beginning and start my climb once again.

I was not planning to remain a public relations officer. The work was too demanding and my hold on the position was tenuous. One had to be energetic and optimistic about mundane matters, full of new ideas every day, selling products, devising programs and providing services. The work did not capture my imagination. It was hard for me to be enthusiastic about alcohol programs, "Quit Smoking" and "Weight Watchers" classes, when I had spent a lifetime immersed in sin and salvation. I was not a spin doctor or a naturally gifted salesman. If I was to succeed, I would need to erupt out of the starting blocks and recover twenty lost years. Chiropodist, surveyor, dentist, property valuer, accountant – what could I do?

I thought, briefly, of following the road to a university post, perhaps in the School of Divinity at Sydney University, but that dream was a passing distraction. I was not leaving a bureaucracy to join another one. I wanted to work for myself and I knew in my heart that no matter how hard I tried, I was not a natural academic. I didn't have the doggedness to go down that path. The other conclusion I had reached late in life, too late to avoid trouble, was that I was not by nature, a team-player. I seemed to function on the outer fringes of any group. I had discovered that I didn't seem to think like many other people. I was too critical, too out-spoken, too theoretical and uncompromising. I disliked committees and meetings and I felt that if I was going to be happy, I would have to work for myself – not in a partnership or for a company, or a firm. I wanted the freedom and flexibility of being my own boss.

I realised I had to return to the books and work hard for a practical degree which would translate knowledge and expertise into a house, perhaps private school fees and a motor vehicle. I would have to buy bread and sugar, perhaps even put fruit on the sideboard and meet the electricity bills. I had no money behind me and needed to work for a regular pay-packet, so there was no way I could indulge in a full-time law degree at the university. I found that the Supreme Court of New South Wales might provide a solution. The judges administered evening lecture courses and supervised half-yearly examinations in a program called the Barristers' Admission Board (the BAB). I filled in the papers and applied for entry.

In this abominable course, everyone, young and old, struggler or gifted, was left almost completely to his own devices. I attended turgid lectures, completed the attendance roll, read the textbooks and presented myself for the pass or fail examinations. No seminars, no tutorials, no counselling for those of us who were constantly failing. Many of the hundreds of students who attended the lectures were public servants or clerks in legal offices – almost all men. Some lived out in the distant suburbs, at the end of the train line, with their exhausted partner and three or four children. They would struggle home by train after a day at work in the office and lectures until nine o'clock at night and begin again, before dawn the next day. There were a few teachers, an architect who wanted to change his profession, a couple of tradesmen, a horde of office clerks – and me. But this "no frills" program suited me perfectly. There was no way I wanted to attend seminars or tutorials, to waste my time with the bells and whistles of education. It was a hard, lonely, bumpy road, but it was a quick and basic path to a professional ticket.

Every six months, after attending lectures four nights a week, many hours of swatting, months of study, weekends in the municipal library at North Sydney, I presented myself for three written examinations, each of three hours duration. Adele tells me that I was very ambitious. I think that I was highly motivated and stubborn. I wanted the best for her and our children.

The Admission Board course permitted me to work during the day to earn a living and to study late into the night. I paid my money, attended the lectures, sat for the examinations and completed the course – without a single day's sick leave from my employer to study and prepare for exams. We needed the Health Commission's pay-packet. I used to sit for the half-yearly examinations in Kensington in the morning and return to work at Chatswood in the afternoon. (In addition, we had started a family and we were renovating a broken-down terrace – mission impossible without the patience and daily support of my partner.)

I began my law course in April 1977 and completed it the same month three years later. It was a hard slog. Nearly every morning for three years, I would rise at about five and study for a few hours while the sun was coming up, while others were showering, shaving, painting faces, eating breakfast and listening to the news. I would kiss Adele goodbye and leave home about eight o'clock on the bus for work in Chatswood. I would listen to the school girls and boys discussing their turbulent social life, as we travelled the by-ways of Crows Nest and Willougby. The tone and content of their conversations provided a startling contrast to the life Adele and I were living in Union Street. What they got up to on the weekends, while I was studying my law books, was a revelation to an innocent ex-priest.

I was doing everything in a hurry. I had no time to lose.

chapter thirty one

1977

ALL OR NOTHING – MAKE YOUR CHOICE

I had abandoned the over-arching, ecclesiastical world of Rome and my youthful hopes had turned to dust. But despite their best efforts, prelates and senior clerics were not going to destroy the faith life I had learnt to cherish and which provided the grid through which I interpreted the events of history and daily life. In order to cope with what lay ahead, I knew that I would need spiritual nourishment – some regular exposure to the challenge of the Gospel message, a quiet space for celebration and thanksgiving, a ritual routine to ensure a sense of continuity. I was determined to cling to my Christian faith and to its noblest traditions.

Many of my colleagues had surrendered their personal faith and the practice of their beliefs, once they had resigned from the firm. The basic tenets of Christianity, the gutsy Gospels and the enduring rich traditions, have often been given the same treatment as the ugly features of the institution – the petty moral distinctions and the trivial dogmatic formulas. Everything was jettisoned. From my point of view, despite their years of rigorous training, these rebellious ex-priests, in their struggle for freedom, failed to spot the diamonds hidden in the rubbish heap. They were not ready to rummage around in search of treasure, to separate substance from trivia or to isolate the essence of the Christian message from haggard, sometimes squalid, appearances.

With some difficulty and with limited success, I have tried to preserve the core of my spirituality. I was aware that I had to keep a light burning in my soul, to treasure the insights and experiences which had enriched my life. Others of my brothers reacted more violently – they would perhaps say that they acted more radically, more honestly, more courageously. That was their right and I understood their reasons, but I felt constrained to negotiate a more tortured path.

So, being determined to attend some regular Eucharistic gathering on Sundays, I was anxious to find a little church where I could pray without fretting and where I could feel safe from rejection under a blanket of anonymity. I was living at the time in an area where Father Haseler was the parish priest but the bullying treatment he had metered out, still touched raw nerves. His church and his form of religion were off my list and I could not return to my home-base at St Joseph's in Neutral Bay. The parishioners there would be, I feared, unwelcoming and judgmental. I may have been wrong.

St Mary's Cathedral, the sacred ground where I had been ordained, could not provide the tranquil space I sought. The cardinal and his clergy knew me and I knew them. The grandiose, pseudo-Gothic building, full of ghosts and shadows, reduced a worshipper to the dimensions of a gnat. There was static in the loud-speaker system and for me it was full of short-circuiting electrical sparks. Too many memories.

I needed a place to worship where I would not feel harshly judged and under threat. I did not expect to be welcomed. At that early stage, I was feeling like an outcast. I needed a sacred space where I could kneel down the back, out of range, and receive spiritual nourishment from the Scriptures. A place where I could approach the table of the Lord discreetly, without rejection, and if I was especially lucky, where I might hear a half-decent sermon. For some years to come, while waiting on the line to receive the blessed bread, I would anticipate refusal. There was always the possibility of some scrupulous, half-mad or black cleric, curious enough to observe who was receiving his bread, crazy enough to withdraw his Master's offer and move on without sharing the sacrament of life and healing with the needy. Those men existed and still do. I was ready for them.

For some few years I attended Sunday Mass at St Patrick's in the city, where the Eucharist had been first celebrated in the convict colony. The church and the community there were not on fire with a spirit of modernity or liberation. Confessions were still processed, in the old fashioned way, around the clock – in and out, recitation of formulas, three Hail Mary's for penance and an act of contrition. The Blessed Sacrament was exposed for adoration in a sparkling monstrance, though no longer around the clock. People spoke in whispers, candle-sticks glittered and altar bells tinkled. The changes in the liturgy inspired by the Second Vatican Council, had been half-done and half-heartedly. Sunday Mass was on the hour, every hour. Anonymous Christians moved in and out routinely, without frills. It was a spiritual fast-food outlet in the city – not very nourishing, but ideal for those too busy to get involved and for those of us on the outer perimeter of orthopraxis and orthodoxy.

Creeping in through the open door of St Patrick's on Sunday mornings was like entering a damp cave. A collection of yellow, low-powered bulbs fought to emit soft rays of light. It was a sombre atmosphere with shadowy corners in the long, narrow body of the interior. Here was a place to hide and to worship. I felt safe and at home, in the corner, at the back. In those early days when I was fragile and scratching scabs, St Patrick's suited me well. Some years later I began to feel at home in the Church at Northbridge where my friend, Neil Brown, was the much loved parish priest and where he celebrated the Eucharist on Sunday mornings. He had made an art-form of inclusion and acceptance. He listened, he heard what was said, but never probed or judged. Later again, I began to attend the Jesuit parish at Lavender Bay where, contrary to the rules of Rome, they sometimes invited me to read. I felt a bit uneasy, but what the heck! I liked Father Peter Quinn. He was not complicated by rules and regulations, by the decrees of the Council of Nicea, or of Chalcedon, by Trent or by Vatican pronouncements. He was a believer and a free spirit. Like St Paul, he would make up his theology and his vision of Christ as he went along. God had given him his Spirit of freedom and Peter was intent on spreading it abroad. Later again, I began to attend St Mary's at North Sydney, always in the hope that Daven Day SJ or Michael Kelly SJ, would be there to nourish me and satisfy my spiritual cravings.

Gradually over the years, I settled into a routine and found my level as a silent layman in the pews. I trod gently – I did not want to interfere or draw attention to myself. I had left the institution behind. I had my own thoughts and I was careful not to be gathered back into her crushing embrace.

chapter thirty two

1977

FACING THE MUSIC

A fter Adele had returned to Toulouse at the beginning of July, leaving me alone in my flat at Epping, I had to face an unpleasant job which had been following me around like a swarm of bees, as I went about my life, shopping, attending lectures and turning up each day to earn my weekly pay-packet. I was still in a poor physical condition. I had skin rashes, headaches and chronic diarrhea – sure signs of chronic anxiety.

A few weeks after she had left me, I drove out of Sydney, round the bends and over the hills of the south coast, to a little fishing community. Even though Adele had not as yet made a decision to return to Australia, I had to share with my parents the decision I had made. I had postponed talking with them, dreading this filial task, but they had to be included. They deserved to know where I was heading. My life at that time would have been for them an open register on which they could read the details of my turmoil. I assume they had been expecting the worst. But I had to tell them myself.

I had spent most of my life away from home and I was not accustomed to sharing bad news with my parents, or they with me. Problems were kept to ourselves. There was nothing to be gained by opening up a Pandora's Box and causing unnecessary worry. As far as I could tell, I had not caused my mother and father any anxiety. Though now that I have experienced what it is like to be a father of a twelve-year-old boy and of a teenager, I imagine they had had sleepless nights and second thoughts about my removal from the family at such a tender age. We had never spoken about that rupture. I had known the path of my life's journey since I had been a young boy and as the years progressed, they had been so far removed from where their son had been, geographically, spiritually and educationally, that it was pointless worrying them about any day-to-day doubts or problems. I am sad to admit that, though they were precious to me, I'd grown up in their absence.

As you already know, during my years of training, the muftis at Manly had marked me down as a risk. They had told me that I appeared to be too close to my family to be able to survive comfortably as a priest. I had to be more aloof, more distant, colder. I had left my family behind and now the life inside the club was all that really mattered. I did not understand what on earth they were talking about. I was away, far away from my family. I did not see myself as particularly close to anyone. I thought I had been thoroughly weaned in the seminary process. At that stage, I had survived more than ten years in the seminary on my own. Anyway, I had thought that being close to my family would have been a good thing and that that was how we all should have been.

I have since come to realise what my superiors meant and I accept that they were right. I was one of those men who looked for affection, who thrived in the comfort of a home, who needed his mother and father, his brother and sisters. I was destined to be unhappy in a single bed, without a family, in the antiseptic atmosphere of a presbytery or a seminary. I had tried hard to sublimate my needs and desires, but it was not working. Despite the years I had spent away from Florence Street and despite the distance which had separated us, I was still close to my parents and siblings. Despite what the system had set out to do, they were important to me and I loved them. The last thing I wanted was to disappoint them. Now, I could sense they were deeply troubled by my predicament. Both were simple, hard-working people; both uneducated in any formal sense. My father was illiterate and although my mother could read and write, she had been taken from school for domestic duties when she was twelve or thirteen years old. They were good people – both deeply involved in the parish at Neutral Bay and later at Milton on the south coast, where their friend, Father Pat Kenna, was the much loved parish priest. They were well-known to bishops and clergy.

My father (everyone called him "Jim") had come to Australia from the West Country – from Galway county. His father had sent him and his younger brother Jack to the end of the world while they were only teenagers. He had laboured hard as a waterside worker and had seen tough times. A union man all his life, Jim was honoured when Big Jim Healy, the president of the Waterside Workers Union, or a member of the clergy, especially a monsignor or a bishop, stopped to talk to him. Those were the days when we showed respect to the bank manger, the local doctor, the solicitor and when we bowed humbly in the presence of authority.

My mother was not so easily overawed. She had grown up in a typical anti-Catholic family and had converted to the Roman faith at the time of her marriage to Dad, at the age of eighteen. Because she had bent her neck to that "Papist nonsense", her English mother, her cranky father and a few of her seven siblings had ostracised her for some years after the marriage. Those were the days when Catholics were second-class citizens and proud to be so. The wounds healed in time and the scars eventually disappeared.

My mother used to make cakes for the nuns and visit the sick and housebound in the parish. In our small semi-detached home in Cremorne, she entertained members of the clergy, especially of the Irish variety. Though they could not afford it, she and dad paid for the four of us to attend school with the nuns in Neutral Bay. They went to Mass and communion every Sunday and put their pittance on the collection plate.

They were simple folk. Neither of them had been blessed with a middle name at their birth (at the time of their marriage in Quambone, they were just "Jim Geraghty" and "Lucy Wiseman"). Later in life I would mix with men whose parents must have entertained high hopes for their sons and who had conferred grandiose middle names on their children – sometimes two. My parents would follow the trend and give middle names to their five children – *Michael John, Maureen Yvonne, Christopher James, Sean Francis and Colleen Mary* – but just ordinary names for each of us. They made sure we were all baptized, neatly dressed, ironed and pressed and never hungry. Throughout their lives my parents were plain "Jim and Lucy Geraghty" – both workers who had survived and raised a family on hard labour and love.

There were difficult times ahead of me – or at least I thought so as I drove down the coast and prepared to discuss my change of plans with Jim and Lucy. I should not have allowed any tawdry concerns to torment me. I should have known my mother and father would be by my side in a crisis. It was only later that I learnt that in defence of her son's happiness my mother had confronted the red cardinal in his den and demanded some real response to the persecution and bullying to which she thought I had been subjected. In the end, the weeks of anxiety and the postponement of the inevitable would reveal more about me than about them. My anxieties reflected my own lack of insight, my insecurity, my failure to appreciate the openness, the compassion of my earthy parents. I had been taken from home before I had leant what my parents could teach me. I had not yet understood that some people love you even when you fail. It was a lesson they never taught me in the seminary. The message I had imbibed was that no matter what I did, it was never really enough and if I failed to please, I would be rejected.

I spoke to Mum and Dad after dinner. They had been expecting to hear from me. I was apprehensive. The right words were hard to find. I told them I had no intentions of returning to the seminary, that I was planning to continue in my job at the Health Commission, at least for a few years. I had started to study law at night and I wanted to complete my three-year course, and perhaps afterwards become a barrister – whatever that meant. It was only a dream. I also told them that the director of the Institute in Paris, where I had been studying, had thrown me a life-line. I had been invited to return to Paris to present my research material as a second doctoral thesis and to lecture in the Liturgical Institute. I was prevaricating.

I had to come to the nitty-gritty. I told them I did not see myself living alone, that my friend Adele had returned home to France and that I was missing her. It probably came as no surprise that I hoped against hope, that she would "very soon" agree to my proposal of marriage.

My parents sat in silence, beside one another, holding hands, while I shared with them. They listened attentively. Then they told me that I had to decide for myself on the direction of my life; that their only real concern was that I would be happy. It was not natural to live alone, they said. They wanted me to believe that they understood what I was going through and that they had known I had been travelling rough for some years. My news had come as no surprise. I was thrilled when my uneducated and proud Catholic father shook his grey curly head, looked me in the eyes and said –

"Well, Chris, you've given many years of your young life to
the Church. Now it's time for yourself."

I went to bed that night singing in my head and rejoicing in my heart. I could not sleep for hours savouring my unexpected welcome home. I had needed to hear what they had to say. These little people had much to teach the clergy and a good deal to teach their son.

As I was driving down the coast in that winter of '77 to visit my parents at Manyana, I should have remembered the generous letter my mother had written to me a year earlier. She had been right. It was going to work out in the end. At least, so far, so good.

chapter thirty three

1977
BOOK YOUR TICKET

Adele had left for an indefinite period. From the day of her departure on Friday 1 July, I was pestering her for an answer to my proposal. The local postman had begun to torment me. One of my anxious letters would dawdle all the way to Toulouse, taking seven or ten days to arrive, beg a reply (which might take an eternal day or two to write) and wander back through the winding corridors of the mail to my post box at Candy Street, Epping. Several times a day, in the nervous expectation of a blessing from Toulouse, I would open the mail-box and look hopefully inside. But it was always empty.

How was I to know that Adele was not at the address in Toulouse which I had carefully traced on the envelope, that she was slaving away, cleaning and polishing her parents' holiday flat on the Costa Brava? There was no landline connection in her parents' house in Spain – she had to walk through the tangle of narrow streets, down the hill to the fishing harbour to find a public telephone. I knew nothing of where she was or of what she was doing. With long periods of silence, with time to ruminate, to smoulder, to imagine the worst, to entertain doubts and become uncertain and unsettled – waiting was agony.

If Adele eventually accepted my offer and agreed to marry me, there were inevitable formalities to attend to. There would be arrangements to be made – time-off from work, travel ticket to purchase and worst of all, I might have to petition the Pope in Rome for permission, to by-pass the priestly promises I had made in 1962 at my ordination and that process might take a little time. Rome could be excruciatingly slow. (I had heard that when the recent German Pope arrived in Rome, he was horrified when he saw the pile of unanswered letters which had accumulated over the centuries. He immediately imported a team of Germanic efficiency experts to clear the backlog. Under his orders, they worked day and night for months, gradually reducing the heap, opening mouldy envelopes and doing their best to deal with the many complaints. After many months they came to the bottom of the stack, picked up the last tattered envelop, opened it with great care and found St Paul's *Second* Letter to the Romans. A member of my class of '62, would wait for years for an answer to his letter seeking a release on parole from the Vatican, though another classmate, a high profile priest who used to be a personality on Sydney radio – one with considerable influence – would receive his papers in a matter of weeks. Rome was unpredictable, but generally slow.)

I would have to renew my passport and arrange injections with the local doctor to satisfy the French bureaucracy. I had the law course to finish, with examinations in mid-September, and I would have to start three new course subjects in early November. My law degree was going to be our financial lifeline, so I needed to keep the studies bubbling along.

Marrying in Sydney would have proved difficult for both of us, so we never contemplated that possibility. Adele would be away from her family and friends, and from her home town, and I would have the problem of involving my family and close friends in a complicated situation, that many would have found unpalatable. I was going out on a religious limb but I didn't want to embarrass my Catholic friends unnecessarily, or put them in an awkward position. Some might have felt bound in conscience to refuse my invitation to attend the wedding, while others would probably have attended but with some hesitation. Given we were going to marry (and that was not yet decided), there was never any question that the ceremony would take place in Toulouse.

Waiting was torture. There was no Toulouse telephone to ring Adele, no neighbour to take an urgent message and my phone at Epping remained mute. Not a word for two weeks in July. I waited, mad with impatience, in the hope that Adele might be moved by some inner urge to dial my number. I was constantly calculating the time on the clocks in Toulouse. Too late. Perhaps not. She would be in bed. Maybe not.

At last an envelope appeared in my box. It was from Spain, from the fishing village of San Feliu. Only a short message on the back of a postcard. Since her return to Europe, she had been depressed. Her father had insisted she go with him to their place on the Costa Brava, to clear her mind and work through her state of confusion by washing floors, blinds, windows, patios, walls, by wall-papering and redecorating three bedrooms, the kitchen, the corridors, a bathroom and a sitting room. She was planning to return to Toulouse in early August. In the meantime, she was lost in activity, trying to put her recent Australian experience back into perspective – and me with it.

Then at long last, after an interminable wait in the ante-room of hell, Adele made her appearance on the end of a Spanish telephone. The twin purr had sounded early in the morning and woke me from a disturbed sleep. She stood in a public telephone box on the Rambla in downtown San Feliu and received an earful of my anxiety. My impatience flowed out across the coaxial cable to the other side of the globe and descended through the earpiece into Adele's troubled heart. She had not received any of my desperate letters. The French postman had begun to deliver them in Toulouse the day after she had left to travel to Spain. Her mother had sent a Spanish note via her fierce aunt in Barcelona, that a *Cristobal* had already sent four letters from Australia. Adele's father was amused that his pagan daughter was receiving messages from someone on the other side of the world called *Christ*. His amusement would overflow into horror when this anti-clerical Spaniard found out who I was and what I had done for a living. But Madame Rodriguez had refused to trust the French and the Spanish mail services, preferring to keep the blue aerograms safe on the mantle-piece in Toulouse, until her daughter's return. We talked until the money ran out. When the Spanish operator eventually severed our connection, my future still remained in the balance. Adele was still thinking. I was to learn over the ensuing years that this woman thought a lot and that she couldn't be rushed.

Then on Monday 8th August, again in the early hours of the morning, she rang a second time and woke me. She had come to a decision. We would be married in October. I was to come quickly. A bomb of excitement exploded in my brain. Juices of joy oozed through my veins. The sun shone in a miraculous sky and the people in the streets around Epping were dancing and smiling. I had feared this call would never come. My feeling of anxiety, which until then had smothered all reason and my terrible foreboding, instantaneously turned into a surge of overwhelming happiness. The world was transfused with delight. Adele told me she was returning to Toulouse, to her home in the *Place des Carmes*, to pack and wait for me. The panic which had dominated my life since she had left Sydney, the feeling of powerlessness, of having no way of influencing her decision when we were apart, had suddenly disappeared.

This joyful telephone call had also come from Spain. As it turned out, I had spoken to Adele sometime *after* she had written a letter to me, but *before* that letter had arrived at Epping. So a few days after our telephone conversation during which she had invited me to come to a wedding, I received the letter she had written *before* our conversation.

"While I am working hard, I am also thinking of you and me;
I have not come to a decision yet, but I will soon, I promise."

When I opened this letter and read it, I was not thinking straight. Her words reignited a high level of anxiety. Had she changed her mind since we had spoken? Was she being tormented by uncertainty? I was back in limbo until I could accept that she had said "yes" definitively and unambiguously. Instead, she was telling me of the misgivings she was feeling about meeting with someone in Toulouse she had known for six years, a young man who had been deeply in love with her and whose affection had not cooled while she had been away in Australia. They had made some plans to migrate to Australia where he would practise as a medical doctor. She had not forgotten the memories they shared and she had many pressures bearing down on her. "I need a few more weeks".

But the question had already been decided, hadn't it? Or had it? Was there someone in Toulouse ready to make a better offer? My prospects could have hardly been worse. I was far away, full of uncertainty and unable to exert any influence on what was happening in the south of France. Eventually I was able to persuade myself that the woman I had met by accident in Germany had agreed, against all odds, to return to Australia and be my partner for life. I was content. Now I just had to purchase an economy ticket to Toulouse.

chapter thirty four

1977
A LETTER OF RESIGNATION

Early in September 1977, and without the usual formal trappings of a letter addressed to a cardinal ("obedient and devoted servant", or "humbly kissing the sacred purple"), I posted a note to the Cathedral to inform head-office that I was on my way.

"Your Eminence,

I promised you I would write when the time came. Now is the time. Recently I visited Fr Eugene Hogan to seek a dispensation from my clerical way of life and its obligations. There is much that could be, and perhaps should be, said but unfortunately while you and I share faith, we live in two totally different worlds … I want to live without the worries and the hassles which have been part of my life for so long … I do not believe that the Lord demands, or that he is honoured by the stresses of the clerical life as I have experienced them. I regard them as quite un-Christian and contrary to the Gospel. I prefer to be my own person, and the Lord's, rather than common property …

I remain,

Yours faithfully, …"

Some few days before I forwarded this letter of resignation, and within days of Adele's agreement to share her life with me, a young priest, Father Mark, who had been one of my students had taken his own life in the presbytery in Auburn. He had been a priest for all of thirteen months and as he died, a young girl in his first parish was expecting his son. I remember Mark well. He had been an awkward young man, rather too serious and inflexible, who had been ostrasiced and bullied by his fellow seminarians. I had watched him as he hovered on the periphery of peer groups, longing to be accepted, seeking to be part of the common life, finding it too difficult to break the simple code of entry. He made me think of my own days in the seminary.

For many of us, the path out of the priesthood and away from the celibate life, was pitted with cruel and painful decisions.

chapter thirty five

1977
PERMISSION PLEASE

B ut it's not so easy to throw off our past and change into new clothes. Recently a senior priest of the Newcastle/Maitland diocese took a courageous life-changing decision when he divested himself of the three, thick, Latin volumes, Summa Theologiae Moralis, written by the Roman moralist, Bernard Nolden. Year after year, it had been used as a textbook by our Moral Theology teacher. This monumental work with all the fine hairy distinctions, all the nuanced ethical positions of St Alphonse Ligouri, all the refined niceties of Jesuitical and Redemporist opponents, with all the varieties of excommunications, the long lists of offences against each of the ten commandments and the five cardinal virtues – a veritable treasure-trove of legal casuistries was the work on which we all cut our moral teeth.

After he had thought and prayed long and hard, the old priest finally decided that his dusty volumes were surplus to requirements. Although he had not opened them for about fifty years, certainly not since the Second Vatican Council, it had not been an easy decision to part with the source of all the moral theology he had learnt. Removing them from his library shelves was like finally accepting that the world had moved on and that the glib answers he had been taught as a boy-priest, no longer seemed so obvious and beyond question.

Finally, he had taken his Nolden down, put a few other exhausted items in his boot – a few starched collars, two treadless tyres, an old kettle, a heap of twisted barbed wire, a faded picture of the Sacred

Heart – drove to the local tip and unloaded his rubbish on top of the pile of other people's junk.

A few days later, a ring on the presbytery bell. One of the local members of the Legion of Mary was at the door holding a heavy plastic bag in her hand.

> "Father, I was dumping some rubbish at the tip yesterday and rescued these valuable books from the pile. Someone has thrown them away. As you'll see, they're in Latin. I think it's Latin and no one else I know reads Latin. I'm sure you can make use of them."

She handed the bag to her parish priest and left. It's not so easy to get rid of your past.

For a moment I hesitated. Many of my fellow priests, some of my friends and classmates, had bowed the head and humbly approached Rome with their begging bowl, seeking permission to marry. Did I need to follow that path? Perhaps I would be fooling myself if I thought that I could make my own decision and, without serious repercussions, throw off the chains of the past.

This highly structured and bureaucratic institution had traced its origin to a wandering storyteller in Palestine. Through the centuries it had gradually established an elaborate system of rules, an extensive hierarchy of officials, a stable of lawyers and public servants, a portfolio of rites and rituals and a complex battery of power handles and control levers. This *one, holy, catholic, apostolic* organization claimed, in the name of that ancient preacher, to exercise control over the lives, the thoughts, the desires, the impulses and actions of hundreds of millions – and over me.

After years of isolation in the desert and a vigorous training program, the institution had inducted young men into the prestigious club of celibate priests forever. Men, like me, had been oiled and consecrated with the indelible mark of Holy Orders. We had been given the power to forgive peccadillos and horrendous crimes, to *transub-stantiate* bread and wine to make Christ present among us and to preach with authority, provided that we agreed to live apart, like marble angels on pedestals.

As part of this celestial world, I had gone ahead, eyes closed, ears pinned back, without a care in the world. But it soon became plain to me that the gentlemen of the Vatican had demanded a high price for admission to their ranks – children forbidden; the joy of a shared bed renounced; the thrill of being held in someone's arms and the comfort of another's company at dinner, at a dance, in the theatre – all were denied. We had to turn our backs on the consolation of a shared life – though the creator had made all his living creatures male and female, with powerful urges which were designed to drive them together. At the time it had looked so easy. In the name of Jesus the homeless preacher, the organisation had laid a celibate burden on callow youths and decreed that there could be, that there would be, no exceptions. Whatever the future held, a decision made in ignorance at the beginning of a young man's life, would determine his deep-down human existence and well-being to the grave.

Then the institution decided that it could make the odd exception. It could permit, for example, married Anglican ministers to function within the Church as ordained priests. It had the power and when it chose, the system would exercise its power in favour of the seriously maladjusted cleric (though sometimes it would refuse to use its power, leaving the tortured soul to dangle). The Church in Rome could dispense and permit the impermissible. But a man could not set himself free before God. His friends could not do it – not even his local Christian community had the power. But a faceless, celibate gentleman in Rome could do it. A bureaucrat, a clerical cockroach in some Vatican corridor, had exclusive control of the magic wand.

For a brief period, Rome relaxed its tight grip on the lives of its clerics and begun, albeit reluctantly, to hand out dispensations to those she thought were demented, sex-starved members of the clergy or those seriously psychiatrically disturbed. The Vatican wanted to regularise these priests' illicit situation, but only those relationships which some of them had established with members of the opposite sex. The taut chain was loosened by half an inch or two. Then suddenly, without warning, the chain was drawn tight again. The men in Rome were again turning the screws clockwise, to close off the drizzle of Vatican permissions. They returned to their policy – "wear the collar or die in sin". Celibacy was something some priests took to hell with them.

In 1977, Rome was handing out dispensations sparingly and slowly. The legal men in the Holy City, with power conferred by God, saw themselves as sub-contracted gate-keepers of compulsory celibacy, as the imperial guards of the indelible seal of ordination. But even when these faceless functionaries were working at their maximum level of compassion, extracting a dispensation from the Curia was as difficult as it had been for a refugee to extract a permanent visa from John Howard's Government. It would take years, maybe three years or more and in the meantime, applicants could go mad.

I had been trained from an early age to seek permission – permission to go to the toilet; permission to start; to stop; permission to speak; permission to enjoy myself; permission to attend a marriage or a funeral (often refused); permission to be sick; to consult a doctor; to have a rest or to write a letter. I had been subject to authority almost all my life. In a world where good order, tidy minds and rooms, neat answers, where conformity and military spick and spanness took priority – a system of permissions and refusals was essential.

I had been in my final year of primary school when I received the call. It was a sticky summer morning in Sydney, at St Mary's Cathedral. The call had come from on high, from Cardinal Norman Thomas Gilroy. I had placed a fatal tick in the box on Brother Spitball's form, to indicate I was interested in becoming a Marist Brother and a teacher. But even though I had served him as his altarboy from the age of eight (every morning, winter and summer, in the early hours of the morning, walking with my sister, Maureen, the hilly mile back and forth to St Joseph's Church, Neutral Bay, before breaking our fast in the kitchen at Florence Street and returning to school for the day), Father John Lander refused my request for a character reference. He said he had had his eye on me; I was a good prospect; I was going to train for the priesthood; he would make an appointment to see the Cardinal. Whoa! The Cardinal! The Priesthood! That was better than being a brother, or the Prime Minister. Nothing was better than being a priest. What a privilege! In my wildest dream I had never imagined that I would be chosen – me. I was blown away and had to rush home to let my parents know.

Within a few weeks, in short pants, I was catapulted into the junior seminary. Twelve years later I was touched by Cardinal Gilroy's soft hands and transformed into a priest. It was a time of supernatural achievement, with all the pagan ritual trappings of triumph and success.

My simple, faithful parents were puffed with pride. I had felt important – and powerful now that my hands were oiled, with my soul indelibly marked forever. My tiny world was complete and I was only twenty-four. I was innocent, ignorant, isolated and as I had been for twelve years, for the whole of my adolescent years, on a pedestal.

Faced with Adele's acceptance, what was I to do? To cover all bases I decided to make some tentative enquiries about being released from my clerical harness. I drove to Ashfield to visit a Vincentian priest who was the officer-in-charge of unpleasant applications and the prosecutor with a commission to prepare the appropriate Vatican dossier. He advised me that I would have to file a detailed summary of my life from birth and complete a number of documents. With an air of satisfaction, the Vincentian Dispensations Officer (the DO) recounted, in abbreviated form, the story of a few of his more notable successes. He had helped a number of escapees, identifying some of the hapless applicants who had been dealing with him in secret. To encourage me, he provided some details of their complicated lives and with all the seriousness of a weather man, he tried to forecast whether they would be successful or not. Like Ricky Ponting, he was proud of his strike rate. This first encounter was unsettling for someone with a paranoid character and a jaundiced view of the clerical rumour-mill.

Father Eugene Hogan handed me three roneoed sheets of paper which I had to complete. The first page was a form letter addressed to the "Most Holy Father" – the Pope, no less –

> "Humbly prostrate at the feet of Your Holiness, I beg to
> submit this Petition for a dispensation from all the obligations
> of Sacred Orders, including that of celibacy".

I was obviously not addressing the itinerant preacher of Palestine. This was someone of imperial status – a Byzantine emperor, the King of England, a Hollywood movie star or the Brownlow medalist from the AFL.

The letter continued –

> "We both, therefore, most earnestly request the favour of a
> dispensation from Your Holiness, for the peace of our
> conscience and the salvation of our souls and also, for the
> good example and edification we must show to our children.

> We are living in a distant city where our marital status is, or
> will be almost entirely unknown – except for some priests and
> our relatives, and very few, very discreet friends.

> We will take all possible means to avoid any unfavourable
> comment or scandal."

I have tried, without a great deal of success, to dredge up from my
imagination a portrait of the gentleman who drafted this daffy epistle.
I can't move beyond the image of a short, fat, oily, groveling, snivelling
flunkey. The scary aspect of this draft request is the importance which
the author, and the Vatican, placed on secrecy and the avoidance of
scandal – reflecting overtones of the covering-up of the exploits of
paedophile priests. I would have to change the wording on this lunatic's
letter if only to make allowance for the fact that Adele was a non-
believer. She was not seeking any favour from His Holiness and in
these peculiar circumstances, she had no concern for the peace of her
conscience or the salvation of her soul. Perhaps this had nothing to do
with the salvation of my soul. In addition, there were (as yet) no
children and we were not living in any distant city. At this stage, the
potential application was not looking good.

What was this pious crap about needing a dispensation *for the good
example and edification we must show to our children*? What planet did
these old men inhabit? They already knew (and I did not) of the
international scandals of paedophilia, which could harm the ecclesial
bride of Christ, and they were sitting on their hands. What other
scandal was worth talking about? Had she been informed, Adele would
have had no intention of taking any "means" at all to avoid such
nonsense.

My letter to the Pope had to set out a brief summary of the
circumstances and reasons for my special petition – this part was left to
the writer's discretion. Then I was to conclude my letter as follows –

> "Begging this favour from Your Holiness, and your apostolic
> blessing upon us both, I am, most Holy Father, your obedient
> and devoted servant in Christ."

The form letter seemed a touch craven. I didn't imagine I could have
truthfully described myself as the Pope's devoted or obedient servant.

Maybe once upon a time, but no longer. Anyway, I thought he was supposed to be my servant.

I turned to the second page. It was entitled *"In Causis de Sacra Ordinatione Eisque Oneribus"* (In Proceedings dealing with Sacred Ordination and Its Duties), and it set out categories of personal details and information about the "petitioner". The Pope would want to know my name, of course; my date of birth; where I went to school; when and where I was baptised and confirmed; what seminary I had attended; when I had first entered the seminary; when I had received the various minor orders (acolyte, porter, exorcist); when I had become a sub-deacon, a deacon, a priest and where I had worked as a priest. The Pope would be keenly interested in these facts from one of the thousands of faceless, needy petitioners. But I did not have to attach any photographs of myself in my clerical gear, or personal character references and there was no need for a Justice of the Peace to affix his signature. The legal documents would come later.

Good Pope John was dead. Rumour has it that he used to read some of these applications himself, endorse his agreement on the documents and add a few warm, compassionate, pastoral comments. But he had gone to God and the cold bureaucrats of the Curia were at their desks with orders from above to close the flood-gates. Many of those lost priests who were refused a papal decree were destined, after years serving in the inner-sanctum, to live their lives in sin outside the camp and then to be tipped into hell for all eternity. These poor sods were to be sacrificed in the empty hope that other unhappy, disgruntled priests, would keep their heads down, their pants on, their shoulders to the wheel and the show on the road.

The third piece of paper which was handed to me dealt with the petition to be dispensed from my promise of celibacy. Father Hogan's useful hints suggested that I provide information about any undue influences or pressures which had been exerted on me as a student; my attitude in the seminary to my studies, the regime and discipline; the difficulties I had experienced with studies and discipline; the difficulties I had had with chastity, as well as the advice and counselling I had received; what instructions I had received on the nature and the difficulties of celibacy; any difficulties I had had with the moral teaching of the Church and with the authority of the Church;

and finally, problems with faith. There was much to be said, which the men in the Vatican would hate.

My petition also had to identify the names and addresses of treating medical practitioners, written statements from them; the name, religion, marital status of any "partner"; and details of children conceived in sin and born to us, including their "date and place of baptism". I was not under the care of any treating medical practitioner at the time and my proposed partner was, of course, "Adela Rosa Rodriguez"; she was a heathen and a spinster. At least that was not going to cause a problem.

I had to provide details of the persons to whom my marital state or otherwise might be known. Finally, two warnings were added –

"In the event of this dispensation being granted, every care must be taken to avoid scandal or unfavourable comment."

"This Petition needs to be detailed, complete, honest and sincere. And very accurate – at a later stage it will be necessary to swear to the contents, in general and in detail."

With some pain I began to construct a summary of my life. I wrote about my parents, each in turn; at some length about my sister Maureen and my reaction to her death; about my brother Sean and sister Colleen. I began to tell my story, but I was quickly losing interest. The process seemed too laborious, too legalistic and surreal.

Before he too deserted the ranks, Father John Davoren (who, as you might remember, had spent some time with Eddy Campion and me in Paris), had been the secretary of the Australian Catholic Social Welfare Commission. In answer to my request and out of friendship, John prepared a six-page, handwritten, confidential, statement of support, to accompany my proposed application. In this statement, John traced a brief history of my journey through the seminary and in the priesthood.

"Christopher is a most conscientious person whose conscience may be overly strict. He has spent so much time in ecclesiastic institutions but does not seem to have learnt how to defend himself against their worst aspects … It is … unfortunate that he has been the victim of what he perceives as a number of serious injustices. It would appear to most observers that his perceptions have been basically valid."

In his statement John told the Pope that as a junior member of the seminary staff, my superior (who was generally considered as "extremely neurotic"), had become "very spiteful towards those he disliked for any reason, however trivial". He dealt briefly with the period after my return from Paris informing the Pope that almost immediately, I had come under fire from some theologically disabled priests and bishops. Rumours and the clerical gossip vine – it had been a painful and destructive time. Two bishops, he said, had secretly banned me from their dioceses (make that three). I had come to public notice once again when a faceless cleric had altered a number of articles I had written for *The Catholic Weekly* and incorporated his own extensive changes.

> "Again the authorities gave no significant sign of concern and appeared only interested in Christopher withdrawing his objections to the treatment he had received, so that "peace" could be restored."

Father Davoren told the Pope that it was obvious that Geraghty had been treated "unjustly."

In conclusion, my clerical supporter recommended that Rome grant the permission I was seeking and, as if to add salt to the raw wound, he suggested that I might be assisted by an expression of gratitude for my "zealous work" as a Catholic and a priest "thus far". I could see the deadly serious, hard-faced men in Rome breaking into laughter.

In drafting my application, it soon became clear that my letter was not going to be the humble, submissive petition which might have encouraged the black bureaucrats in Italy to sign a dispensation. Anyway, my Holy Father in Rome would probably not have been the least interested in what I had to say. As the paperwork was being shuffled from one delay to the next, from one pigeonhole to another, I could see "RECUSATIO –NEGATIO" being written in red across the cover of my dossier.

chapter thirty six

1963-1993
TIMES WERE A-CHANGING

When he was a young energetic priest in Sydney, by a horrible misfortune some ten years or so after his ordination in 1952 and about the time of my own ordination, Father Bert fell in love with one of his pretty young parishioners and Bernadette happened to be the nubile daughter of an influential member of the right-wing of the Australian Labor Party.

Time has witnessed great changes in the Australian political scene. Now, the conservative Liberal Party is chocked with Catholics, mainly Jesuit trained from exclusive private schools, but in the late 50's and early 60's, Labor was the only political party to which any self-respecting Catholic would belong.

At the time, Bishop James Carroll was an auxiliary bishop assisting Cardinal Gilroy in the Archdiocese of Sydney and a luminary in the back passages of the Labor Party. He was certain to be displeased with Bert's situation.

Guiltily, secretively, the young couple had gone ahead to plan their future happiness. In the hope that Rome might grant him a compassionate ticket-of-leave, though dispensations were as rare as snake legs in those days and with Bernadette's help, Bert had purchased the wedding ring.

Father Bert solicited the support of his closest clerical friend and with Father Brian, he had tiptoed in to see the devious, but influential, bishop. They had high hopes that they might be able to persuade him to support an application for a special dispensation all the way from Rome. When you are in love, the whole world, even the Vatican, seems soft and romantic and membership of the Labor Party had to carry some weight. But it was 1961 and the Roman Catholic Church was still rigid in its discipline and infallible in its dogma. In those days we believed that the Church had not moved much since Jesus had ascended into heaven; that God was a terrifying judge; and that hell was a place of eternal and horrific punishment where Protestants and bad Catholics went. The little delegation, Bert and Brian, reminded the bishop that Father Tom Connolly had recently scored a Vatican pass, but from what I heard, Bishop Carroll denied this fact (though it later proved to be correct) and dispatched our two friends back to their parishes without a hope in Hell.

Even the Labor Party connections were not persuasive enough to move the bishop to action. The man with the episcopal ring and the keys of the kingdom was not ready to be as accommodating as he would later prove to be, around the time of my crisis, when another young priest informed him that he'd met the love of his life and was planning to jump overboard and swim ashore. By that stage the bishop had developed some theological wriggle-room to deal with the ever-increasing problem of desertions. But in the early 60's, when the inner lives of priests like me and Father Bert were still deeply rooted in the earth of holy submission, Bishop Carroll was toeing the party-line and playing on-side. The factory was still turning out a good product and the mass exodus of Manly priests had not begun.

The bishop was a trained canon lawyer from Rome and he knew how important the rule of law was for the good governance of the firm. In accordance with the law, he had delivered his edict – Bert was never to cast his doe eyes on the girl who was disturbing his life and loins, the girl whose father was so well known to the bishop. Under episcopal directions to vacate the parish where he had been ministering and take up an appointment in a parish far away, on the fringe of the diocese, Father Bert packed his few belongings and with a heavy heart but without looking back, he had moved west.

Some years later, in 1977, about the time when I was tormenting myself about permissions and dispensations, the same Bishop Carroll, now raised to arch-episcopal status, was confronted with a similar situation. In the meantime, he had grown old and cunning. He had had his eye on a young Sydney priest and he was grooming him for the big time. He wanted to make sure his protégé moved quickly up through the ranks of the clergy. He was bishop material, but he had met and fallen for a pretty girl in the office – another problematic union made in heaven. Like Father Bert, the young priest (let us call him *Joseph*) was in the process of deciding to resign from the clergy club and to marry the girl of his dreams. But when Bishop Carroll learnt of these plans, he was determined to prevent Father Joseph from straying off course. In the true Labor tradition, he was prepared now to do "whatever it took".

The Archbishop invited Father Joseph and his sweetheart to share a meal with him at an exclusive restaurant in Watson's Bay. He had reserved a table in the corner, in the shadows – Jimmy worked best in the shadows, unobserved. He knew how to avoid the public gaze. Nearly everything he did was surrounded with whispers and secrets and while he preferred the telephone, this situation demanded a personal appearance. He was hoping that with his soft voice and his gentle, persuasive smile, he could convince the couple to accept his compromise plan. They ate *à la carte*, drank fine wines on the Archdiocesan account and chatted. At one stage, *between the fish and the mud-cake*, the Archbishop invited Joseph's angel to dance. He had a reputation. He was an elegant, sophisticated gentleman, *à la Cary Grant*, and he had a way with the ladies. He was seeking to persuade his partner, while she was in his arms, to warm to a cunning plan he had devised. He accepted that they were in love and that they wanted to share their lives together. Unlike many of his religious brothers, this Archbishop accepted there were some forces in creation that the Church could not control. The attraction between a man and a woman was dizzying. His dancing partner told me that there on the dance floor, James Carroll offered to set her up in a soft nest somewhere in the eastern suburbs. The Archdiocese would pay the rent and Father Joseph could visit her discreetly, secretly and without complication. He could continue to wear his Roman collar, drive to the firm's offices in the city, function there throughout the day as a priest of the Archdiocese and, if he chose, and as often as he liked, return to his friend's little pad in the evening. It was a fairy story to win the heart of every romantic. I don't know whether it was true or just a used-car-salesman's trick, but to convince his partner, the Archbishop told her that he had done the same for other priests in trouble and that the law of celibacy was only a Church regulation which had come into force as late as the twelfth century. This was a new slant. I had never been told during my years of training that this celibacy business was not to be taken all that seriously.

Father Joseph's promising career would remain on track, the Archbishop's important work would continue uninterrupted and when they had had enough of grinding and rubbing, they could simply resume their independent lives as if nothing had happened. It would be an exciting interlude in the long journey of life, a memory to warm their hearts into old age. But the cunning old fox's plan never saw the light of day. The young ones thanked their host but would have nothing to do with his generous offer. His plan would necessitate Father Joseph and his beloved to live a lie. Their love for each other would have been tainted. They would never have been free to look at one another, face to face and rejoice in their union.

When Joseph and his wife told me their story, I had already moved on – and so had they. I had seen a thing or two. I was not scandalised to hear of an Archbishop, worldly-wise and wily, who could find room to step and dance within the nut-cracking system of institutional prescriptions. But I was surprised – and amused. Even within the inner-sanctum of the hierarchy, at the giddy centre of ecclesiastical power, politics trumps principle, ends can justify the means and practical considerations can overpower the dictates of heavenly orthodoxy.

Some years passed. While Father Bert had continued in his priestly ministry, experiencing who knows what tensions, his friend, Bernadette, had married and settled into suburban life, with children and a mortgage. He never forgot her but there had been no contact – no touching, no notes, no telephone calls. The world assumed that the relationship had grown dry and fuzzy like ink on blotting paper. But the girl he loved had married someone who would blur her life with sadness. At odd times she had to suppress a sudden surge of anger when she thought what life might have been if the Church had not intervened, if the bishop had supported them or if they had simply let their hearts guide them.

One day the husband had packed his belongings into boxes and left the home, forever. There had been no discussion, no warning or explanation. He had had enough.They had never been happy and as he went, Bernadette breathed a heavy sigh of relief.

In the early 90's, Bert's clerical friend who had accompanied him years before to petition the bishop, happened to hear a whisper that Bernadette's husband had summarily deserted her. Sometime later, when they accidentally met in the street, she asked Father Brian to let her old boyfriend know where she was and how she was. And he did.

Bert and Bernadette were married within weeks. No problem, no dispensation, no beg-your-pardons. Bert was not going to make the same mistake a second time. On Sunday at mass, when he announced his retirement and his wedding plans, the parishioners wished their parish priest bliss and happiness and a whip-around produced a healthy nest-egg for the newlyweds. At their simple secular wedding ceremony, Father Bert, now grey with age, put his hand in his pocket, fumbled around a little and, with a cheeky smile, fitted a wedding ring on his bride's finger. Her face broke into a radiance of joy. It was the same ring he had purchased some thirty years before, the one they had chosen in anticipation of a forbidden union.

The Archbishop was not alive in 1993 to save Bert the second time, to repeat his prohibition or to propose his compromise plan and keep the show on the road. But by then, Bert had become a senior and a more hardened performer.

In 1977, in the midst of turmoil, I was not aware that I could approach Archbishop Carroll to participate in his crafty plan to keep promising priests in service. Perhaps he would not have seen me as a man with a promising future in his Church. I did not know of his unofficial massaging of rules which would allow some members of the team to play off-side. Had I known at the time, instead of being amused as I am now and knowing myself, I would have been outraged. Some might say that this blatant example of the disconnect between an institution's public policy and its underhand machinations, was typical of the unprincipled right-wing Labor politics in New South Wales in which Carroll was enmeshed. Anyway, like Father Joseph's sweetheart, Adele was not a girl who would have countenanced the bishop's solution.

chapter thirty seven

1977
THERE ARE ALWAYS CONDITIONS

When Rome reluctantly decided that a member of its priestly caste, who was planning to defect or who had already handed in his keys and gold pass, had been sufficiently unhinged when he was ordained, or that he had been pathologically too immature at the time to make a proper decision, or that he had been under heavy pressure from his family to join the ecclesiastical ranks, or that he exhibited a sexually charged deviant personality disorder – in brief, when Rome decided that there had been something seriously wrong with the candidate at the time the bishop had placed his soft, waxy hands on his head and when all the papers had been thoroughly examined and the decision made, the Pope's little man in the Vatican signed the order and mailed out the dispensation, not to the nervous applicant, but to his bishop. But that wasn't where the matter ended. As a matter of policy, like any local council authority, the bureaucracy always attached a list of conditions to its final document. While these might have varied from year to year or from Pope to Pope, the conditions of discharge have tended to be less offensive as Rome continued to dip her virginal toe into the muddy waters of the twentieth century.

I should not pretend to any special expertise as to what conditions the Vatican attached to her dispensations. As you already know, I am an expert in the area of excommunications – I completed a six-month course on the subject at Manly and at that time, there was no course available on dispensations from Holy Orders. The subject was taboo.

Manly priests did not defect – they all stayed happily on the job. Any discussion contrary to the party-line was unimaginable.

I cannot list all the possible conditions which were imposed on successful applicants, nor can I track the history of each of the different conditions. This vast subject would make an interesting thesis for a doctorate in Canon Law. Someone might have already published his research but life is too short to care.

The standard conditions which were attached to any dispensation, seem to have been that the unfortunate ex-priest was not allowed to – attend Mass in any of his old haunts; publicly read any of the lessons in the liturgical celebration; assist in the distribution of communion or teach in a Catholic university or school. He was not permitted to serve on the parish council, or act as a catechist in the local state school. Of course, Rome could say what she liked, but it was up to the locals to obey and many parish priests were so frazzled and frantic for assistance that any half-serious pastor, would take no notice of the conditions imposed by the imperial personage across the seas. Any half-sensible pastor welcomed assistance wherever it could be found – and the situation grows worse as each year passes. Some are now discussing the possibility of welcoming ex-priests back into the ministry to "say" Masses again and to hear confessions – if ever the faithful decide to return to the shadows of the confessional.

But it was not always thus. Archbishop Thomas Vincent Cahill ordained his nephew John in the same year as Cardinal Norman Thomas had smeared the oil on my hands in Sydney. The year was 1962. I can only imagine that it would have been extremely difficult to have been a blood relation of tubby Tommy Cahill. Six years later, in that historic year of 1968 when the world was full of *The Beatles*, *The Rolling Stones* and revolution, Tommy was the official celebrant at his poor nephew's wedding in the cathedral church in Goulburn. He had been enthroned Archbishop of Canberra and Goulburn the year before and was using his own cathedral for this disreputable work. Someone had to do it and it was better to keep the shame in the family.

While it took me fifteen years to negotiate my path out of the priesthood, Tommy Cahill's nephew had been quicker off the mark. He was one of the many who, in the shadow cast by the Second Vatican Council, had charged headlong over the cliff as though possessed by the prince of demons. Rome was distributing a few dispensations and attaching what she considered, were reasonable conditions – conditions such as Jesus might have demanded if he had thought of the priesthood, of Holy Orders and compulsory celibacy.

Archbishop Thomas Cahill had been educated and ordained in Rome and had become a gifted church lawyer. Some commentators have described him as "an unspectacular conservative", pedantic, colourless, odourless in his buckle shoes, with red buttons and piping on his cassock, and a red cummerbund around his ample belly which never seemed to rattle or vibrate in fits of laughter. He was deadly serious – and a very important person. While he agreed (reluctantly) to officiate at the wedding for his nephew and his bride in his own cathedral, he insisted that the church doors had to be closed and locked and that the groom's parents (the bishop's own brother and sister-in-law) be forbidden to attend. No invitations, no guests and no celebration. The wedding of a priest was a supernatural catastrophe which had to be covered in secrecy and shame. Furthermore, the dispensation was granted on condition that Father John agreed to be banished from his home state of Victoria – not just from his parish or his diocese, where the people knew him, but from the entire state. He agreed and the happy couple was to raise their family of nine children on the other side of the Nullabor Plain.

But Uncle Tom's treatment of his nephew was not unique. Bishop Bernie Stewart of Sandhurst dealt with Father Jim and his bride Mary in the same generous manner. The bishop agreed they could be wedded in one of his churches, in the presence of two witnesses and no guests. The church had to be locked and the ceremony had to take place after sunset. The couple were informed that the "special permission" from Rome would be withdrawn if anyone was to find out the time or the place of their "unfortunate union".

By 1977, almost ten years later, when I was contemplating filling in the papal forms, dispensations had dried to a trickle. The Vatican had become concerned that priests might take advantage of her generosity and that they would depart in droves. Defection had become contagious. The disease was spreading and Rome had to take preventative steps to contain it. While she was engaged on this mission, she was also apparently revising the conditions attached to her rare permissions to "play off-side". To ensure maximum transparency, these conditions were expressed in Latin.

In 1977 and thereafter, one of the conditions set out in the dispensation was that the wedding had to be conducted *"sine pompa vel externa apparatu"* – without pomp or fanfare. Michael Harfield, a classmate of '62, married Kerry Doyle, a Miss Australia, in the chapel of Santa Sabina and a crowd of Sydney socialites had gathered to parade like birds of paradise, in their feathers and finery. The Vatican had delivered the groom's dispensation in record time, within a few months – Michael had been a media personality and had become well-known among the bunyip aristocrats of Sydney. The authorities needed to get him off their books and out the door as quickly as possible. The conditions attached to Michael's release were the least of Rome's worries and contrary to Vatican policy, the wedding went ahead amid much pomp and ceremony.

I don't know what the other conditions were in 1977. I presume the standard ones applied. The dispensation would arrive with a list of conditions, but without any congratulatory telegram from Rome – no best wishes from the diocese, no little cheque to help the happy couple on their way. It was all very clinical, very legal and covered in shame. But the standard conditions imposed by His Holiness were the least of my concerns. I had no intention of becoming re-entangled in the institutional life of the Church – reading lessons in church or distributing communion. The standard conditions would not have troubled me since I was planning a wedding overseas, in Toulouse, and the absence of guests, as well as the sunset clause, would not have caused me a moment's loss of sleep.

In September 1977, I did not know much about my future wife but she was an object of fascination. I did understand, however, that she would have found intolerable and incomprehensible any conditions the Vatican might have sought to impose on an occasion which was meant to be joy-filled. I never mentioned the subject to her.

chapter thirty eight

1977
BUGGER THEM

This was a big one – to submit to bridle and saddle, or to run free. I now had to choose and live with the consequences.

One of my clerical brothers, a former seminary student of mine, had thought that the whole Vatican permission process was a nonsense and without a care in the world, he went ahead to wed his heretic bride in his future father-in-law's backyard.

> "I was living with this left wing, bolshy female who was worldly and bright. In my own mind I had left the priesthood behind. I had made my decision. I didn't need anyone's permission to leave – I had already left. I had had a happy childhood. My parents had not made me go into that fucking seminary where most of the teachers were crazy. I was not a sexual deviant and my parents had loved me. I was not mad. So I really had no valid grounds for a dispensation. They could go to buggery. I simply refused to play the game. Going for a dispensation is like asking the referee to allow you to play offside. It's like colluding with the oppressor. They only had the power if I gave it to them and I wasn't that stupid. I never felt that I was going to Hell and I didn't believe in Hell anyway. They carry on with a lot of crap in the name of Jesus."

The decision was an easy one for him, but I was a more complex character.

In September 1977, I was on the crest of a huge wave out the back, looking down the face of an imaginary wipe-out, not knowing whether I had the courage to ride it to the beach, or whether I would be broken on the theological reef, just beneath the surface. I had only moments to decide whether I would keep paddling, or whether I would back off and wait for a gentler ride. I felt the thrill and the horror of the big wave beneath me. I hesitated and for a moment, I wasn't sure what to do. Then I took off and gathered speed.

In the end I decided to follow a side-path, away from the highway to heaven which had been made smooth by the dictates and dogmas of an institution, a highway which had been flattened by rules and permissions, by formulas and safety nets. I took a narrow, stony, hilly, pilgrim track. I decided to journey alone (as I had always really done), finding my own way, without any heavy baggage to slow me down. It is what each of us is condemned to in the end.

I had been dancing with the devil long enough. It was time to change partners and learn a different step. For too long I had followed the dictates of those who pretended, often on quite flimsy grounds, sometimes on no grounds at all, to speak in the name of and with the power and authority of Jesus. Dogmas, devotions, formulas, indulgenced ejaculations (these are not what you're thinking), divinity, sin, good and evil, this and that – it was as if they had the whole of life and reality by the throat, as if they had no problems and no doubts or second thoughts. But towards the end, when life (if it's ever going to) has to begin to make sense, when we are cleaning out our drawers and jettisoning the objects we have not used for years, when reality has to be stripped bare and when the unalloyed truths which govern human existence must emerge, like cattle from the scrub – I have found the freedom to think for myself, to accept and to reject, and the ability to glimpse the precious jewel hidden in barren ground, to see the bones buried in flabby flesh.

So I decided in the end that *they* could go to buggery. I was not going to dance to their dirge. My letter to the Pope was never sent. I had decided that the process which Rome had devised to remove unwilling priests from the payroll, was demeaning. In the course of writing my story, I began to see that the whole exercise was mad. I did not need their permission to live my life and I had more important things to do.

I had looked back long enough and it was time to look to the future. Adele had finally agreed to share her life with me. Over the telephone from Spain, she had whispered a simple "yes" and together we set about planning a wedding.

chapter thirty nine

1977
PREPARING FOR A WEDDING

No member of my immediate family was invited to our wedding. It seems strange now that I remember, but I did not even suggest to any of them that they might like to attend. I simply announced that I was leaving for Toulouse to get married.

My mother wrote one of her simple, poignant letters to welcome Adele into our family. It was dated September 18th, a month or so before we were due to exchange vows, and in it she told her daughter-in-law-to-be that she could see that her son was "tremendously happy". She introduced my sister Colleen and her family and my brother Sean, Diane (his wife at the time) and their three "beautiful children". She described herself and my father as "simple folk who are getting on in years". Her words were to-the-point as always and unusually warm.

> "Jim is seventy and rather wonderful – and a charmer. He is always busy and gets great joy in doing things about the place."

(In later life, Adele would regularly chide me for my lack of handyman's skills and for not taking more after my father. She claimed that she used to dream about marrying a man who could make things, fix things, hang pictures straight or drive a nail. In this regard, I proved a complete dud.)

It is a thrill to read what my mother thought of my father. As I remember, as a young boy, their early relationship had been rocky – disturbed by money worries, with the responsibility of four young children, upset by the death of their first-born, Michael, and by the unpleasantness created by some of the members of Mum's family. But they had weathered the storms. Over the years I had watched them grow together and for the last thirty years of their lives, they had loved one another tenderly, treating each other with gentleness. I used to watch them sitting together at Manyana, looking at a program on television in the evening, holding hands.

In her letter to my wife-to-be, my mother described the family home as "very simple but very warm and welcoming" and that proved to be the truth. Everyone was welcome in Jim and Lucy's home. There was always a lot of people coming and going in our household, cups of tea and homemade cakes. She concluded her letter by sending her love and greetings to Adele and her parents and wishing both of us "all God's choicest blessings". I was moved to tears when I came to learn of this nuptial document. My mother was a woman of few words, but she usually hit the mark.

Before the curse of the Geraghty women took her away in March 1999, there were things I needed to say to my mother. I had the bright idea of writing a letter to her, telling her what I thought of her, how important she had been to me and how much her children had loved her. Despite the images of strength she emitted to the world, she was a woman who was fragile and uncertain of her value. When I wrote to my mother, she was very ill. I sent my letter off by post and waited. Just days before her death from breast cancer, I visited her. Weak and wasted, with that distant Death look on her face, she looked up from where she was sitting in my sister's family-room. Her ghost-like eyes searched my soul as she said –

"I received your letter, Chris."

Nothing more was said. I knew she had read it and that it had warmed her heart. After the many years she and I had corresponded by letter, the idea of writing this last letter came to me as a blessing straight from the angels. It was my farewell to a woman who had been a good and generous mother.

By the end of September, the North Shore was a mass of colourful flowers – pinks, whites, purples and crimsons. Flowers were everywhere with vines cascading over fences, into the streets, flopping over verandahs and mingling together in flower beds. These colours would be gone by the time I returned with my bride from Toulouse. The world changes and the moment passes, however much we might want to freeze the experience. Loved ones die and petals drop to the ground, but the mystery of life continues. The flowers and their soft colours would reappear the next year and the next, and the world would be renewed and life would go on.

I celebrated my thirty-ninth birthday on the third of October, completed my law examinations on the tenth, arranged a four-week holiday (two with pay, two without) and flew away to Paris, on to Toulouse, for a wedding.

chapter forty

1977

THE WEDDING

In October 1977, on the twenty-second, Adele and I married in the city of the pre-Christian tribe of Volques Tectosages, the Gallo-Roman city built on the banks of the Garonne River, the capital of the Visigoth Kingdom of the fifth century, the city of Crusaders on their way to Jerusalem and of pilgrims on their journey to Santiago de Compostella, the centre of the Albigensian heresy and the home of the Dominicans where the remains of St Thomas Aquinas are buried.

I had dreamt of the hugs and kisses waiting at the end of my long trip from Sydney and there she was – smiling and radiant. The love of my life, perfect in my dazzled eyes with her smooth arms around me. Warm kisses, soft lips, silken skin.

After family greetings in a busy airport in the middle of a crush of strangers, after brother François had kissed me several times on both cheeks and squashed me in a bear-hug, we collected my luggage and squeezed tight into François' vehicle. François' ten-year-old daughter, Valerie, kept staring at me through her thick lenses, curious to see her aunty's boyfriend and puzzled to meet someone who couldn't speak proper French. I had no idea where we were going, but as we hurtled through narrow streets in the centre of old Toulouse, I was happy to have Adele by my side. After three tortuous months, I cared about nothing else.

In January 1951, while I had been packing an old suitcase in anticipation of the first of many train trips to the junior seminary at

Springwood, baby Adele had been coming, as a gift from the heavens, into the small apartment on *Rue des Prêtres* in the centre of the medieval district of Toulouse. It was providential. My future wife had been born to an immigrant family living on the top floor above the *Street of the Priests*.

Angels sang. The Rodriguez cats meowed in chorus on the roof above. Shepherds had gathered with their flocks as her auntie Rosa glowed with pride over the crib. This little person, minus her lucky teeth, had been perfect when she made her first appearance on earth. The soft, professional hands of the male nurse, Monsieur Boucaud, who was living with his family in the apartment below, had delivered baby Adela in the Age of Aquarius. Alphonse Rodriguez had summoned his neighbour to attend when his daughter, uncharacteristically, had begun to hurry her arrival. He had to roll up his long sleeves and attend to the birth of a baby girl whom they called "Adela Rosa" after her maternal grandmother "Adela" and her own mother "Rosa".

Mother Rosa had been a pretty woman in her salad days. In the photographs with her young family she appears beaming, with an open, natural smile, but her attractive features had crinkled and withered in later life. When I first met her, my mother-in-law-to-be was a tiny, nervous, worried lady with sharp features and grey hair. Dark, suffering circles framed her eyes – haunted look, like an owl. Her load was heavy, caring for her disabled grandson. It crossed my mind that Adele's mother had not laughed loudly for a long time.

While her mother spoke Catalan at home and a broken version of the French language when she went abroad to shop, Adele's father conversed in a happy mixture of French and Castilian. He was short, balding, and rather stout. A smiling man with a wink of conspiracy, a glint in his eye as if he knew everything and worried about nothing. He appeared to have an insatiable enthusiasm for books and historical magazines such as many autodidacts, who were robbed of a formal education in their youth, develop late in their lives. While he read, he smoked fat cigars one after the other which he selected from one of the many boxes secreted under his bed, hidden away from his troublesome daughter. He appeared to be a happy man – relaxed, uncomplicated, earthy and, like his daughter, facing anything just as it came. No wonder Adele was so fond of him.

As young honchos in and around Barcelona, Alphonso and his brothers were determined to resist the unconstitutional coup of the Catholic dictator and had fought on the side of the Republican Government. Like many Spaniards (but unlike the Catholic hierarchy in Spain) the Rodriguez men had harboured a bitter hatred of Franco and his regime. Having observed the scandalous partnership between the sanctimonious general and the upper echelons of the Roman Church, Alphonso and his brothers gloried in outbursts of anti-clericalism. So intense was his loathing of the dictator that Adele's father had refused to return to his homeland until the dictator had died and gone to Hell. Years later, in 1975, on hearing the exquisite news of the General's death, the eldest brother organised a reunion of Franco-haters. He became so excited in the course of his Dionysian dancing and drinking that he suffered a heart attack and died, leaving this world in an ecstasy of joy. I was marrying into an anti-clerical, revolutionary family.

The day before the wedding, at a time when all the buses and trains in Toulouse were on strike, three of my clerical friends arrived in town. From what they had said in Sydney several months before, I had half-expected two of them to turn up – three was a bonus. Father Lex Levey and Father Michael Bach had received their holy orders the same year as me. The three of us had been good friends since our days in the minor seminary at Springwood and I was happy to have them by my side on such an important occasion.

The wedding day dawned. Adele had arranged that we would be married at midday in the *Hotel de Ville* and the panic bells began to ring about 10 o'clock that morning. She had flowers to collect and she had to submit herself to the hairdresser, whom her mother used to patronise. The salon was conveniently placed a hundred metres along the narrow street, opposite her home. After she had finally escaped the attentions of the beauty salon, Adele had made her way on foot down through the Saturday shoppers to her parents' home. As the guests were gathering in front of the *Hotel de Ville*, in the vast open space at the centre of Toulouse, Rose-Marie, who was also a daughter of Spanish immigrants to France and a friend from university days, drove the two of us to *The Capitole* to meet up with the wedding guests. I gazed admiringly at my bride-to-be as she stepped from the car. She was looking radiant in her cream suit, an elegant navy-blue blouse and an ample, stylish, cream hat. Close to her beautiful breast, she was holding a bouquet of tiger lilies bound together with colourful ribbons and bows. My wife-to-be was stunning.

Adele introduced me to the deputy mayor of the city. Out of a sneaking regard for one of his better students, Monsieur Franco had agreed to officiate at her wedding. He had been the founder and the general commander of the School of Languages that Adele had attended at Toulouse University, where Rose-Marie, Brigitte, Laurence from Bordeaux, the ebullient and handsome Monique from Paris, Marie-Helene, the diminutive Martine and of course Adele, had all learnt to be simultaneous translators. The girls would later describe to me how Monsieur Franco used to preen himself and parade like a peacock in the presence of his harem of young women. In their good-humoured and knowing way, and while in full bloom, they had had no trouble keeping him at a cool distance.

We sat side-by-side, enveloped in a pair of plush red velvet Louis XIV throne chairs in the *Salle des Illustres* and listened to a brief secular monologue on marriage and the family. Huge and extravagant paintings of fierce, bloody battles, of buxom mythological figures and immense mirrors, were hanging on the walls. We sat together under a painted ceiling of peaceful, pastoral scenes. Heavily embroidered curtains framed the French windows, which opened onto balconies and looked down over the vast, paved square at the centre of the city.

Acting on behalf of the Fifth Republic of France and wrapped in a tricolor, Monsieur Franco was anxious to make this a grand occasion. His imperial bearing throbbed with the special regard he entertained for the pretty girl he had taught. My clerical witness, Father Michael, sat beside me in his beige summer suit, while Father Lex hovered uncomfortably at the back of the pack. In the circumstances, this was not an occasion which he felt free to celebrate with joy but at least he was present and I understood this as a sign of friendship.

Adele and I held hands and promised to love one another and to be faithful to each other in our hearts. I pledged, as far as it lay within my power, to make my partner happy, to work tirelessly for her, to struggle and strive, to study for her, to hold her tightly in my arms and to cherish her. To commemorate the solemn occasion, the celebrant presented us with an embossed marriage booklet and a silver medallion, which I would keep on my desk in chambers at the Bar and later on the Bench. We signed the register to seal our future and then travelled in a disorderly procession of cars, out into the countryside to a charming restaurant, to celebrate our union with our friends. At one stage, the wedding celebration was interrupted by a single message from Australia. It read "Jubilation – Felicitation – Celebration – Congratulation – Edmund Campion". It was such a nice touch. Heaven only knows how Ed came by the privileged information which allowed him to lob a message into the centre of Toulouse. His sources were faceless and as usual, well-informed.

The next day, for a few days of private pleasure, a French train carried the two of us south, to spend our first night in Carcassonne and then on towards Spain. I was beginning to enter into the unknown world of my new companion and wife. As we sped south, Adele was entertaining me with stories of her family on holidays in the Mediterranean sun.

We were making our way to her parents' flat in a fishing village on the Costa Brava. Adele's father had purchased the property while she had been with me in Australia and it had been there, that she had retreated to consider my unpromising proposal of marriage. San Feliu de Guixols was set between an exclusive Mediterranean beach, la Conqua, to the north (one which we later often visited with the boys) and another fishing village which was protected by a large fort on the headland at Tossa de Mar.

Joined to Adele, I relaxed into floating, dreamy days in a Spanish village which had long remained undisturbed. We walked the shady lanes and promenaded arm-in-arm among the locals on the provincial Rambla, as the hot Mediterranean sun was setting late in the evening. We strolled on the beach and looked in the windows of jewellery stores and fashion boutiques. To feed my young wife's shoe fetish, we shopped for footwear in a tiny shop in the centre of the old village. The shoe boxes were stacked floor to ceiling, four and six deep, leaving a tight path with irregular, teetering walls of boxes from the entrance, for the octogenarian sales-lady, dressed in Spanish black, to shuffle up and down, moving boxes in search of the requested styles and sizes. Like a competent librarian, like our Sydney solicitor in the midst of his bursting files and piles of papers on chairs and on the floor, she knew exactly where every item in her charge was to be found.

After two or three days in heaven, Adele and I packed a few essentials in an overnight-bag, boarded one of the many buses which pass between Barcelona and the Costa Brava and she took me visiting her Spanish relatives. They all wanted to see the man Adele had chosen as her life companion, the man they had heard about on the Rodriguez grapevine, the priest from the other side of the world. And I wanted to meet my in-laws and to see where Adele had come from. Aunts, her father's youngest brother, cousins, a retired American pilot who had married cousin Victoria and who had flown secret recognisance flights over Russia during the Cold War – stories and delicious scandals from both sides of the family. I had suddenly become a participant in a different world and dancing to a different tune.

Finally the train returned us to Toulouse. Adele had a few, fleeting days to whisper farewells to her brothers, her beloved father, her frail mother, to family members and close friends – Brigitte, Rose-Marie and Danny. There was luggage to pack and a few pieces of valuable antique furniture to send on ahead by ship – a beautiful, Louis XIV, in-laid desk and a stately armoire. The craftsman's hands of Adele's father had restored both to their original splendour. They would be with us throughout our married life as heart-warming reminders of her family on the other side of the world.

My new parents-in-law watched anxiously from their little window on the top floor, as François tried to start his reluctant car. François' coquettish wife, Marcelle, and Adele, teamed up with me to push for a short distance along the *Street of the Priests* before the motor grumbled back to life. We jumped in and looked back to catch a glimpse of Adele's mother at the window, half relieved, still worried and saddened, waving a farewell to her only daughter. The frail motor vehicle, packed to bursting with luggage and bodies, disappeared into the Toulouse turbulence and spluttered to the train station near the *Canal du Midi*. (This was François' first car. There was to come a time when he would own six or seven flash cars – several MGs, a Jaguar coupe, two Deux Chevauxs, English Mini-Minors, an Aston Martin – and a garage business to boot. There were prosperous days ahead of him, but, like me, he was only a penniless student at the time of our marriage.)

We landed in Sydney in the middle of November and made our way by taxi, to my bachelor pad in Epping. The few plants I had left on the balcony had survived. The lady in the flat above had offered to water them while I was away. It had transpired before I left for Toulouse that she and I had a mutual friend. As luck would have it, or as providence had arranged it, she had been a nun in Newcastle, had left the convent some months before my departure overseas and had rented the little flat immediately above mine. She was keeping company with an ex-priest, also from Newcastle, who had also recently left the ministry. As time passed, they married and settled in their home town where, like Adele and myself, they raised a family and found joy in one another's presence.

chapter forty one

1978
SEIZING EVERY OPPORTUNITY

In late 1978, a year after our wedding and despite a number of job applications, I was still employed at the Health Commission on a modest salary and struggling to meet the mortgage repayments. I was on the verge of completing my law studies. With a bit of luck and a lot of sweat, they were going to be behind me in March 1980, by which time I would be out on the highway, in the fast lane, seeking a job in the law, somewhere – anywhere. But there were no school chums I could call on, or rugby mates, or university classmates. I had no female friends in the law and most of my male friends were priests or ex-priests and no help. No half-loyal Catholic lawyer worth his spiritual salt, would raise a flag to give a spoilt priest a start in the law – or so I thought. If I could gain a toe-hold, I was confident that I could scramble up the rock-face using my enthusiasm and brute strength.

In November '78 I sought advice from a friend who had abandoned a good practice at the Bar to become a young judge. I had drafted a rather turgid letter, setting out my background, and my experience such as it was, and seeking employment in a legal firm. There was no way a public relations officer like myself could have put a positive legal spin on my application, so I needed expert advice and perhaps a leg-up. I was hoping that some firm of solicitors might take pity and offer me a start, even before I had completed my studies. I was looking for some basic legal experience as well as some professional contacts, which might help eventually when I made my mad leap to the Bar. Of course,

I was dreaming. My judicial friend studied my draft letter, re-worked it and commented on it in the scrupulous, pedantic manner which I would later come to recognise was characteristic of lawyers. he corrected a few grammatical errors and the punctuation. I was grateful when he offered to act as one of my referees. I did not have to continue to rely only on Father Bach's standard character reference.

On the back of my draft letter, my friend scribbled a list of eight firms for which he had done legal work as a barrister and to which, he advised, I should forward my application together with his recommendation. I followed his advice to the letter. I posted my letters to all eight firms and sat back expectantly, waiting for the replies to come in. I waited and waited. Weeks went by and months. No-one. Not one.

Of course, I should not have been surprised by the silence. They were all running a business and I was not going to make any of them a pile of money. I was not familiar with the ways of the world. I was still living in the world of angels and fairies, ignorant of the forces which drove business and the law. I had nothing tangible to offer them, and no plan B.

In January the following year I came across a note scribbled on a sheet of my public service memo pad, which had remained hidden for a few days on my untidy desk at Chatswood. Someone from Channel 10 was looking for me. Over my time with the Health Commission, I had had regular contact with journalists at the various television stations and I had been circulating a monthly newsletter, pumping out regular news releases on health issues and following them up with telephone calls. Richard Colville was a bit secretive on the telephone when he suggested we have lunch. The director of news, Tom Barnett, was looking for someone with legal knowledge to join his team of senior reporters (Burston, Colville and Edmundson), who presented regular special reports during the news hour. When he offered me the job, he had no idea of the width and depth of my legal prowess and I had no idea what a journalist did day-to-day or what they wanted me to do, so we were even. Here was another world about to open up, either to embrace me warmly or to swallow me. I signed a contract for one year and began my new career as a television journalist at Channel 10 in late January 1980. Money had been tight in the Geraghty household, so the marked improvement in my pay-packet each week was a joy to behold.

But by the end of the first year I was ready to move on. Twelve months was enough to realise that the controllers and manipulators of our little minds, developed programs and their news bulletins on the assumption that their viewers were almost brain-dead. Nothing could possibly be too stupid, too mundane and trivial for their audience. In my naivety, I was surprised to discover that many journalists, with a few notable exceptions, were indifferent to what was happening in the world or in their city. During the twelve months that I was in the busy newsroom at Channel 10, I never sighted a copy of a news revue, or any overseas journals, or foreign newspapers. Not once did I hear a conversation which touched on any major social issue, on any political, philosophical or religious topic. I had come out of a world of religion where religion was almost never discussed, where many of the teachers and preachers hardly opened a book, maybe never read an article in a theological journal. Why should journalists be any different?

The main topics of conversation, in the newsroom or on the road with the camera crew, made this ex-priest feel awkward and isolated. For example, we would discuss in technicolour detail how much alcohol each had consumed the night before; who had famously wrestled the news director to the ground in the local public bar; how someone had spewed his manly intake of alcohol all over the front garden or on the restaurant floor; whether the wife had complained; how she had locked the door in anger when he had arrived home as the sun was rising – and of course, who was screwing whom. The level of conversation in the newsroom was abysmal. I felt that to be a happy member of this competitive team (and after the distance I had to cover, I wanted to be part of the action), I had to assume the guise of a hollow show-pony. Alcoholic vomiting seemed compulsory. I remember a number of conversations before the evening bulletin on Fridays, about attractive discounts for journalists at city brothels. I heard a whisper that one of the occasional camera-men on the road was moonlighting after work, filming pornographic videos to pay off his mortgage. Others were meant to live by a strict code of ethics, exposed and harshly judged by us if they fell short. But journalists and their camera team were in a category of their own. It was amazing to live in the world behind the news.

I was uncomfortable in the television paddock, like a refugee who had just arrived in a strange country, without money, without the ability to speak the language and with no knowledge of the culture or geography. I was trying to survive. I had grown up in a hot-house, in a filing cabinet, and had been suddenly released into wild, cut-throat mountain country. I concede that my assessment of the glitzy world of television may have been a bit distorted. Not everyone fitted into the hedonistic culture. There were good people in the newsroom who were less conspicuous, but my sudden exposure to this heathen world was a shock and the bastards and sharks were visible.

I gritted my teeth for the twelve months and as soon as my contracted time had expired, I made my escape. I had been out of-place among the weary, bored journalists who got their evening news stories from the morning newspapers and talk-back radio. I was later amused to discover that one of the news-readers at the time (a pleasant, poised young woman who stood apart from the crowd) later accepted the difficult position as public relations officer for the internationally famous theologian and climate-change scientist, Cardinal George Pell.

After I had completed my law course in December 1980 (while I was making my appearance on the evening news bulletin), I was again on the move. Letters went out to various city firms. I was not interested in finding legal work out in the suburbs. I wanted to land a position with one of the big firms in town. I had my sights set on going to the Bar and in my ignorance, I thought that a big city firm, once I had proved myself, might feel some loyalty towards an ex-employee. I hoped that they would send me a barrow-load of lucrative briefs once I had spent a few years toiling to make a fortune for the partners. I was wrong. Again naivety and innocence prevailed. Anyway, most of my letters were ignored. But I was surprised when the Catholic lawyers at *Freehills* granted me an interview but after they had cast an eye over me, they judged me unsuitable. Who could blame them?

Three smooth partners of *Blake Dawson's* also looked me over – Cameron, Eyers and Somervaille. They were much younger than me and, as a general policy, like all the major city firms, they used to search out the top-guns graduating from the most prestigious universities and I was certainly not in that league. I had a diploma in law from some two-bit night school run by the Supreme Court of NSW and I knew nothing. Why they decided to look me up and down was beyond me, but they did and they offered me a junior position which I accepted without a second thought. I was on the ladder – on the bottom rung, willing to learn how to be an employed solicitor, ready to make large sums of money for the partners of the firm and a pittance for myself and Adele. (I should also acknowledge that the city firm of *Hall and Hall* granted me an interview and eventually offered me a job working with their senior partner. I was to catch up later with the partner who had interviewed me. As life moved on, we had become colleagues on the District Court bench. Judge Margaret and her husband Warwick, who had also been a partner of the same firm, sometimes teased me over drinks about my failure to accept their attractive offer of working alongside their senior partner, as his dogs-body or personal assistant. I was reluctant to tell them that I had heard on the grapevine that their senior partner was considered a difficult man to work for. Perhaps Margaret had hoped that an ex-priest might have had the long-sufferance and submissive attitude necessary to deal with the gentleman in question, but I had problems of my own.)

I was on the road at last. I put in three years at *Blake Dawson's* where I made some good friends and learnt the tools of the legal trade – the shortcuts, the tricks, the ethics and etiquette. I had the great advantage of good teachers who were proud of their profession. I will mention only one of them – an atheist who has since gone to God. I mention him because he was particularly generous towards me and to others on trainer-wheels. John McDarra, partner No 12, tutored me in how to act professionally in the legal world. He was the solicitor who sent me my first brief when I eventually found my way to the Bar – a brief to act for an insurance company against an employee of the City Council who had popped a haemorrhoid (one, one only) while working out in the city gym and who was claiming worker's compensation payments. The worker won and I lost.

The winding, rocky path of finding a place in the world, had eventually led me to the Bar for eight or nine years, and from there to a bench of colourful judges for sixteen years.

chapter forty two

2008
LEARNING TO DANCE WITH A NEW PARTNER

We were living in McMahons Point, in an old terrace, with a cat and two young children. I was well advanced into my fourth decade and labouring away as an advocate at the Sydney Bar. I was reading briefs on the dining room table late into the night, forever anxious whether the judge I would face on the coming day would be a bully, a pedant or a lawyer. Some of them were pleasant and seemed to remember what it had been like, before they had become infallible. Adele was spending her days washing nappies, shopping, preparing meals, sweeping paths and making beds. The surge of mad infatuation had calmed. We had moved into overdrive as the revolutions that drove our communal engine had dropped back a notch. The shrill, flute whistle of our honeymoon period could be heard in the distance, almost drowned out by the sweet, mellow sound of the cello talking to the saxophone and by the sound of children crying. We had settled comfortably into married life.

It was Adele's suggestion that we should take lessons in vertical dancing. I had never learnt the art. It was not something the grey men in charge had thought to teach the seminarians in my day. Singing in a choir, yes, and public speaking and debating received some little attention, though not much. Some of us were allowed to show an interest in performing on stage if we wished, but I had been too frightened of making a fool of myself. But dancing was not permitted. Swirling and twirling in carefree circles around a dance floor to the sound of *Frankie Valli and the Four Seasons* or *The Bee Gees* until giddy with delight, was beyond the world of my imagination. I was resigned to the fact that I had no rhythm in my blood. Even as a young boy I had been tense and rather self-conscious.

Adele thought it might be good for me to learn to dance. I needed some form of relaxation and dancing was an activity we could do together.

She had danced as a teenager in Toulouse and it was obvious, even from the way she walked and her body bounced, that rhythm had been woven into the seams of her flesh. But from my early days as a priest apprentice, I had been deprived of any sensual or musical stimulation. Popular music, loud bands, Elvis, The Beatles, Johnny Cash, Jacques Brel, Edith Piaf, Johnny Halliday, The Rolling Stones and Mick Jagger, had been as much part of her world as the Catholic catechism had been of mine. She and her brother François had thrived in the milieu of modern music.

When we went out on social occasions, in a dinner suit and formal dress, and the music began to play, she and I would sit at the table like dummies. The others were having fun but because of the gaping holes in my education, I couldn't bring myself to take my partner's hand and glide out seamlessly onto the dance floor. I am sure Adele understood. She never complained, but she waited her opportunity and suggested that we attend classes.

We paid our money at the community centre just down the hill from our home and begun to learn to dance Jive and Rock-and-Roll on Monday evenings. I was well out of my comfort zone but the teacher carefully explained the basic manoeuvres and patiently watched us as we practised moving our feet about, forward and backwards, this way and that, always following the predetermined, canonical patterns. I gave the teacher my full attention, but while I was concentrating on my feet, my upper body was as stiff as a corpse. When we joined hands and my turn came to dance a few steps with Adele, she said it was like rocking and rolling with a stuffed gorilla. Eventually however, I had her passing under my raised arm, twirling about, dragging my hesitant arm down, or out in front of me. It was torture, but I thought I was getting the hang of the basic steps – though coordinating my feet movements with the arm movements was not always possible.

During the lessons, I was pleasantly surprised to make contact again with a friend who had been working in the religious department of the ABC when we had last met. I had known her in an earlier life, when she was a high-powered nun in the Parramatta Mercies, teaching in Archbishop Jimmy Carroll's parish of Woolahra. We had worked together briefly when we were both on the ecclesiastical stage. Now we were learning to make our way in another world and acquiring skills late in life which others had mastered as teenagers.

When I joined with her on the dance floor, took hold of her diffidently and greeted her smilingly, she pretended I was a stranger. I made a tentative attempt to prompt her memory, but since she was sending out frigid vibrations, I withdrew and pretended that I was confused and that I had made a mistake. She was struggling, like me, to make her way in a foreign world. Maybe she was searching for a partner. She disappeared from the course soon after that, in mid-stream, before we had come to the backward shuffles and pirouettes.

After each class, before I could forget what I had learnt, Adele would hurry home to record a detailed description of each manoeuvre. In her neat handwriting, in a plastic folder, she preserved her notes on the foot movements, the hand and arm movements, coming together, pushing apart, twirling, circling – all that we had been taught. I never perfected the art of throwing my partner casually over my left hip, or passing her between my parted legs while holding her lightly under the arms. Some of the manoeuvres were just not possible.

When I came to the end of our course of lessons, the teacher took hold of me and led me out onto the floor. We danced a little together and after a few twists and twirls, we grinded to a halt. The teacher looked into my eyes and advised me that I would have to have some private remedial lessons. I was not pleased and this was not what I had expected to hear. I was looking for encouragement and had thought I was doing quite well. I had accepted that I would never be a Fred Astaire, but I was not as bad as some of the others. Adele was still pushing and pulling at me, complaining that I was going the wrong way or not leading her as she expected – as a gentleman was supposed to. She has never been satisfied with anything less than perfection. She has always been a stickler for the rules and regulations and she thinks that rules should be followed religiously. There is never any excuse for disobeying the regulations. She expected precision and perfection, while, by temperament, I had tended to be somewhat more flexible. I am by nature, a bit sloppy. The clash of our different approaches to life in general was being worked out on the dance floor.

Anyway, I knew what the teacher was hinting at. It was not a question of private remedial lessons. I dropped his clammy hand there in the middle of the floor, turned my back and walked home. I knew what he wanted, and I was not prepared to deliver it. I was happy at home.

I never reached an elevated level of dance proficiency. My efforts were only ever rudimentary. Every time we had to attend a function which included dancing – wedding receptions, the Bench and Bar dinners or the judges' annual conference – Adele would bring out her old notes in the plastic sleeve and together we would try to decipher her script. Like the Dead Sea Scrolls, they became more tattered and difficult to read as time passed.

She used to insist on a few painful practice sessions in the kitchen before I had a chance to make a fool of myself in public. I never really mastered the art, but I used to have fun trying. As the years passed, I learnt to relax, laugh and pretend I could do it. I could hold Adele, or one of our lady friends, close to my body, smile at her and talk a little as we moved around the floor, though not always in harmony with the music. Adele used to whisper directions as we danced and I used to count the rhythm under my breath, but I was worlds away from where I had been as a stiff and celibate cleric dancing with the devil. I was no casanova, but I was a surviver.

From time to time a group of us from the neighbourhood would organise a dance party with our friends. We used to hire the local ANZAC club hall, decorate it with streamers and flags, hire a band and throw a party. Adele agreed that this would be a good way to celebrate my seventieth birthday. We sent out invitations, hired the venue, organised an open bar tab and engaged the services of a band of world-weary guitar players and a manic drummer. *The Swinging '60s* played *The Beatles* songs and the music of *The Rolling Stones* – tunes on which everyone at my party, except me, had been weaned. The musicians played their heart out, puffing and sweating until midnight. There were four hundred of us clamped together on a large dance floor, all laughing and dancing, shaking bottoms and gyrating, pressed close and having fun. During a break to catch our breath, the crazy lead singer dripping sweat, took hold of me by the shoulders and shouted in my ear –

"Happy birthday, mate. This is the best fucking night I've been to in years."

I was flattered.

Everyone joined in – judges, barristers, neighbours, old parishioners from my past life, ex-priests and their wives. It was a magic way to celebrate a birthday and to show off my dancing skills.

By insisting that I learn to dance a little, and in many other ways, Adele was responsible for turning my life around to face the sun. When I had first met her in Brilon, I had already come to realise I was screwed up and screwed down. But with patience and persistence, my dancing partner had created a new world for me.

chapter forty three

2011
A LIFE OF MY OWN

The Roman Church in which I had lived had come to present itself as an exclusive club for the washed and saved – like a Masonic club, an RSL or Leagues Club, or a Commonwealth Bank full of bonds and valuable real estate. To remain a member one had to keep the rules – all of them. One had to accept the sub-culture and the trappings, the uniforms, the badges, the language and every detail of the club's code of beliefs. We all knew that if someone did not accept all the rules and the whole of the belief system, there was no alternative but to leave.

It was only later in life that I slowly began to see that the Roman Catholic Church was never meant to be a club. It was more like an extended family with a large, intricate family tree, a loose grouping of people, a type of vast movement. I also began to find a deeper understanding of the person of Jesus and of the message he and his followers had preached. Slowly, and reluctantly at first, I began to discover that life was about celebration, searching and the experience of being free and personally responsible. I began to suspect that God was a rumbling, mysterious, smouldering presence in a vast cosmos and that Jesus was an itinerant preacher-rebel who had been touched by the divine, rather than some meek and mild, pious, conservative voter.

Almost against my will, I came to see that the Church in the Vatican, which claimed to be a community of Jesus followers, was not ministering to the poor, welcoming the frail, embracing the wounded or gently crutching the fly-blown. The institution appeared as though it was ruled by old men in long dresses, with no smiles; men caught in the net of dogmatic formulas, with no common-sense; tiny men so conflated that their mothers would not have recognised them. I began to hear the belly laughs of God thundering down the centuries, earthquaking through the universe. I had to decide what was important – not to the bishop or the Pope, not even to my mother or father, not to my clergy classmates, but to me. To me before God, to me as I was, in all conscience, present to myself. Ultimately, I had to find my own way through the maze of life.

Over the years, ever since my re-internment at Springwood as a teacher, my faith life had been subjected to a radical realignment. I had made my way out of that terrifying world of faith in which God was ready to listen to, but seldom answer our every trivial prayer. A world in which everything, every dogma and formula, every act and ritual movement was of supernatural importance, in which badges, frills and magical words were all critical indicators of my orthodoxy. Eating meat on Friday, missing Sunday Mass, masturbating, sexual assaults, bashings and murders, were all mortal sins and inevitably led to punishment forever in hell. I had come to realise that there were grades and shades, that there were real people and important events, there were straw people, clowns and puppets and then there were myths, metaphors and legends. Life was not all black and white. I learnt that I could live with greys and gaps in my belief system and happily survive. There was a hierarchy of beliefs and values, and a very complex, twisted web woven by the criteria of orthodoxy and orthopraxis. I began to feel comfortable ignoring petty parts of the Church's code of behaviour and peripheral passages in its thick book of beliefs. Given the educational opportunities the institution had given me, I had been able to refine my personal belief system to a manageable size.

For a long time, God had ceased to be a massive hard-edged figure in my life. I had a profound belief in the existence of a being – a personal force outside myself, deep within myself and one which was at the centre of my existence. There was a power, a presence which pervaded my world, but one which I could not grasp hold of or put a face to. Mysterious. Unknowable. From my Christian tradition and the sacred literature, I had inherited some useful metaphors which allowed me to fumble in the shadows – father, creator, shepherd, rock, warrior, mother, lover, friend, protector – but none were adequate. These images gave me the power to probe the realities surrounding my life and to explore the mysterious territories beyond the horizon. But this Being always remained the Secret One, the Hidden One.

In my search, I might eventually discover a freedom, like a bird floating on the wind, but it was only a freedom within my world. I was such a tiny person in a little world of my own, facing the unknown, confronted by the incomprehensible, by the terrifying mystery of reality and its possibilities.

I remained fascinated by the figure of that rough and ready, vagrant wanderer, often tired and dusty, who used to disappear into the desert to meet with his Father. Jesus used to speak his mind without the need of glib formulas – no dogmas, no theological statements, without the support of thrones and funny hats. He spoke in parables and epigrams. According to him, God was not easy to find. Face to face, in real life, she was not filtered, pasteurised and packaged, and yet he spoke about this distant being as though he was just over there, as though he could commune with him intimately. Every now and again, when I was reading our sacred literature, I would fall on a text which was breathtakingly radical. It would appear that the founder at the head of the Christian movement, was ready to countenance attitudes and values which would undermine public order. Harsh criticism of religious leaders. A freedom to override rules that the priests and lawyers would have us believe were God-given.

Throughout my life I have learnt to love the message of Jesus and the ramshackled community of his followers whom we have dared to call the Church. I have loved her for her lifegiving liturgy, her hymns, her local rites and simple ceremonies, her celebration of life in all its moments of fulfilment and of tragedy, for bringing all kinds of people together, for blessing, consoling and burying them. But I am irritated by her ancient formulas of frozen truths, her rigidity, her evil methods of control and torture and her suffocating infallibilism.

I love her when I see her looking after the poor, helping to heal wounded sinners, paying silent attention to the elderly and the sick, visiting prisoners in gaol. But I am saddened by her anxiety to exclude, by her conceited triumphal pride, her denial of natural justice, her paranoid secrecy, her savage excommunications, her subjection and rejection of women and her neglect of our black brothers and sisters of Redfern.

I love her for preserving the memory of Jesus in the Gospels, for her constant search for the face of God in her sacred literature down the ages. She is justly proud of her kaleidoscopic collection of sermons, letters and poetry, recorded stories of saints and sinners, her spiritual and mystical writings, her doctrinal controversies, theological treatises, recorded dreams and visions, her apocalyptic ravings and philosophical tomes – in Greek and Latin, Aramaic and Syriac and all the languages of the world. She can glory in a richness of religious experiences as colourful as a peacock in full bloom. But she has persecuted heretics and her own theologians, ravaged followers of Islam, burnt people at the stake, imposed heavy burdens of conscience on the frail and claimed exclusive property in the divine.

I love some of her saints, but not all, some of her councils, but not all, some of her leaders, but not all. I love Father Pedro Arrupe, Archbishop Oscar Romero of El Salvador, Bishop Helder Camara, Bishop Pedro Casaladáliga of Säo Felix in Brazil, Cardinal John Henry Newman and Ted Kennedy of Redfern, but not Pacelli, Octtaviani or Ratzinger or Karol Wojtyla. I loved the portly Pope John for his courage, his simple trust in the Spirit of God, his expansive humanity, his optimism and his infectious warm inclusiveness. I love Irenaeus of Lyon, Thomas Aquinas, Paul the Apostle, Thomas More, Francis of Assisi and Teresa of Avila. I admired Augustine of Hippo for his faith, his fine intellect, his pastoral carefulness and his unbounded energy. But I find hard to accept some of what has been taught over the centuries in his name and under his theological banner. I cannot warm to St Bernard of Clairvaux, or John Vianney, or Therese of Lisieux, or Bernadette of Lourdes. The canonization of the founder of *Opus Dei*, Monsignor José María Escrivá de Balaguer, seriously devalued for me the currency of the canon of saints and the inclusion of Pope Pius XII with all his baggage, in the official list of saints and martyrs, would be an act of hubris and stupidity. I do not suggest that he is not at peace with God, but in his earthly life, as far as I can see, he showed few of the qualities which would recommend him as a folk hero to the modern world or a figure to emulate in our lives.

I admired the Polish Pope, John Paul II, for his physical and spiritual strength, his involvement in the world, his Tarzanic energy – but I could not entrust my salvation to him. He favoured bigots and religious fascists and refused to move against criminal members of the clergy like Father Marcial Maciel of the Legion of Christ. He allowed himself to appear as a superstar celebrity traversing the world stage in his popemobile. He forbade without encouraging, proclaimed but did not listen. He found fault, centralised and excluded. I couldn't see the Jesus of the Gospels reflected in him. But then who could detect the image of Jesus in some of the Renaissance popes? I wonder how they could have risen through the ranks, to the top of a religious movement, to be the representative on earth of our Jesus of Nazareth.

I love my Church's elegant medieval buildings – Chartres, Notre Dame, Bourges and St Sernin in Toulouse – but her shrines dripping with superstitious piety do not move me. I hate her pomposity, her pretensions, her lavish wealth and her displays of worldly power.

I love the compassion of her founder and some of his many followers but shudder when faced with the cruel rigorism, the dry legalism of the institution. I warm to the revolutionary spirit of Jesus but I am horrified by the destructive conservatism of his Church. Jesus embraced everyone, publicans, sinners, the poor and the marginal but his Church raises barriers, excludes and excommunicates. I am embarrassed by the blood on her hands, the cold eyes of her torturers, the stiff necks of the holy hypocrites but I love the dirt under her fingernails, her callused hands, her welcoming smile and the crusted knees of her sinners.

I have loved some of her modern thinkers (Congar, de Lubac, Teilhard, Bof, Kung and Curran) but I eschew her crass dogmatism, her fear of change, her support for fascist governments and the failure of her leaders to read *the Signs of the Times*. The whole world knows, the little people in the pews, even the middle managers all know that she needs to change her underwear, buy a new dress and powder her face if she is to entice men to dance with her. She needs to smile and sing, to venture out into the sunshine and breathe the air of the twenty-first century. She has allowed herself to become dowdy, flabby and a little ridiculous.

I cherish her mystic tradition, her poetry, her reverence for the past but grieve when confronted with her fear of the future and her mistrust of the Spirit of God. She preaches the Gospel, but does not seem to listen to it. She has ears but does not hear; nerves but does not tremble. She fashions burdens for others, commands people to remove gnats but covers herself in fine clothes and jewels and hides criminals from the eyes of justice.

I love my Church when she comes to life under the power of the Spirit of God but I have learnt to resist her deep suspicion of God's creation, her mistrust of the human body and her fear of human genitalia as instruments of intimate love.

I came to accept that I needed to celebrate my life in the world and my beliefs – in dirges and requiems, in dance and song, in joyfulness, in ecstasy, in extravagant praise. I needed to rejoice in my life and be thankful in God's presence. I wanted to simplify my faith world so that it would not be cluttered with dusty dogmas which had lost their lustre.

I did not want to feel that to be a believer and a follower of the Catholic traditions, part of me had to inhabit a parallel universe. I came to dislike the feeling of living a dual spiritual life in which one part of me was in conflict with another, where my faith was continually crashing up against my common sense, against my sense of right and wrong, my rudimentary understanding of historical development, cultural forces, scientific discoveries and advances. I wanted to live an integrated, human and believing existence. I wanted to be able to say what I really believed, to be responsible for my own life, my thoughts and deeds – sometimes terrible, sometimes murky, often hesitant, sometimes pure and transparent. I was anxious to find a life of my own.

chapter forty four

1993-2012
BACK DOWN TO EARTH

"We are all of us naked beneath our clothes".

Heinrich Heine

It was a hot Sydney Monday in February. The bitumen was melting in the streets and a furnace of haze lay over the city. Satan himself was sweating as he went about his work. Judges and barristers were decked out in their finery, solicitors and friends in clammy suits and ties, ladies in summer frocks and hats, were perspiring inside foundation garments and pantyhose – we had all gathered to celebrate my swearing-in as a judge of the Compensation Court of New South Wales. I was already in my fifty-fifth year.

After the sweltering court ceremony, full of speeches and laughter, after the cups of tea and sandwiches with friends and fellow judges, Adele and I were moved to deliver the fresh leftovers to the patrons of St Vincent de Paul at Wooloomooloo. We were feeling pleased with ourselves and it had been an occasion to remember. My legal career was taking off in an unexpected direction, into the exclusive and eminent ranks of the independent judiciary – a substantial salary, an attractive pension on retirement, an honorific title, free public transport and comfortable chambers. People were going to stand when I made my appearance in court in my wig and robes, just as they used to when I walked out in my alb and chasuble onto the sanctuary. The new world promised security, status and a good life for me and my family. I had to be careful to keep my feet on the ground and remember where I had come from. That my father had been a union man toiling, often on the midnight shifts, for Patrick's on the wharves, sometimes passed over in the pick-up because he was a Catholic. Now the court I was joining was full of Catholics – O'Meally, Moroney, O'Toole, Burke and Moran. Catholics had found their place in the Australian sun – still in the ranks of the working class, the unions and the Labor Party.

As I walked up the grotty harbour-side, back-lane towards the Matt Talbot refuge, a large tray of fresh sandwiches in my arms and my beautiful wife by my side, I was feeling pretty contented. It was still hot and sticky and sweat was snaking down my face. The white shirt under my best dark suit was soaked. Trickles of perspiration were finding a path down my legs inside my creased trousers. But we were on a mission, sharing what we had (well, our leftovers), doing one of those enhancing acts of charity when virtuous people give a small proportion of their super-abundance and feel justified. I had fallen victim to the artificial hype which surrounds such occasions.

It was mid afternoon. As we walked along, both holding a tray of tasty goodies, we passed two untidy men sitting side by side in the gutter outside the refuge. They appeared to be regular clients of the establishment, just the ones who would enjoy our contribution to their daily needs and be thankful for our generosity. They looked unwashed, ragged and grimy – shoes without socks, mouths without teeth. They were probably waiting for a feed. As Adele and I passed by, dressed in our best clobber, I heard one old hobo say to his mate –

> "Look at those fucking idiots, will ya. Don't ya fucking feel
> sorry for 'em. Look at 'em dolled up in all their gear. I
> wouldn't be them for fucking quids."

I have often thought of those two old, unkempt philosophers and remembered what had passed between them as Adele and I had entered their territory and processed up the lane. Every one of us has his own peculiar perspective on the world. I had my own way of relating to and interpreting what was for me reality, and they had theirs.

I do not suggest for a moment that there are not judges, or doctors, or priests for whom we, whoever we are, should not feel compassion and sympathy. But I was amused and pleased to be reminded that whatever I thought I was at that moment, I was, according to those on the ground, still a paid-up member of the frail family of humanity. Though I have often needed to be jolted back into the real world and reminded of who I really was and where I had come from, there was no need on that day to feel sorry for me or for Adele. Our life together, luckily, was proving more than satisfactory.

Throughout the years of our marriage, my wife continued to live in a world radically different to, and often hostile to the world inhabited by the Pope and his celestial team. It was as though they were holding out in a parallel universe on Mars, while she was grounded here on earth. She lived her life surrounded by mountains and rivers, and in the midst of animals and enfleshed human beings. In contrast, churchmen had their minds focused on constructed images of heaven and hell, of angels and demons, souls to be fought for, of sacred signs and blessings, and on fuzzy images of a mysterious triune God, who could be addressed respectfully and who was listening attentively. I had lived in that world for a great part of my life but at the age of nearly forty, I had elected to escape from the rarified atmosphere of outer-space and to wander about on *terra firma*, in the landscape where Jesus had lived. I had made the exhausting trip from Mars to earth, but I was determined to hold fast to the enriching elements I had discovered in an earlier existence. I tried to be a believer living in the real world, rather than a stranger on earth waiting to be transported to an alien land above the clouds. In Toulouse, Adele and I had harnessed ourselves together as a team. But for some years I continued to carry a cumbersome, ill-fitting yoke which kept bruising my flesh and irritating my thin skin.

My marriage proposal had been both an act of desperation as well as a moment of sheer inspiration. In accepting my crazy offer, Adele had gambled her life on an unpromising late-starter. Some of our friends, those on the inside, those close to me, as well as her friends, and especially her parents, were no doubt convinced that this marriage was a mistake from the beginning and doomed to failure. After a fairly public failure in my first life when I danced with the devil, I was making a second attempt just at the time when this pretty French girl was on the cusp of a career, on the edge of a life with a dancing partner who was brand new. She was twenty-six. I had spent the years since her birth in 1951 under clerical orders, either in the seminary or not far from it. She was beginning and I was beginning again – and from behind scratch.

I have no regrets that I lowered my guard and threw in the sweaty towel. After I had removed the boxing gloves and climbed out of the ring, I entered a different world. With Adele by my side, I began to mix in a circle of friends and colleagues who were, by and large, not too interested in religion. Atheists, agnostics, anglicans, religious and secular Jews, ex-Catholics, lapsed Catholics and journeymen – though a few of our friends had kept up their membership in *The Holy Romans*. There have been many interesting conversations and interchanges which would have eluded me had I remained in the tiny sphere of the clergy, or had I married into the culture in which I had lived my whole life. My wife and our friends, my colleagues in the law and my mates in *The Men's Support Group* at the local pub, have challenged me to review my beliefs, to examine my responses to difficult ethical questions, to revise my dogmatic or prejudicial attitudes, to live among men down in the pit where the action is and to grow as a human being. I am inclined to think that I have had the best of both worlds.

I have never been tempted to retrace my journey. I came to know that even after a lengthy apprenticeship, I didn't fit the mould. Now that I have lived my life, now that I have found the freedom to think my own thoughts, to have my say and dismiss what others might think or say, why would I go back into an organisation controlled by old men, where women travel in the third-class carriages and where the driver insists on siting in the rear and travelling backwards?

Like the Labor Party in New South Wales, like many large institutions, despite the drive and vision of its founder, despite the light he lit on the hill, despite the noble intentions of good, holy men and women, the Roman Catholic Church has allowed itself to become fat and crippled with arthritis, with too little exercise, young talent and new ideas discouraged and the local branches allowed to wither. Like the defunct Communist Party, the candidates for high office are selected carefully by the old members of the central committee who do not represent the rank and file. Middle management, even members of the Papal cabinet, are forbidden to speak their mind and are reduced to mouthing empty spin and ugly focus-group formulas. But the perks of office are too attractive to resist – free flights, hire cars, allowances, favours, high places at table and guarantees of future preferment. Jesus is weeping, the people are angry or indifferent, while the old Party has lost its way. Yet it seems determined to continue on in the vain hope that life is cyclical and the mad belief that the leaders are infallible, that they should never admit mistakes, that clerical crimes should be covered over and that God will put all things right again.

I did not want to live my life as a lonely cleric any more. It took years for me to admit it to myself, but I was craving for someone to hold me tight in a loving embrace. I longed to live a life, a tiny life, but a life of my own.

Adele and I have been happy together. Over the years, and without too much stress, I discovered that Adele's beauty and dignity were not skin-deep (though on the surface, they were breathtaking from our first meeting in Germany). I found that the qualities I admired seeped deep down into the heart and soul of the woman who had placed her money on a bolter. How such a careful, prudent girl came to take the gamble is a question I have never been able to answer. She has helped an inmate escape from a dark place. She was waiting at the prison gate when he broke out with only the clothes he was standing in. His pockets were empty. They walked away hand-in-hand and made a life together.

My mother had been right – it did all work out in the end. Let me conclude with the prayer of wonder and praise which we used to say in the seminary before we went to sleep, as the lights were going out –

"Benedicamus Domino – Deo Gratias".

www.ingramcontent.com/pod-product-compliance
Lightning Source LLC
LaVergne TN
LVHW051452080426
835509LV00017B/1742